SketchUp for Interior Design

SketchUp for Interior Design

3D Visualizing, Designing, and Space Planning

Lydia Sloan Cline

WILEY

Cover Design: Wiley

Cover Image: Large image and two on the second line: Courtesy Matthew Kerr, IIDA, ASAI, Zimmerman Architectural Studios, Milwaukee, WI. Second from the top in right hand column: Courtesy of Terry Sandee, REDGRAPHX, Inc. Top right corner image courtesy of author.

For general information about our other products and services, please contact our Customer Care Department within the United States at (800) 762-2974, outside the United States at (317) 572-3993 or fax (317) 572-4002.

Wiley publishes in a variety of print and electronic formats and by print-on-demand. Some material included with standard print versions of this book may not be included in e-books or in print-on-demand. If this book refers to media such as a CD or DVD that is not included in the version you purchased, you may download this material at http://booksupport.wiley.com. For more information about Wiley products, visit www.wiley.com.

Library of Congress Cataloging-in-Publication Data:
Cline, Lydia Sloan.
  SketchUp for interior design : 3D visualizing, designing, and space planning / Lydia Sloan Cline.
     pages cm
  Includes index.
  ISBN 978-1-118-62769-3 (pbk.); 978-1-118-80493-3 (ebk); 978-1-118-80507-7 (ebk)
  1. Interior decoration—Computer-aided design. 2. Interior architecture—Computer-aided design. 3. SketchUp. I. Title.
  NK2114.C59 2014
  747—dc23
                        2013026541

Printed in the United States of America

·10 9 8 7 6 5 4 3

Contents

Foreword

Modeling software is rapidly replacing traditional two-dimensional drafting software as the vehicle for designers to create and communicate. SketchUp has emerged as the modeling program of choice in many diverse fields as a result of its low price and relatively short learning curve. This book is for the beginner who wants to get up and running with it fast.

Why Read This Book?

You may be wondering why you should read a SketchUp book, when there is so much content online. My answer is that the online content, while very good, is not organized. If you don't know what the software's capabilities are, you don't know what to ask or search for. This book leads you through SketchUp in an orderly manner. Its intent is to acquaint you with its many capabilities. Toward that goal, tools and functions are briefly described under their own headings and then used in step-by-step examples.

SketchUp's most popular functions are introduced early, to enable you to quickly do what you want to do with it. Some tools are revisited later to show more complex options. By the time you finish, you'll have been exposed to most of the tools, one or two options for each, and some different approaches for solving modeling problems. You'll then be pointed to a site where you can ask your increasingly complex questions. End-of-chapter links to high-quality online content are also given as a guide through the ocean of Web information.

What's Covered?

Coverage is specific to the interests of interior designers and interior architects: how to model interior spaces, study scale and proportion, test different ideas, present solutions, plan spaces, and generate architectural floor plans, elevations, and sections. There are also examples that show SketchUp combined with other software programs and hand-rendering tools for maximum utility and flexibility.

Knowledge of other drafting software is not needed. However, it is assumed that the reader has basic architectural drafting knowledge, such as what floor plans, interior elevations, perspective, and isometric and section views are. This book shows how to use SketchUp to create those drawings; it doesn't discuss what they are. If you could benefit from a drafting refresher, some resources are listed at the end of this Foreword.

Since PCs are standard in the interior design and architecture fields, screenshots are from a PC. Where operations on a Mac are different, Mac screenshots are added. Pro (the pay version of SketchUp) is also discussed, because Pro is cheaply available to students and schools. While all tools in Make (free) and Pro work in the same way, Pro has additional features needed in a professional work capacity.

Extra Goodies

On the Wiley site there are video tutorials of the book's projects; look for the [] symbol on the page. There is also a Homework folder full of files for completing the end-of-chapter exercises and recreating the projects yourself. Download and save the whole folder at once to your desktop so everything will be available when needed. Instructors have an additional folder with answers to the end-of-chapter questions, some project models, and high-resolution images of SketchUp drawings for showing classes how SketchUp is used in the practice of interior design and architecture.

So, let's get started!

The site that contains the videos is: www.wiley.com/go/sketchupforinteriordesign

Further Resources

Cline, Lydia Sloan. *Architectural Drafting for Interior Designers*. Clifton, NY: Cengage, 2007.

Cline, Lydia Sloan. *Drafting and Visual Presentation for Interior Designers*. Upper Saddle River, NJ: Prentice Hall, 2011.

What Is SketchUp and How Do Interior Designers Use It?

What Is SketchUp?

SketchUp is a *polygonal surface modeling program* (Figure 1–1). *Polygonal* means that everything SketchUp creates is made out of polygons (flat shapes bordered by straight lines). *Surface* means that everything it makes is hollow. *Modeling* means that it makes models, which are three-dimensional (3D) digital drawings composed of lines and faces (planes). Collectively, those lines and faces are called *geometry*.

SketchUp is also a *vector* program, meaning it creates vector files with an *skp* extension. A vector file is a collection of lines and curves that scale up or down without loss of quality. Examples are pdfs (Adobe documents) and dwgs (AutoCAD documents). This is as opposed to a *raster* file, which is made with individual pixels and loses resolution quality when enlarged. Examples are jpgs and gifs.

SketchUp is strictly a desktop application, not a Web-based one. It works on both the PC and the Mac. Files made on one platform transfer easily to the other.

Objective: This chapter discusses what modeling is, what SketchUp is, and how it's used by interior designers.

Concepts and Functions: SketchUp Make, SketchUp Pro, model, solid/surface/wire/polygonal model, polygon, geometry, vector, raster, BIM, attributes, dynamic component, reports, solid modeling tools

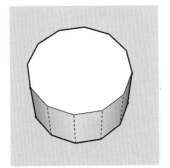 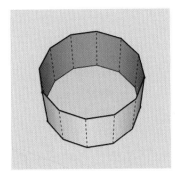

Figure 1–1: All SketchUp models, including circles, are made of polygons and are hollow.

Who Uses It?

SketchUp was written as a user-friendly alternative to the complex modeling software common in the architectural field, its original user base. Previous owner Google made it free to the public, which wildly expanded its popularity beyond the original architect user base. Now interior designers, game developers, filmmakers, woodworkers, catalog illustrators, packaging designers, landscapers, and more use it too.

Is It Easy to Learn?

It's probably easier than other industry-standard modeling programs, because it has fewer features and is somewhat intuitive. But "easy" is relative. Like everything else, it still takes practice—you probably didn't make great pencil sketches right away, either.

Know that there are many ways to do the same thing in SketchUp, and no one "right" way. Some ways take a few more steps, but if you make learning it the first priority, efficiency will follow.

What Is SketchUp Used For?

SketchUp is used to electronically sketch ideas three-dimensionally—to "get your doodle on." It's the closest you can get to pencil and tracing paper for thinking out ideas. Since you can "sketch" loosely (meaning without inputting numbers), this software helps you think spatially. Height/width relationships become easy to see; for example, a hallway that seems wide in a floor plan may reveal itself as dark and narrow when the vertical dimension is added. As with a physical foam-core model, a digital model can be studied from any direction. However, SketchUp one-ups the foam-core model with camera tools that let you stroll through the digital model at eye level. Finally, SketchUp models can make the jump to the construction documentation process when the LayOut feature are added.

SketchUp has evolved into two programs: a free, noncommercial one called Make and a commercial product called Pro. Both are owned by Trimble, a company that makes positioning technology products.

The Difference between Traditional CAD Drawings and Models

With traditional computer-aided drafting software such as AutoCAD, the mouse is an electronic pencil with which you basically replicate the hand-drafting process. Three-dimensional (3D) drawings made with AutoCAD are really a collection of two-dimensional (2D) entities that give the illusion of three dimensions. A model, however, is a true 3D object that the viewer can "orbit" around and view from any position. Two-dimensional (orthographic) views are generated from it (Figure 1–2).

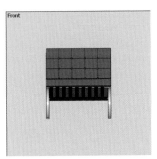

Figure 1–2: The user orbits around a model to view it from any position. Two-dimensional (2D) views are then generated from it.

AutoCAD is not a prerequisite to learning SketchUp; the two programs operate differently. If your computer drafting experience to date is limited to traditional 2D software, you will find that modeling requires a different approach. You may also find that you never want to go back to 2D software once you see the advantages of 3D.

How SketchUp Displays the Model

By default, SketchUp displays the model as a 3-point perspective. That is, all parallel lines converge to left, right, and top or bottom vanishing points. However, it can be set to display as a 2-point perspective, as an *isometric* (3D view in which parallel lines remain parallel), and orthographically (plan, elevation, and section views).

Types of Models

It's helpful to understand the different model types before you learn SketchUp, because this may affect how you plan to use it. Knowing a software program's strengths and limitations affects the time spent on a piece and its resultant quality.

There are three types of models: solid, surface, and wireframe (Figures 1-3).

Solid models are just that: filled solid inside. They contain data such as interior volume, mass, and weight. This enables you to perform tasks such as specifying a constant wall thickness or connecting and curving adjacent edges. Solid model file sizes are large, so they may run and regenerate slowly. *3ds Max* and *form·Z* are two solid modeling programs popular with architects and interior designers.

Surface models are hollow with a thin skin, composed strictly of lines and faces (planes). You can create complex curves and forms, but only surface data—e.g., area—is stored. A surface model doesn't recognize geometry as specific features; for example, where a solid model would recognize a staircase and perform relevant calculations, a surface model just sees the staircase as lines and faces. Surface models are used when the designer is primarily concerned with external form and appearance. Their file sizes are generally smaller than those of solid models, so they run faster. Besides SketchUp, another popular surface modeling program is *Rhinoceros 3D*.

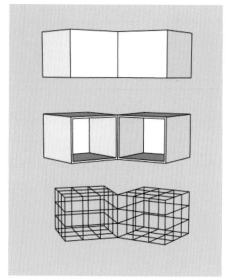

Figure 1–3: Solid, surface, and wireframe models.

Wireframe models are the simplest. They only contain information about the object's edges and intersections. As the name implies, this model appears constructed from wires. Its file size is very small; hence, it runs quickly. Wireframes can be created or displayed with any modeling software.

BIM, or *building information modeling*, refers to a particular, data-rich type of solid model plus a collaboration process. A popular BIM program used in the construction industry is *Revit*.

No model type is "best"; all have unique advantages. For example, designs that require a constant wall thickness are better drawn with a solid modeler. Designs that require curved, sculpted surfaces are better drawn with a surface modeler.

Older and newer versions of SketchUp can work on the same computer, but Make and Pro cannot. Only one can be installed.

What SketchUp Make (Free Version) Can Do

The free version of SketchUp can do almost everything the commercial version can, such as:

▶ Make complete interior and exterior models

▶ Add color, texture, shadows, and geolocation information

▶ Apply styles that simulate art media, such as pencil and watercolor

- Make, download, and edit components
- Download and use dynamic components
- Download and use plugins (add-on software)
- Create (low resolution) raster files and animations of the model
- Import raster files of floor plans to trace, and of real-world materials to apply
- Export the model to 2D image formats

Pro has additional features that working professionals need.

What SketchUp Pro Can Do

- *Import AutoCAD (dwg) and Revit (rvt) files* (Figure 1–4). This turns them into SketchUp geometry, which enables precise modeling from existing floor plans (tracing a raster file may be time saving but is not precise). Layers and blocks are also preserved.
- *Export SketchUp models into formats that can be directly imported into AutoCAD or Revit.*
- *Create presentation boards and design documents from the model.* This is done with LayOut, a feature that installs with Pro as a separate program (Figure 1–5).

COURTESY MATTHEW KERR, IIDA, ASAI, ZIMMERMAN ARCHITECTURAL STUDIOS, MILWAUKEE, WI

Figure 1–4: An AutoCAD floor plan imported into SketchUp Pro and partially modeled.

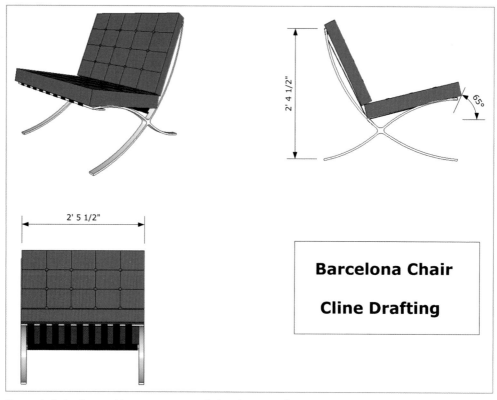

Figure 1–5: LayOut enables you to create a design document from a model.

▶ *Make custom line weights and styles, giving the model a hand-drawn appearance* (Figure 1–6). This is done with Style Builder, a feature that installs as a separate program.

▶ *Export high-resolution animation and raster files.* These are more suitable for printing and presentation than the low-resolution files the free version is limited to.

▶ *Create and edit dynamic components.* These are models programmed to store information and perform specific actions (Figure 1–7). For instance, staircases can add steps when height is adjusted, and cabinets can store price and parts information and open doors with a click.

▶ *Perform additive and subtractive modeling tasks*, or what engineers call *Boolean operations*. This saves steps, making for a faster workflow (Figure 1–8).

▶ *Generate reports* such as materials takeoffs (e.g., how much paint to buy based on the area of walls in the model).

▶ *Receive upgrades, maintenance, and support on technical problems via e-mail and phone.* Such support is for installation and licensing issues, not tutorials on the software.

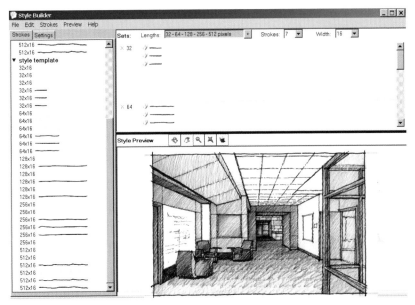

Figure 1–6: Style Builder creates models that look hand-drawn.

Figure 1–7: Clicking on this dynamic cabinet component makes the door open to show storage options.

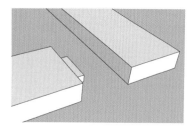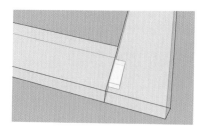

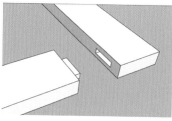

Figure 1–8: With solid modeling tools, a tenon is pushed into a block of wood, then pulled away, revealing a clean mortise joint automatically created.

Purchase Pro

A single, nonexpiring license for Pro costs $590, which includes a year's maintenance subscription. Upgrading to new versions after one year costs $95. Offices can buy single-user and network licenses. A single license installs SketchUp on any computer, but only one can run it at a time. With a network license, you pay for the number of seats or *instances* desired (with a 50-seat minimum required for a first purchase). The software can be installed on as many computers as wanted, and the license resides on a server. You can run as many instances of SketchUp as you bought seats for. Network licenses can't be used off-site because SketchUp must detect the license before starting. Thus, if you wanted to bring a laptop to a client presentation, a single-user license would be needed.

Purchase a Pro Educational License

Students enrolled at accredited schools can purchase a $49 educational version that expires after one year. It is fully functional and doesn't watermark images, but it doesn't permit commercial use. Upgrades during the license's year are free. You can also repurchase the license after expiration if still a student. Obtain it through SketchUp's network of educational resellers; see Further Resources at the end of this chapter.

How Designers Use SketchUp

Following are examples of ways SketchUp can be used by interior designers and interior architects, both by itself and as part of a larger workflow.

▸ Solidify a pencil-and-tracing paper floor plan by tracing over it, and then model the traced plan (Figure 1–9).

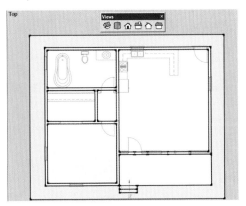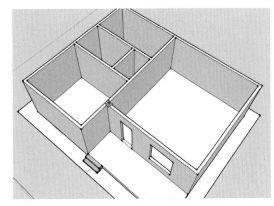

Figure 1–9: Tracing an imported plan and then modeling from it.

▸ Import models of specific manufacturer catalog items and use them to space plan (Figure 1–10). This enables seeing if there's enough room for the furniture before presenting to the client. The SketchUp model scan serves as a 'fit' drawing.

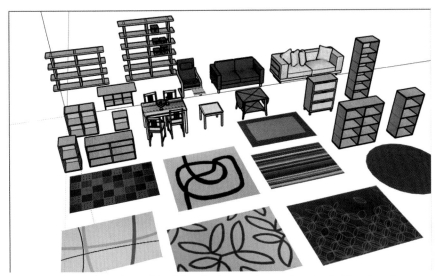

Figure 1–10: Ready-made models of Ikea furniture and rugs, downloaded free from the 3D Warehouse.

▶ Change the model style to give it an artsy look (Figure 1–11) and make high-resolution PDFs for marketing materials.

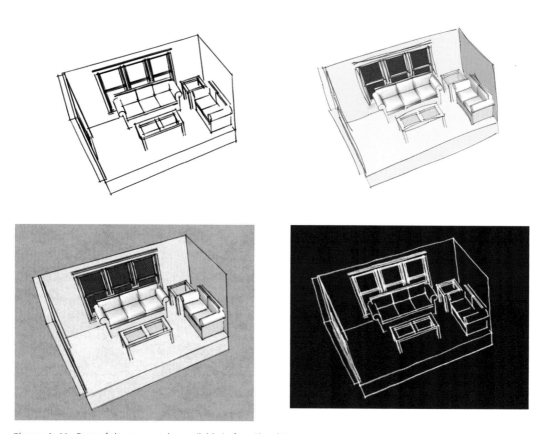

Figure 1–11: Four of the many styles available in free SketchUp.

▶ Use a SketchUp model as an underlay over which to trace ideas and adjustments. Print up plans and 3D views of the model, hand-color and scan, and then import them into Photoshop for lighting and text enhancement (Figure 1–12).

▶ Show animations and slide show scenes of different options (Figure 1–13). This enables clients to see how the design works before committing to it. Their favorite photos and wall art can also be incorporated.

Courtesy Matthew Kerr, IIDA, ASAI, Zimmerman Architectural Studios, Milwaukee, WI

Figure 1–12: A SketchUp model was printed up and then used as an underlay for tracing and marker work.

Figure 1–13: Incorporate photos into the model. The tabs at the top are preset scenes of the house for a slide show.

▶ Send the model to hands-on clients who want to make suggestions directly on it. Since the software is free, they can download it themselves and experiment with colors, materials, and appliances.

▶ Import images of the textiles specified in the design to display in the model (Figure 1–14).

- Show models of case goods to the tradespeople who will make them, enabling them to see exactly what's wanted. Then use the LayOut feature to make construction documents from the model. LayOut can also make quick drawings for bid and permit purposes.

- Maintain a library of manufacturer-supplied dynamic cabinet components. Change the components' size and configuration as needed, and get instant prices based on each option.

- Use Style Builder to give an "open to changes" look to the drawings. This makes them appear less like a finished product while also conveying a specific personality and brand identification.

Interested? Come on over to Chapter 2, where we'll discuss what's needed to run SketchUp, put it on your computer, and explore its workspace.

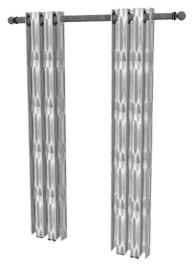

Figure 1–14: Textile pattern applied to a drapery model.

Summary

SketchUp is a surface modeling program used by interior designers for space planning, conceptual design, and client presentations. Users can think through an idea, study design options, and present them creatively. SketchUp has a free version called Make and a commercial version called Pro, which contains functions needed for professional work.

Further Resources

Buy an educational license for Pro here: www.sketchup.com/buy/eduresellers.html

Buy Pro (noneducational) here: https://store.sketchup.com/

Cline, Lydia Sloan. *Drafting and Visual Presentation for Interior Designers*. Upper Saddle River, NJ: Prentice Hall, 2011.

Obtain a free eight-hour trial of Pro: www.sketchup.com/intl/en/download/index.html

The Official SketchUp Blog: http://sketchupdate.blogspot.com/

@SketchUp on Twitter

SketchUp on Facebook: www.facebook.com/#!/sketchup

Getting Started

I n Chapter 1 we discussed what SketchUp is and saw ways interior designers and interior architects can use it. Now we'll discuss what's needed to run it, and peek at its workspace.

Hardware, Operating System, and Browser Requirements

SketchUp is a graphics-intensive program. The more detailed your model, the more processing power it needs. A late-model computer and operating system is needed, specifically:

PC: At least 2+ GHz processor, 2+ GB RAM, 500 MB of available hard-disk space, and a 3D-class video card with 512+ MB of memory or higher. Video card driver must support OpenGL 1.5+. SketchUp Pro requires .NET Framework version 2.0.

> *Operating System*: XP, Vista, Windows 7, 8, and the Internet Explorer 7.0+ browser.

Mac: At least 2.1+ GHz Intel processor, 2 GB RAM, 500 MB of available hard-disk space, 3D-class video card with 512+ MB of memory or higher. Video card driver must support OpenGL 1.5+.

> *Operating System*: Mac OS X 10.7, QuickTime 7, and the Safari browser. Boot Camp and Parallels are not supported.

A keyboard and three-button mouse, with the third button a scroll wheel, is the easiest and most efficient way to use SketchUp. A one-button mouse or laptop track pad is doable but difficult. Three-dimensional modeling requires much more on-screen movement than 2D drafting. A scroll wheel lets you make that movement faster than clicking icons or keyboard shortcuts. Mac users, your one-button mouse can be swapped with any manufacturer's two-button/scroll wheel mouse.

Objective: This chapter discusses what's needed to run SketchUp, how to download and open it, and tours the workspace.

Concepts and Functions: three-button mouse, video card, tablet PC, graphics tablet, digital pen, computer tablet, Space Navigator, splash screen, workspace, menu bar, axes, scale figure, origin, measurements box, instance, viewer, template, Photoshop, Dropbox, Save, Save As, Save A Copy As, Save As Template, backup files

▶ If your scroll wheel doesn't orbit or pan, the mouse settings may need adjustment. PC users, go to **Control Panel>Hardware and Sound>Devices** and choose **Printer>Mouse**. Mac users, go to **System Preferences>Keyboard** and choose **Mouse**. Look for a ***middle click*** wheel setting. If this option isn't there, you may need to install a more recent mouse driver.

The Video Card

The *video card*, also called a *graphics card*, is an electronic board inside the computer that sends information to the monitor. The ones installed in most off-the-shelf PCs and Macs are for general use, not the higher demands of modeling software. Hence, they display SketchUp models with a low-resolution, jagged appearance. Stronger cards, such as the NVIDIA GTX 600 series, are made to handle modeling software's demands. They're typically installed in the computers of college drafting labs and companies that make software models. Higher-end, off-the-shelf computers such as the Dell Precision also have them. If your goal is to print SketchUp models for construction documents and marketing purposes, and make animations for presentations, consider the video card when buying or upgrading a computer.

Figure 2–1 shows screenshots made with a low-end and high-end video card. Most of the figures in this book were made with a high-end one. You might try to discern which ones weren't.

Figure 2–1: The left screenshot was made with a standard card; the right with an NVIDIA GTX-620 card.

The Space Navigator 3D Mouse

A mouse option for both the PC and Mac is Logitech's *Space Navigator* (Figure 2–2), designed for modeling software. It works similar to a game joystick, combining SketchUp's *Zoom*, *Pan*, and *Orbit* navigation tools into one. It also tilts, spins, and rolls. The Space Navigator can be used alongside the traditional mouse.

Figure 2–2: The Logitech Space Navigator 3D mouse moves through the model more efficiently than the traditional mouse, and can be used alongside it.

Speaking of joysticks, you can actually use a Wiimote controller (remote from a Wii game) as a 3D mouse, too. Free GlovePIE software needs to be installed to do this; see Further Resources at the end of this chapter.

Use a Tablet PC

Although SketchUp was designed to work with a keyboard and mouse, there are some alternatives. One is a *graphics tablet* (not the same as a computer tablet) and digital pen. The tablet's buttons can be programmed to perform multistep functions that otherwise take multiple keystrokes to perform, and the pen may cause less wrist fatigue than a mouse. Examples of graphics tablets are Wacom's Graphire, Intuos, Cintiq, and Bamboo. Pens and graphics tablets are also useful with Photoshop, which some designers import files of their models into for further development.

SketchUp can be operated in a limited manner on a Windows tablet PC. Third-party viewer apps exist for the iPad, iPhone, and Android tablet (Figure 2–3). Those apps let you view, walk through, and even annotate the model. This is useful for an on-site presentation, e-mailing, or opening from a Dropbox (online hosting) account. Adding PDF files generated from LayOut can turn a tablet PC into a portable portfolio! But heavy-duty modeling is best done on a computer with a keyboard and two-button/scroll wheel mouse.

Figure 2–3: A SketchUp viewer app on an iPad.

Download SketchUp Make

It's time to point your browser to **www.sketchup.com** and download the program (Figure 2–4). You'll be asked what you'll use it for—select *Personal* for the free version—and what your specific interest, operating system, and e-mail are. The software downloads very fast, even with a slow Internet connection.

Figure 2–4: The SketchUp download process.

SketchUp installs in Windows Programs and Mac Finder/Applications. Three shortcuts (Figure 2–5) automatically appear on the PC desktop. On the Mac, the SketchUp icons appear in the dock. Right-click, select **Options>Show in Finder**, and then drag the three icons from the Finder window to the desktop, if you want.

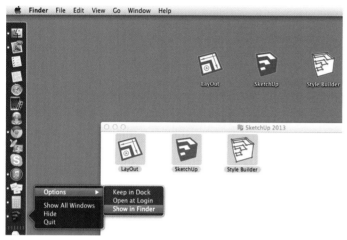

Figure 2–5: On the PC, three shortcuts appear on the desktop after installation. On the Mac, the icons can be dragged from the Finder onto the desktop, if desired.

By default you're given 8-hour trial versions of Pro, Style Builder, and LayOut. After 8 hours of use (the clock isn't ticking while the software is closed), Pro reverts to Make, and the other two stop working.

Click on the SketchUp icon to launch. A splash screen appears (Figure 2–6). As an aside, it has no exit buttons, so if you didn't mean to open it, click **ESC** to cancel. At the bottom is a collapsed window called *Template*. Templates are files with default settings, such as measurement units. Click it.

The template window opens (Figure 2–7), showing multiple choices. Choose *Architectural Design – Feet and Inches*. In this template, all length numbers entered will appear in a feet and inch format. Every number you type means inches, so you don't need to include the inch unit ("). But SketchUp recognizes dimensions in any format as long as you include their unit after the number (e.g., mm, cm, m, or (') for the foot sign).

Finally, click *Start Using SketchUp*. Figure 2–8 shows the screen. Figure 2–9 shows the PC and Mac menu bars and the Getting Started toolbars right underneath. The menu bars are slightly different; Mac users, note that yours starts with a **SketchUp** entry.

Figure 2–6: The splash screen with the collapsed Template window at the bottom.

Figure 2–7: Choose the Architectural Design – Feet and Inches template.

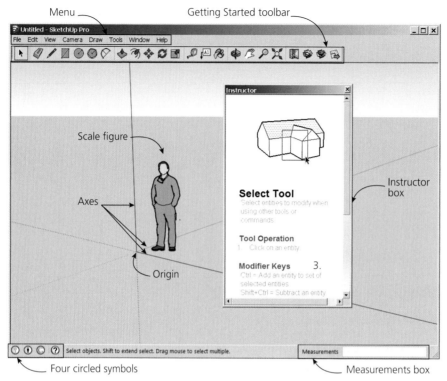

Figure 2–8: The SketchUp screen.

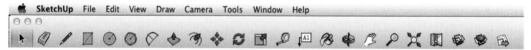

Figure 2–9: The PC and Mac menu bars.

The Workspace

The workspace contains:

The menu bar: This is a horizontal bar at the top of the screen that houses tools and functions. It has eight categories: *File, Edit, View, Camera, Draw, Tools, Window,* and *Help.*

▶ File: Contains functions that let you open, save, print, import, and export files.

▶ Edit: Contains standard cut, copy, and paste functions plus SketchUp-specific ones such as making groups and components.

- ▶ View: Contains functions that alter how the model looks, such as making it monochrome or wireframe.
- ▶ Camera: Contains tools that change your position relative to the model—e.g., inside it at eye level—and let you view it in 2D as well as 3D.
- ▶ Draw: Contains tools that create the model.
- ▶ Tools: Contains tools that edit the model.
- ▶ Window: Contains dialog boxes through which the model's properties are altered.
- ▶ Help: Contains information about, and links to, websites about the software.

Once you start using *extensions* (discussed in Chapter 9), a *Plugins* category will appear. This contains controls for extensions, add-on software that enables SketchUp to do more things.

The Getting Started toolbar: The horizontal bar under the **menu** bar containing icons that activate tools.

The modeling window: The large area where you create the model.

Three axes: These are the height, length, and depth lines along which SketchUp draws. Their intersection is called the *origin*. The height (y) line is blue, and the ground lines (x and y) are red and green. The axes lines are solid in the positive directions and dotted in the negative. Every point has a coordinate (group of numbers) that describes its location: (3,4,5) means 3 units along the x/red axis, 4 units along the y/green axis, and 5 units along the z/blue axis (Figure 2–10).

A human scale figure: This figure helps you gauge sizes, helpful when you're just "sketching," not inputting dimensions.

The measurements box: A field in the lower-right corner of the screen in which all inputted numbers appear. If you don't see it, it's probably hidden behind your Windows taskbar. Maximize the SketchUp screen or drag it higher on the desktop.

Instructor box: This window contains a brief tutorial for the tool currently activated.

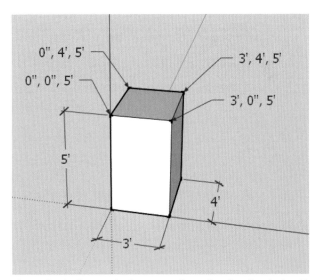

Figure 2–10: Every point has a coordinate that describes its location along the axes.

Four circled symbols in the bottom left-hand corner of the screen: These make pop-up screens appear. Re-click the circles to make the screens disappear.

- ▶ *?* activates the Instructor box.
- ▶ *G* logs in to your Google account (if you have one).
- ▶ *Human figure* gives information on the model, such as its properties.
- ▶ *Light bulb* gives the model's geographical location (if one has been specified).

The Measurements Box

Typing numbers is how you make SketchUp models accurate, and those numbers appear in the measurements box. Such numbers include line lengths; circle diameters; rectangle sizes; number of polygon sides; number of copies; distance to move, offset, or push/pull something; and rotation angles. You don't have to type them there, but that's where they'll show up. Some tools cause default numbers to appear there, which you'll over-type as needed.

The nature of the number that appears in the measurements box depends on which tool is activated. The number could mean inches, degrees, or number of sides. Line lengths are entered like this:

- ▶ *2'* means two feet
- ▶ *2'8* means two feet, eight inches. There is no space between the numbers or symbol.
- ▶ *2'8 1/2* means two feet, eight and one-half inches. There is a space between the eight and one.

As we cover different tools, how they're entered in the measurements box will be discussed.

Run Multiple SketchUp Files at the Same Time

On a PC, clicking **File>New** prompts you to save the current file. Upon saving, the file closes, and a new *instance* (open copy) of SketchUp opens. Clicking **File>Open** also prompts you to save the current file, and then navigates to another one.

To run multiple *instances*, which are copies of SketchUp software, right-click on the desktop icon and select *Open* or click on the icon of the file you want to open. Know that although you can run multiple instances, you can't run multiple files under one instance.

On a Mac you *can* have multiple files open in one instance. Clicking **File>Open** or **File>New** opens a new file without closing the current one. Since this mimics how most other software operates, its benefit is familiarity. Otherwise, it's irrelevant unless you're working on a network license, where the number of instances open must equal the number of licenses purchased.

Save Options

Under **File** there are four *Save* options. *Save* does just that—it saves the open file. *Save As* replaces the open file with a new one. *Save A Copy As* leaves the current file open and makes a closed copy at a location you choose. *Save as Template* makes a template out of your file. The file is saved with an *skp* extension. Files made in earlier versions of SketchUp can be opened in later ones, but files made with later versions cannot be opened in earlier ones. They must be saved as an earlier version first; do this by scrolling through the *Save as type* field at the bottom of the Save dialog box (Figure 2–11).

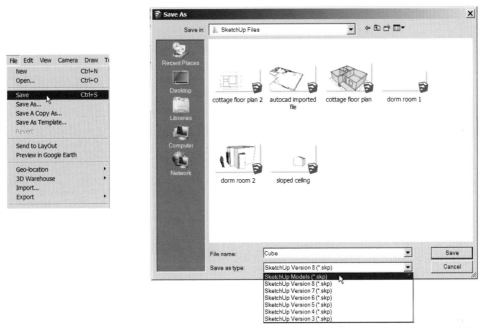

Figure 2–11: There are four *Save* options. SketchUp files can be saved in their current version or an older one in the Save dialog box.

Being so graphics-intensive, SketchUp occasionally crashes, so save often. You can program it to automatically save at a time increment of your choice at **Window>Preferences >General > Autosave**.

PC users exit the software at **File>Exit** or by clicking the *X* in the upper-right corner. Mac users go to **SketchUp>Quit SketchUp** to exit the software; clicking the red button in the upper-left corner just closes the active file, not the software (recall that you can have multiple files open in one instance).

We haven't saved this file yet, so do it now. Call it *Cube* and choose where on your computer to save it. Perhaps make a folder called *SketchUp files* and put all work from this book in it.

Backup Files

Backup files are automatically made in the same location as the *skp* file as long as the *Create Backup* box is checked at **Window>Preferences>General** (on the Mac, *Preferences* is under the **SketchUp** menu. They have an *skb* extension. Don't delete backups until done with a project, because they're useful if (oh, the horror!) the skp file gets corrupted or accidentally overwritten. SketchUp's backup files are unique in that they're the *previously* saved version of the model, not the last saved version. This is handy if you mess up a model after a save and need to backtrack a bit. Convert the *skb* file into an *skp* file by just overtyping the *b* with a *p*.

SketchUp also creates Autosave files at specific time increments after the last save (again, you can set those). That file is deleted once you save again or exit. If SketchUp crashes, the Autosave file remains, giving you almost up-to-date work.

Next up: Navigating around the workspace! Join me in Chapter 3, where we'll start learning tools.

Summary

SketchUp can run on a Windows, Android, or Apple platform. It requires a late-model computer and operating system and an IE or Safari browser. It's optimally used with a three-button mouse and keyboard, but can operate on Windows and Android tablets in a limited manner. Viewer apps are available for the iPad. Students can purchase cheap educational Pro licenses. Once SketchUp is installed, the user chooses a template and then proceeds to the workspace. SketchUp can run multiple simultaneous instances, but only by clicking a file icon, not by clicking **File>Open**. Four Save options exist, and the automatically created *skb* backup file is unique in that it preserves the next-to-last saved version.

Further Resources

Download a free SketchUp viewer for Windows and Mac devices: www.sketchup.com/products/sketchup-viewer

Download software to make a Wii controller work as a mouse. http://glovepie.org/glovepie.php

Info on the Space Navigator: www.3dconnexion.com/products/spacenavigator.html

Video about getting started with SketchUp: www.youtube.com/watch?v=OPkv9tRuO-c

Viewer app for SketchUp models for Apple and Android devices. http://limitlesscomputing.com/SightSpace

Viewer apps for SketchUp on the iPad, iPhone, and iTouch. www.viso3d.com/, http://limitlesscomputing.com

Exploring the Interface

I n Chapter 2 you installed and launched the SketchUp software, and saved a file called *Cube*. Open it, as we're going to
maneuver around the workspace now.

Select or Change a Template

We selected the *Architectural Design – Feet and Inches* template
in Chapter 2, which we'll continue to use. Each time you open
SketchUp, it defaults to the last template used. Change it
anytime by clicking on **Window >Preferences>Templates**
(PC) or **SketchUp>Preferences>Template** (Mac) and selecting
a new one (Figure 3–1). Your current template won't change,
but after exiting and reopening the program, the new one will
appear. Making a custom template is also possible and discussed
later in this chapter.

Add the Large Tool Set

The Getting Started toolbar doesn't contain every tool. There
are a lot more. On the PC, click **View>Toolbars**. This opens
the toolbar window, which shows them all (Figure 3–2). Check
the box in front of *Large Tool Set* to make that toolbar open
(Figure 3–3). On the Mac, click **View>Tool Palettes>Large
Tool Set**. Then run the mouse over each icon to read its *infotip*, a
pop-up menu that describes what it is and does.

Large Tool Set duplicates most of Getting Started's tools and
has a few others. We'll work with both toolbars open, and for
brevity, will mostly access tools through them throughout the
book. But they can also be accessed through the **Camera**, **Draw**,
and **Tools** menus at the top of the screen if you so choose.

Explore. Click on the menu items and read the submenus.
Shortcut fans can find a list of keys that activate tools at
Window>Preferences>Shortcuts (Figure 3–4), and assign
their own shortcuts. Now let's play with some of those tools.

**Objective: This chapter discusses
the SketchUp desktop and how to
maneuver around it.**

Tools: Select, Rectangle, Push/Pull,
Pan, Orbit, Zoom, Move, Undo

Concepts and Functions: desktop,
infotip menu bar, Getting Started
toolbar, Views toolbar, Standard
toolbar, Large Tool Set, human
scale figure, modeling window,
auto-select, measurements box,
axes, inference engine, inference
lines, dialog box, transparent tool,
Escape modifier keys, plan, elevation, perspective, paraline, isometric, selection window, crossing
window, template file

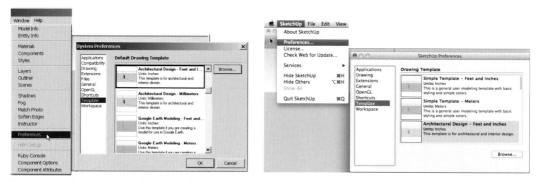

Figure 3–1: Clicking on **Windows>Preferences>Templates** (PC) or **SketchUp>Preferences>Templates** (Mac) takes you to this screen, where you can select a template.

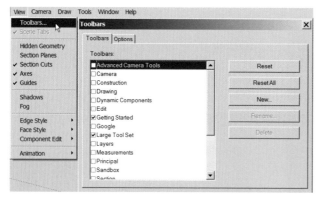

Figure 3–2: At **View>Toolbars**, add the *Large Tool Set* to the workspace.

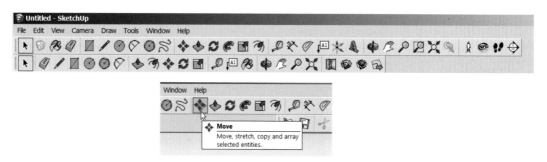

Figure 3–3: The Getting Started toolbar, Large Tool Set, and the Move infotip.

SketchUp for Interior Design

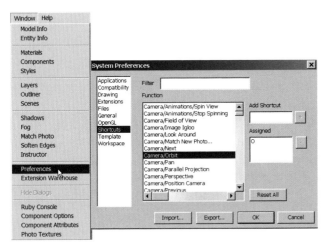

Figure 3–4: Activate tools via keyboard shortcuts.

The Select Tool

The *Select* tool (Figure 3–5) looks like an arrow. It highlights objects for editing. Click on it to activate it.

Figure 3–5: The Select tool.

An *Instructor box* appears each time a tool is activated. This is a dialog box that displays information about that tool (Figure 3–6). Links inside it take you to the SketchUp Knowledge Center. Clicking on a different tool changes the information in the Instructor. If the Instructor distracts you, go to **Windows>Instructor** and uncheck it. When you want it back, recheck. You can also make it appear and disappear by clicking the circled question mark in the lower-left corner of the modeling window.

With the *Select* tool activated, click on the human scale figure. A blue box appears, meaning that the figure is highlighted and ready for editing. Right-click inside that box and choose *Erase* from the context menu that appears (Figure 3–7). He's gone! No

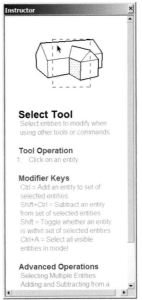

Figure 3–6: The Instructor box contains information about the activated tool. Turn it on and off at Windows>Instructor.

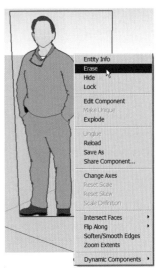

Figure 3–7: Right-clicking on a selected item brings up a context menu.

worries, go to **Edit >Undo Erase** and bring him back. Undo reverses the last action, and you can undo all actions one at a time until the last save. Then erase him again. You can always re-import when needed.

The Rectangle Tool

The Rectangle icon looks like a square (Figure 3–8). Click it.

Now click the cursor anywhere on the modeling window, drag, and release. You've just drawn a rectangle (Figure 3–9).

Figure 3–8: The Rectangle tool.

The Inference Engine

While dragging the rectangle, you may have noticed a diagonal dotted line appear and disappear (Figure 3–10). That's SketchUp's *inference engine* at work. The diagonal line appeared when the rectangle's proportions were dragged into a square shape.

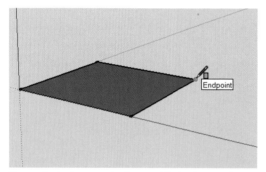

Figure 3–9: A rectangle drawn with the Rectangle tool.

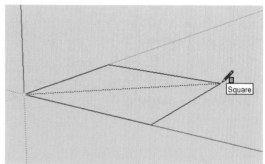

Figure 3–10: A diagonal inference line indicates that the rectangle is currently a square.

The inference engine is a geometric analysis feature that enables you to draw accurately. Depending on how and where you move the cursor, it assumes, or *infers*, the specific points, planes, and directions you want. You hover over the approximate location of the midpoint, endpoint, edge, or intersection, and then the actual midpoint, endpoint, edge, or intersection appears as a colored dot or line, and a *tooltip* will appear, a pop-up box with the inference name. Tip: Sometimes the inference you want won't pop up immediately. In that case, "encourage" it by moving the cursor over that area for a few seconds.

The inference engine enables you to make accurate models without having to constantly input dimensions. There are three kinds of inferences: *point* (e.g., to an endpoint or midpoint), *linear* (along the three axes), and *planar* (on the model's faces). To clarify planar inferencing, SketchUp "snaps" to a plane when it cannot snap to a specific piece of geometry.

But instead of abstractly discussing inferencing, we'll discuss it as we use it. For now, just go to **Edit>Undo Rectangle** (Figure 3–11), and then redraw the rectangle as a square by watching for the diagonal inference line and clicking when it appears.

The Push/Pull Tool

The *Push/Pull* tool (Figure 3–12) adds volume to, or subtracts volume from, faces by extruding (stretching) them. It's also an *auto-select* tool, meaning that when you move it onto a face, the face is highlighted. Not all tools highlight faces; generally, you have to highlight them in a separate action with the Select tool. Click the Push/Pull icon and then move the mouse onto the square you just drew. See how the face becomes dotted? That means it's selected and ready to edit.

Click, hold, drag the cursor up, and let go. The square is now a cube (Figure 3–13).

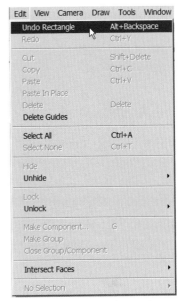

Figure 3–11: Every action can be immediately reversed with the *Undo* function in the Edit menu.

Figure 3–12: The Push/Pull tool.

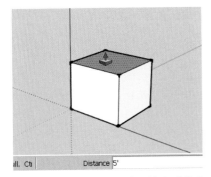

Figure 3–13: A cube made with Push/Pull.

Be aware that when the face being extruded is adjacent to another face, it will pull that face along (Figure 3–14). To keep the adjacent face intact, press and release the **Ctrl** key (**Command** on the Mac) right before performing the push/pull action. A plus sign will appear.

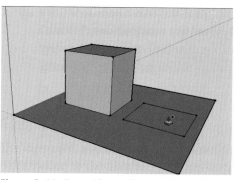
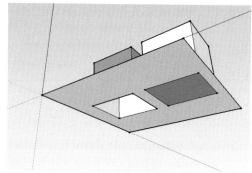

Figure 3–14: To avoid extruding an adjacent face, press and release **Ctrl** (**Command** on the Mac) right before push/pulling. Look for a plus sign. On the right graphic, the first extrusion was done without pressing the **Ctrl** key; the second extrusion was done while pressing it.

Input Numbers

To make the cube a specific size, type its dimensions while you model it. For example, after drawing the rectangle, type 5′,5′ to make it 5 feet on each side. The first dimension goes along the red axis; the second dimension goes along the green. Typing must be done immediately after releasing the cursor; if you perform any action in between, it won't work. Right after push/pulling, type 5′ to make it that high. Altering its dimensions later is covered in Chapter 4.

Since SketchUp's default is inches, the foot symbol must be included or you'll get a 5-inch-tall cube. SketchUp draws at a 1:1 scale, so the 5′ is true size.

Note that while 5′ appears in the measurements box in Figure 3–13, you don't have to type inside that box. You can type anywhere on the screen. Also note that even though we're using a feet/inches template, you can input other formats as long as you include their units after the number. Likewise, if you were working in a meter unit template, you could input feet and inches by adding their symbols. To change the units in a file you're working on, go to **Window>Model Info>Units** (Figure 3–15).

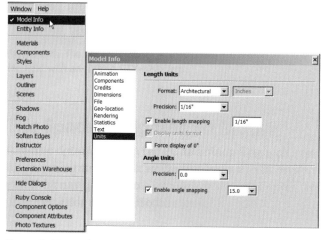

Figure 3–15: To change the model's units, go to **Window>Model Info>Units**.

The Pan and Orbit Tools

The *Pan* tool looks like a hand; click on it (Figure 3–16). Then click on the cube, hold, and drag it around the screen. You're panning, that is, moving it around the desktop. Now click on

Figure 3–16: The Pan and Orbit tools

the *Orbit* tool, the red and green arrows left of Pan. This whirls you, the viewer, around the cube; the cube itself doesn't move. Play with this tool—orbit on top, below, and behind the cube (Figure 3–17). If you hold the **Shift** key down while orbiting, you'll temporarily pan. The most efficient way to orbit is to hold the mouse scroll wheel down and drag it around.

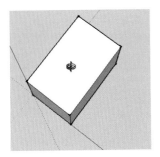
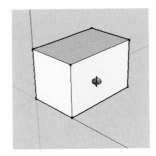

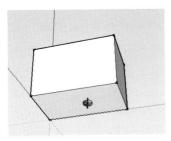

Figure 3–17: Orbiting around the cube.

Pan is useful to move geometry away from anything overlapping it, such as other geometry or *dialog boxes*, which are pop-up windows that appear with certain functions. Orbit is useful for spinning a model around to view it from all angles.

Pan, Orbit, and Zoom are *transparent tools*, meaning you can activate them while using another tool and then pick up the other tool where you left off. For instance, if you're drawing something with the Pencil and click on Orbit, the Pencil icon will become gray. When you click the Pencil to reactivate it, it will resume drawing in the location it was at before you clicked Orbit.

Modifier Keys

Modifier keys are keys pressed while using a tool to make it do something else. Examples so far are pressing the **Shift** key while orbiting to temporarily pan, and pressing the **Ctrl** key while push/pulling to keep a face intact. Here are PC and Mac modifier key equivalents:

PC	MAC
Alt	Command
Ctrl	Option
Enter	Return
Shift	Shift

The Escape Key

The **ESC** key quits an operation. It cancels dialog boxes, closes buttonless splash screens, closes menus, and quits functions. If you're in the middle of something and need to get out, just hit **ESC.**

The Zoom Tool

The *Zoom* icon is a magnifying glass to the right of the Pan icon (Figure 3–18). Zooming in brings you close to an object, which lets you home in on small details. Zooming out brings you farther away, which lets you see the big picture.

Figure 3–18: The Zoom tool.

Click the Zoom tool onto the model, hold the cursor down, and drag it up and down to zoom in and out (Figure 3–19). Even better, just rotate the scroll wheel on the mouse. The icon to Zoom's right—the magnifying glass with three arrows—is *Zoom Extents*. Clicking it makes the whole model fill up the window.

If you click Zoom Extents and your model hides off in a corner, it's because you've got little pieces of geometry you drew earlier still lurking around. Find and erase them, and your model will come back. Clicking Zoom Extents is a good way to locate small pieces that seem to have become lost.

The Views Toolbar: Generate Orthographic Drawings

You've probably noticed by now that the cube you modeled appears in perspective. That is, it looks the way the eye sees it: Parallel lines converge to vanishing points; it looks smaller when farther away and larger when near. Three-point perspective is SketchUp's default mode. However, you can make the model appear as a *paraline* view, which is a view in which parallel lines don't converge. Click on **Camera>Parallel Projection** (Figure 3–20). Now you see the cube as an *isometric* view (Figure 3–21), a type of paraline drawing in which the horizontal lines slope at a 30° angle.

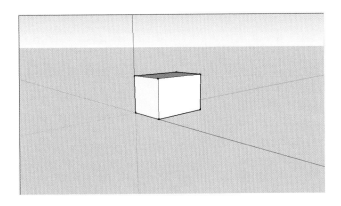

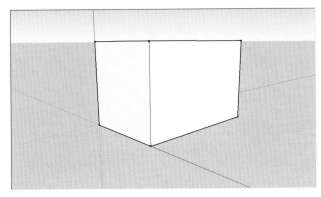

Figure 3–19: Zooming out (top) and in (bottom).

Figure 3–20: Click on **Camera>Parallel Projection** to see the model in a paraline view.

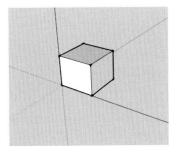

Figure 3–21: The cube seen as an isometric view. All parallel lines slope at a 30° angle.

Keeping parallel projection on, we're now going to do something that makes modeling software really shine. We'll generate orthographic views from this cube, specifically top, front, and side views—or in architectural drafting terms, the *plan* and *elevations*.

On the PC, click on **View>Toolbars** and check the *Views* box. A new toolbar appears with icons that look like 2D views of a house (Figure 3–22). On the Mac, go to **View>Customize Toolbar**. A tools dialog box appears on which tools and toolbars are stored (Figure 3–23). Drag the Views toolbar from this window into the Getting Started toolbar (Figure 3–24).

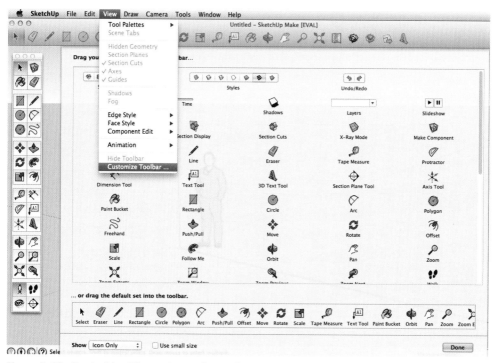

Figure 3–22: The Views toolbar.

Figure 3–23: On the Mac, **Views>Customize** Toolbar brings up a tools dialog box.

Figure 3–24: On the Mac, drag the Views toolbar into the Getting Started toolbar.

Clicking on the View toolbar's icons generates top, front, right, back, and left views (Figure 3–25). To return to the isometric view, click the View toolbar's first icon, the one whose tooltip says *iso*. Finally, click **Camera>Perspective** to return the model to a perspective view.

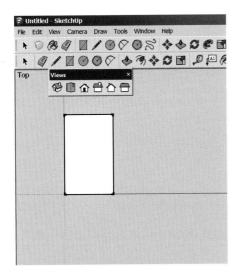

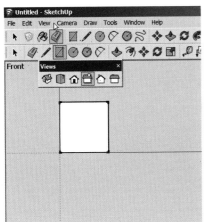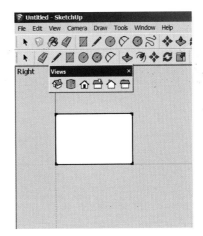

Figure 3–25: Top, front, and left side views generated from the model.

Select with Selection and Crossing Windows

Geometry must be selected before anything can be done with it. An efficient way to select it is by dragging a window around it (Figure 3–26). Activate the Select tool by clicking on it. Then click on the screen, hold the mouse down, and drag it from the upper-left corner to the lower-right. Let go. This creates a *selection window*. All geometry entirely within that window will be selected for editing. Now drag the mouse from the lower-right corner to the upper-left corner. This creates a *crossing window*. All geometry touched by that window, whether entirely inside it or not, will be selected. The cube is now highlighted—as evidenced by blue dots on its faces—and ready for editing.

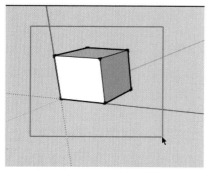
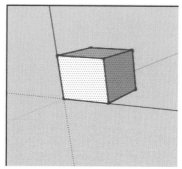

Figure 3–26: A selection window is dragged from the upper-left corner to the lower-right corner, and highlights everything inside it. A crossing window is dragged from the lower-right corner to the upper-left corner and highlights everything it touches. Blue dots indicate a selected face.

▶ As discussed in Chapter 2, SketchUp requires a strong video card. Performance issues with a weak one may include an inability to make selection windows and infotips not appearing. A quick fix is to go to **Preferences>OpenGL** and check *Use hardware acceleration*. What you're doing is bypassing the video card and making SketchUp do the calculations itself. Be aware that this will also slow the program down when you are working on large models.

Select by Clicking, Right-Clicking, and Holding the Shift and Control Keys

Click the Select tool once on a face to select it. Double-clicking selects a face plus its edges. Triple-clicking an edge or a face selects all attached geometry (Figure 3–27a). Holding the **Shift** key down brings up a +/- sign, indicating that you can add or remove individual pieces from the selection. Holding the **Ctrl** key down brings up a + sign, indicating that you can add individual pieces to the selection. Finally, you can just right-click on a selection, choose *select*, and pick from the options (Figure 3–27b).

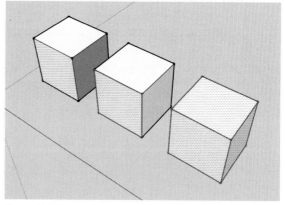

Figure 3–27a: Single-click to select a face. Double-click a face to select it and all its edges. Triple-click an edge or face to select everything attached to it.

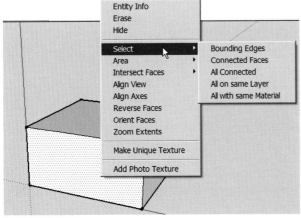

Figure 3–27b: Right-click the selection, choose *select*, and pick from the options.

The Move Tool

The Move tool (Figure 3–28) relocates selected geometry. Activate it. Then click on the cube and move it around! When you move parallel to the axes, lines that color-coordinate with those axes appear. They're *inference lines*, telling you that you are indeed parallel to the axis. Figure 3–29 shows the cube moving along the red axis.

Figure 3–28: The Move tool.

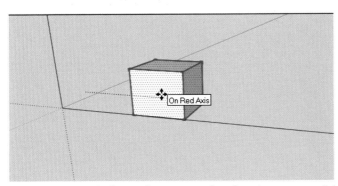

Figure 3–29: A red inference line appears when the cube moves parallel to the red axis.

Customize the Desktop

What if you don't like where the toolbars are? What if you don't like their shape? Personalize the workspace by customizing the toolbars and changing their locations.

Customize Toolbars on the PC

On the PC, toolbars can be undocked and moved by grasping their handles, the double lines at each end. Change their shape by stretching their edges. Remove a toolbar from the modeling window by unchecking it in the Toolbars window. Even the Measurements window can be moved by checking it in the Toolbars window and then dragging it where desired. Toolbars can also be moved off the workspace and onto the desktop to free up more modeling room (Figure 3–30).

Figure 3–31 shows how to make a custom toolbar. Open the Toolbars window and click *New*. In the pop-up box, type the name of the toolbar and hit **Enter**. The new toolbar is now listed with all the others. Drag and drop tools from other toolbars into it (the Toolbars window needs to remain open while you are doing this). This enables you to have only the tools you use taking up space on your screen.

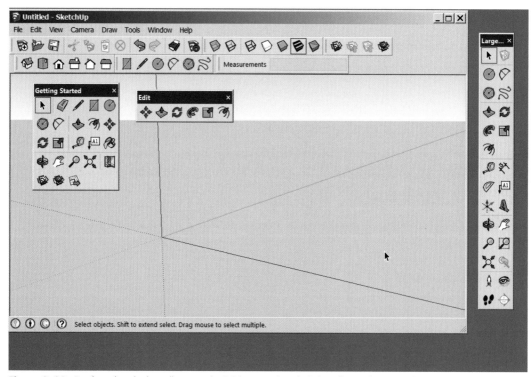

Figure 3–30: Dock and undock toolbars on the PC by grasping their handles and moving them. Stretch to resize. They can also be moved off the workspace.

A useful toolbar to activate is *Standard*, which contains the Windows utilities *Save*, *Cut*, and *Copy*. We'll be activating other toolbars as needed throughout the book.

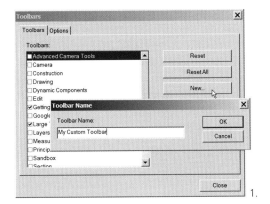
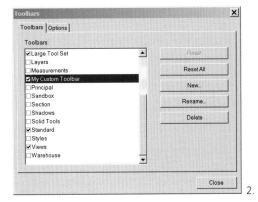

Figure 3–31: Make a custom toolbar by clicking **View>Toolbars** and choosing *New*.

Once you close SketchUp with the toolbars in their new docked positions and shapes, it will remember them each time it opens, as well as any screen size changes. To restore a native (original to the program) toolbar to its original state, highlight it and click *Reset* on the toolbar window. To alter the memory of toolbar placement and screen size, make the desired changes and then go to **Window>Preferences>Workspace** and click *Reset* (Figure 3–32).

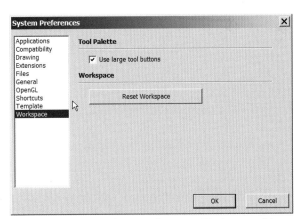

Figure 3–32: At **Window>Preferences>Workspace** click *Reset Workspace* to restore the native toolbars.

Customize the Getting Started Toolbar on the Mac

You can add, delete, and relocate tools on the Getting Started toolbar. Right-click on it and choose *Customize Toolbar* (Figure 3–33) or go to **View>Customize Toolbar.** The tools dialog box we saw earlier appears; drag individual tools from it into the Getting Started bar. Delete icons from Getting Started by dragging them out (they can always be retrieved from the dialog box again). Drag tools left and right to relocate. You can also drag additional toolbars from the dialog box onto the workspace. Note that the tools dialog box must be open while performing all these actions. Click *Done* to set. Toolbars on the Mac cannot be docked.

To restore Getting Started to its original state, remove all its tools, and then drag the *default set* toolbar at the bottom of the tools dialog box into it. SketchUp will remember any other modeling window changes made, such as screen size and location of other toolbars. To change that memory, make the desired changes and then go to **SketchUp>Preferences>Workspace** and click *Reset Workspace* (Figure 3–34).

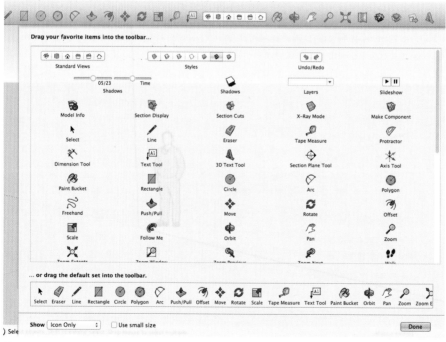

Figure 3–33: Mac users customize the *Getting Started* toolbar by dragging tools out of it or into it.

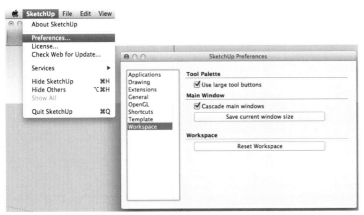

Figure 3–34: To change the memory of the workspace settings, make the desired changes, go to **SketchUp>Preferences>Workspace**, and click *Reset Workspace*.

Make a Custom Template

A *template file* is a predesigned file of default settings. You may want to create a file of custom settings once you start SketchUpping in earnest. Here's how:

1. Select **File>New** to open a new SketchUp file.

2. (Optional) Go to **Window>Model Info** and adjust whatever settings there you want, such as dimensions (discussed in Chapter 8).

3. (Optional) Go to **Window>Preferences** and adjust whatever settings there you want, such as the default image editor (discussed in Chapter 7).

4. (Optional) Go to **Window>Style** and adjust whatever settings there you want, such as color sets, shadows, and sketchy edges (discussed in Chapter 8).

5. (Optional) Draw anything you want all your models to have, such as a customized scale figure, or erase the scale figure if you don't want it.

6. (Optional) Add and alter toolbar sizes and positions.

7. Go to **File>Save As Template** to save this file.

8. Enter a name for this new template file and save. A thumbnail graphic will appear with the native (original) ones at **Preferences>Template** (Mac users, remember that, for you, the path is **SketchUp>Preferences**. PC users go to **Window>Preferences**).

9. (Optional) Check the *Set as Default Template* box. This will make it load each time you open SketchUp.

To delete that template, PC users go to **Preferences>Templates** and click the *Browse* button. That takes you to the directory where templates are stored. Find it, right-click, and delete (Figure 3–35). Mac users, follow this path: **Macintosh HD>Users/Library>Application. Support>SketchUp 2013/SketchUp.Templates**.

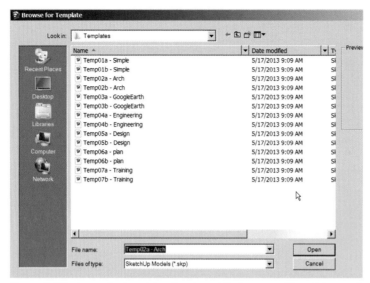

Figure 3–35: Access the templates directory at **Preferences>Templates**, and browse for the one to delete.

The Help Function

Stuck? Click on **Help>Knowledge Center**. The Help function is online; there is no local help. There's a search box there, but you may have better luck just typing your question directly into Google. It has probably already been asked and answered multiple times on one of the many online forums that discuss SketchUp.

Manage Dialog Boxes

Earlier we looked at the Instructor box. It's just one of many dialog boxes; see a list of more at the **Window** menu (Figure 3–36). As you use them, you'll quickly discover that managing them becomes an issue. Multiple open dialog boxes take up space, block out the model behind them, and frequently need to be moved out of the way. Click on the top bar of a dialog box to collapse it; click it again to expand. Stack multiple boxes together (Figure 3–37), and they'll move as a group. Keep a collapsed stack of frequently used boxes off to the side, maybe on the computer desktop.

Now that you can maneuver around the workspace, it's time to model something. Join me in Chapter 4, and we'll make some furniture.

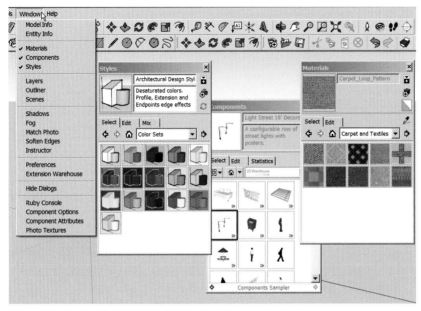

Figure 3–36: The Window menu shows a list of dialog boxes. Three of them are open here.

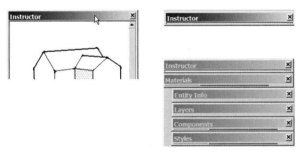

Figure 3–37: Click the top bar of a box to collapse it; click again to expand. Stack multiple collapsed boxes together to take up less room and move as a group.

Summary

Personalize the workspace with modified toolbars and custom templates. Combine tool use with the inference engine for quick, accurate modeling. The Select tool highlights geometry, which then can be edited. The Pan, Zoom, and Orbit tools maneuver around the modeling window; Rectangle makes faces; Push/Pull adds volume; Move relocates; and Esc gets you out. Generate 2D views with the Views toolbar, stack dialog boxes to manage them, and take questions directly to Google for quick answers.

Further Resources

The Push/Pull tool: www.youtube.com/watch?v=miC1hvWQjlQ

SketchUp channel on YouTube: www.youtube.com/user/SketchUpVideo

1. This exercise will get you comfortable with the SketchUp interface. Open the Eames Chair (Exercise 3–1) file in the Homework folder (this file was downloaded from the Trimble 3D Warehouse).

    www.wiley.com/go/sketchupforinteriordesign

    ▶ Use *orbit* to move around it and *pan* to move it around the modeling window.

    ▶ Zoom in and out of it.

    ▶ Change its view in the Camera menu from perspective to paraline, and then activate the **Views** toolbar.

    ▶ Click on the **Views** toolbar's icons to see the chair's different orthographic views.

    ▶ Click on the *iso* icon to return it to a 3D view, then click **Camera>Perspective** to return to a perspective view.

    ▶ Click the Select tool on the chair and notice the blue bounding box that appears. That will be discussed in Chapter 4.

2. Open a new SketchUp file. Customize the toolbars, and then save it as a template file. Close it, and then find and reopen it.

Modeling Furniture, Cabinetry, and Accessories

In Chapter 3 you maneuvered your way around the modeling workspace. Here you'll learn what a surface model consists of and how to use SketchUp's most basic modeling tools. You'll create a table, bookcase, and clock.

Faces and Edges

Open the Cube file made in Chapter 3. The cube, like all surface models, consists of *edges* and *faces*. Collectively, those edges and faces are called *geometry*.

Edges are lines. They're always straight and have no thickness. You can apply styles that make them appear thick, but that's just a display trick. Faces are coplanar surfaces, meaning flat like a piece of paper. They're bounded by at least three edges and also lack thickness. The front, called the *normal*, is white; the back is blue.

You can't have a face without edges, as the Eraser tool will now demonstrate.

The Eraser Tool and Erasing

The Eraser tool (Figure 4–1) only erases edges. Click it onto an edge to remove it. You can also drag the Eraser by holding the mouse key down to continuously erase multiple edges. However, the fastest way to erase a bunch of things at once is to select them and hit the **Delete** key.

Figure 4–1: The Eraser tool.

The Eraser doesn't erase faces. Instead, highlight the face with the Select tool, right-click, and choose *Erase* from the context menu. Figure 4–2 shows an edge and face being erased. Make sure when right-clicking that a tool is active, not Orbit, Pan, or Zoom, as they have different context menus.

▶ The second box on the top in Figure 4–2 could be the start of an interior perspective.

Objective: This chapter uses SketchUp's basic drawing and editing tools to create three models.

Tools: Pencil, Freehand, Eraser, Tape measure, Scale, Offset, Arc, Rotate, Circle, Component, Pencil

Concepts and Functions: edge, face, normal, geometry, rubber banding, fill, stickiness, group, nested group, bounding box, make a component, component axis, local axis, definition, instance, redo, grips, guide lines, guide points, shadows, hide, editing box, attributes, materials browser, collections, flip along axis, setting axis colors, cursor crosshairs, entity info box, Escape key, taper a leg, linear and radial array

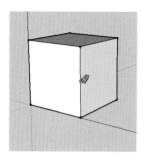
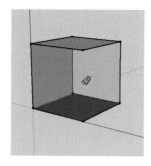

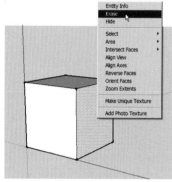
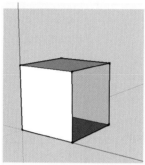

Figure 4–2: Erasing an edge makes the faces disappear. Erase faces by selecting them, right-clicking, and choosing *Erase* from the context menu. Or select them and hit *Delete*.

Go to **Edit>Undo** and click as many times as needed to restore the cube. Note there's a *redo* option also, in case you undo too many times. Or just drag a crossing window around it, hit **Delete,** and redraw it.

The Pencil and Freehand Tools

The Pencil, also called the Line tool, draws straight lines, which, in a model, are really edges. The Freehand tool draws irregular lines in any direction. Those irregular lines are actually curves, which, in SketchUp, are multiple line segments that behave as a single line (Figure 4–3).

Activate the Pencil and draw a line on the top of the cube from midpoint to midpoint. Find those midpoints by hovering over them until the cyan midpoint inference appears. Click, draw to the opposite side, and click on the midpoint inference again (Figure 4–4). Always draw parallel to the global axes unless the item you're modeling is skewed to the axes for a reason. Hold the **Shift** key to lock the Pencil along an axis.

Figure 4–3: The Pencil and Freehand tools.

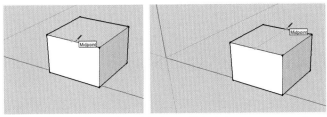

Figure 4–4: Hover over the midpoint until the inference appears, then click and drag the Line tool to the opposite midpoint.

The Pencil "rubber bands," meaning that the endpoint of one line is the start point of another. Clicking the **Esc** key exits the Pencil, as it does all other tools. If rubber banding annoys you, go to **Preferences>Drawing** and unclick *Continue line drawing* (Figure 4–5) to turn it off.

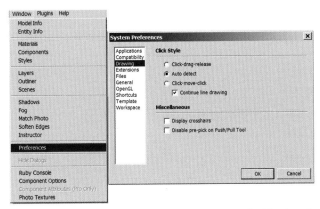

Figure 4–5: Adjust the settings to make the Line tool rubber band or not.

Note that in Figure 4–4 the line between the two midpoints is green. That's the inference engine telling you the line is parallel to the green axis. Once you click on the second midpoint, the line returns to black.

The Move Tool

The Move tool (Figure 4–6) relocates geometry. Activate and click it anywhere on the line you just drew. The Move tool is auto-selecting, meaning that it highlights geometry just by touching it. Now move the mouse straight up. When a blue inference line appears, you're moving parallel to the blue axis. Hold the **Shift** key down while using Move to lock the movement along an axis. Click the line at a random height to make a gable roof (Figure 4–7).

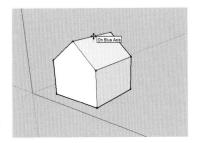

Figure 4–6: The Move tool.

Figure 4–7: Drag the line up with the Move tool to create a roof ridge.

Stickiness

When you moved that roofline, it took the planes on both sides with it. That's called *stickiness*—the fusion of objects that touch. Stickiness lets you do great things like create a gable roof simply by moving a line up. It can also be frustrating if you don't know how to work with it, because it will deform objects you didn't mean to deform. As an example, let's make an add-on to the house and then try to move it. Activate the Rectangle tool. Click it on the front and back corners of the house, as shown in Figure 4–8 (note the green endpoint inferences and tooltips that appear), and then move it any distance to the right to make a rectangle. Note that the rectangle *filled*, or colored in. That means a face was created. Next, push/pull the rectangle up until the blue midpoint inference point appears. Click on that point (Figure 4–9).

Drag a selection window around the house (Figure 4–10) to highlight it. You'll inadvertently select geometry you didn't mean to; in this case, four lines and one face on the block got selected. Press the **Shift** key. This brings up a plus and minus sign, meaning you can add or subtract individual pieces from the selection (Figure 4–11). Click the Select tool onto four lines and one face. This deselects them, leaving only the house highlighted.

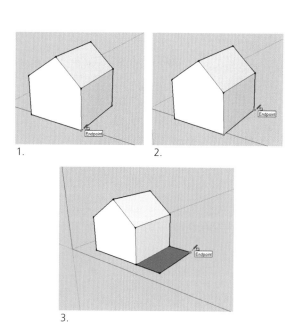

1.

2.

3.

Figure 4–8: Click the Rectangle tool on the front and back corners of the house, and then to the right, to make a rectangle.

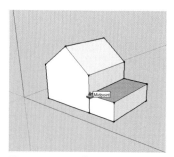

Figure 4–9: Push/pull the rectangle up to the house's midpoint.

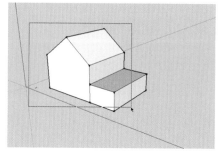

Figure 4–10: Drag a selection window around the house.

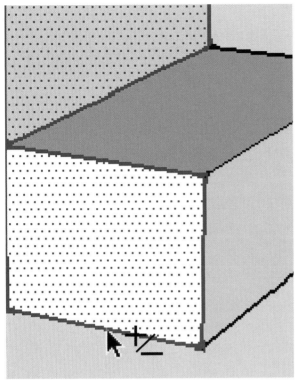

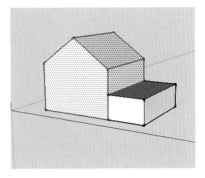

Holding the Shift key down while using the Select tool enables you to select and deselect individual pieces.

Now click Move on the house and do just that—move it around. See what happens? The house sticks to the block, causing the block to deform (Figure 4–12). Not good!

Click **Edit>Undo** to restore the block and house to the way they were before moving the house.

Groups

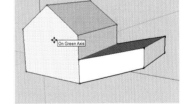

Figure 4–12: Moving the house causes the block fused to it to also move, resulting in deformity.

Here's how to manage SketchUp's stickiness. Make a *group*, which is a collection of loose geometry inside an invisible shell. Any geometry can go in a group: edges, faces, text, dimensions, cutting planes. Groups can even contain other groups, which collectively are called a *nested* group.

A group is isolated from the rest of the model's geometry, so it doesn't stick to anything. In addition to solving the stickiness issue, groups let you manipulate—move, rotate, scale, paint, etc.—all the pieces inside them as a whole. Copies of groups are independent of each other.

Make a Group

Activate the Select tool and reselect the house (deselect any part of the block that gets caught in the selection window). Right-click on it and choose *Make Group* (Figure 4–13). A blue *bounding box* appears. This is the invisible shell that encloses the loose geometry, and signifies that it is indeed a group.

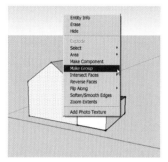 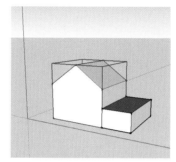

Figure 4–13: Select the house, right-click, and choose *Make Group*. A blue bounding box appears around it.

Everything in that box is in the group. To deselect, click somewhere off the group. Now click the Move tool on the house again, and move it around. It easily moves without taking the block along (Figure 4–14).

The bounding box should be about the same size as the geometry inside it. If it's much bigger, you inadvertently included something else in it. Right-click on the group and choose *Explode* from the context menu. This returns the group to its individual edges and faces. Then carefully select and group it again.

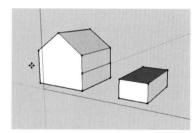

Figure 4–14: Groups don't stick to other geometry.

Edit a Group

Separating the house and the block left a line on the house, a common occurrence. It should be erased if not needed, because a line divides a face into two faces. Confirm this by push/pulling the top and bottom parts independently. Keep your model "clean" by removing unnecessary geometry.

We can't apply the Eraser directly to the line because that will make the whole group disappear. Instead, double-click on the group to open its *editing box* (Figure 4–15). Everything outside the group turns gray, and cannot be selected. Everything inside the box is fair game, so erase the line now. Close the editing box by activating the Select tool and clicking somewhere off the group.

You can draw a line on a group outside its editing box, but that line won't be part of the group and will get left behind when you move the group, unless you specifically select it, too. Loose geometry and groups can occupy the same space, which can be confusing when you're first learning SketchUp. It's easy to think you're adding lines to a group when you're actually drawing them over the group. We'll discuss this in more detail in later chapters.

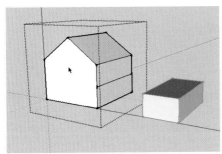
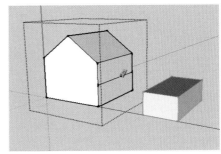

Figure 4–15: Changes to a group must be made inside its editing box, which is activated by double-clicking.

Causes of a Non-Filling Face

Before we start our project, let's discuss a common modeling problem: tracing a perimeter that won't fill. No fill means no face. If you're not sure if a face has formed or not, click the Select tool on it. A face will become covered with highlighting dots. No dots mean no face.

The following are the causes of a non-filling face:

The model is very large or very small. SketchUp doesn't deal well with either, and other problems may arise with extreme sizes, too. If that describes your model, make it smaller or larger and see if that helps. You can always scale it to size later, which we'll discuss in this chapter.

A line is unconnected. See if this is the case by clicking **Window>Styles>Edit** and checking the *Profiles* box to turn profiles on, or by increasing the profiles number. That makes any line not connected to others on both sides appear thinner than lines that are connected on both sides.

Overlapping geometry. See if this is the case by making the model transparent at **View>Face Style>X-ray**. Zoom in closely to look for small overlapping pieces.

The face is not coplanar. This is because:

1. The endpoints aren't aligned. They may be misaligned just enough to form a subdivided plane, one where a face forms if a diagonal line is drawn across it. See if SketchUp supplied a hidden diagonal line by clicking **View>Hidden Geometry**. Alternatively, click the Text tool on each endpoint, hold the mouse down, and drag. This creates a leader line and text field in which each point's *x*, *y*, and *z* coordinates

appear (Figure 4–16). A coplanar face must have endpoints that share an identical *x, y,* or *z* coordinate. Exactly which one depends on the face's orientation.

Or

2. *One line isn't parallel to the rest of the lines.* Assuming you're modeling parallel to the global axes (the best way to model), set all lines so they match the color of their parallel axes. Any line not parallel will be black.

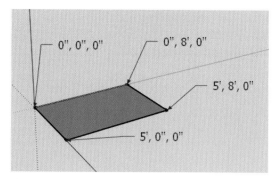

Figure 4–16: Click the Text tool on a face's corners to reveal their coordinates. This horizontal face's endpoints have the same *z* coordinate, indicating coplanarity.

Best Practices

Start your model on or near the origin. Certain tools simply operate better there, plus SketchUp sometimes gets glitchy when the model is far from the origin.

Model in the upper-right quadrant. Number coordinates are positive there, making inputted numbers and calculations easier.

Align the front of your model (the longest side) with the red axis. This makes it work best with the Views toolbar.

Model all lines (edges) parallel to the axes. This facilitates accuracy, coplanar faces, and, again, works best with the Views toolbar. This is so important that we're going to color-coordinate the lines of our first project with the axes to help develop your "feel" for when you're modeling along the axes and when you're not.

Color-Coordinate the Model's Lines with the Axes by Changing the Edge Style Setting

Styles are display settings that change the model's appearance. Line color, thickness, and endpoint size are examples of those settings. More are discussed in Chapter 8.

Figure 4–17 shows how to change the color of lines (edges) to coordinate with their parallel axes. Click on **Window>Styles** to open the Styles dialog box. Click the *Edit* tab to bring up the edit panel. Then click the first icon, *Edge Settings*. At the bottom of the panel is a Color field. Scroll to *By axis.* This will color-coordinate the edges with the axes they're parallel to, and take effect immediately. Note that the roof's sloped lines remain black. This is because they're not parallel to any axis.

1.

2.

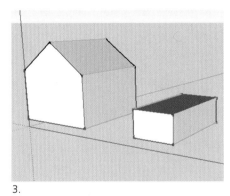

3.

Figure 4–17: Click **Windows>Styles** to open the Styles dialog box, then the *Edit* tab, then the *Edge Settings* icon; then scroll to *By axis* in the Color field. The model's edges will immediately color-coordinate with the axes they're parallel to.

Another aid in modeling accurately is activating the cursor's crosshairs. They color-match the axes, too (Figure 4–18), providing instant visual feedback when lines aren't parallel to the axes. Go to **Preferences>Drawing** and check *Display crosshairs*.

 ## Model a Table

So! It's time to implement these tools and techniques. Let's model the table in Figure 4–19. Go to **File>Save** and choose *Save As*. Type *Table* in the pop-up screen. This will save and close the Cube file and make a new file active

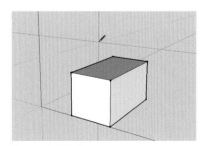

Figure 4–18: The cursor's crosshairs color-coordinate with the axes, providing instant visual feedback when lines aren't parallel to the axes. Activate them at **Preferences>Drawing**, and check *Display crosshairs*.

called *Table*. It will have the same settings as Cube, including the color-by-axis setting. Drag a selection window around the house and block, right-click, and choose *Erase* to clear the screen.

Model the tabletop (Figure 4–20). Activate the Rectangle tool, click it on-screen, and type *6',3'*. The first number goes along the red axis, the second along the green (don't forget to type the foot symbol, since the default is inches—and remember, you can type anywhere on the screen). Next, push/pull the rectangle up a little bit and let go. Immediately type *2"*. The top will adjust to a 2" thickness.

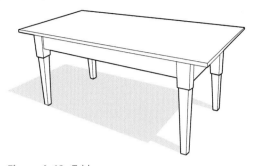

Figure 4–19: Table.

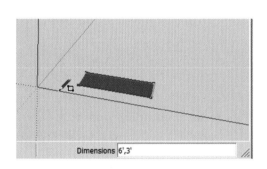

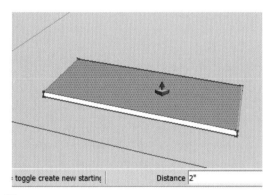

Figure 4–20: Make a rectangle 6' × 3' and push/pull it up 2".

Make the tabletop a group. Drag a selection window around the tabletop, right-click, and choose *Make Group* (Figure 4–21).

We could use some guide lines for leg placement.

Guide Lines and Guide Points

Guide lines are dashed, infinite-length construction lines. Guide points are marks at specific locations. Both can be made anywhere on the screen. Neither is part of the model; they're strictly for construction purposes. They can be hidden, erased, moved, and rotated. The Tape Measure is needed to make them.

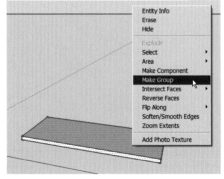

Figure 4–21: Select the tabletop, right-click, and choose *Make Group*.

The Tape Measure Tool

The Tape Measure (Figure 4–22) measures lines and creates guide lines and guide points.

Measure a line by clicking the Tape Measure on the endpoints. Create guide lines by dragging a model line with the Tape Measure to the desired guide line location. Create guide points by clicking the Tape Measure on an endpoint or midpoint and then clicking on the desired guide point location.

The Tape Measure also scales the model bigger or smaller. Click it on two endpoints, type the desired size, and hit **Enter**. Be aware that the whole model will resize, not just the item you clicked on. To affect only that item, group it and rescale inside its editing box.

Click the Tape Measure on two of the tabletop's endpoints, and 6′,3′ should appear in the Measurements box, confirming your dimensions. The measuring tape functions like an inference line, changing colors to match parallel axes. The Measurements box dynamically displays the length of the measuring tape as the mouse moves.

Click the Tape Measure on a line, move it away, and click again. A dashed line appears. Click the Tape Measure on an endpoint or a midpoint, and then click anywhere on or off the model. A guide point appears. Too many can interfere with inference engine accuracy, however, so erase them when they're no longer needed. They can be erased individually or all at once at **Edit>Delete Guides**. If you think you might use them again, hide them at **Edit>Hide**.

Draw guide lines. Orbit under the table, click the Tape Measure on an edge, move the Tape Measure to the right, let go, and immediately type 2″. A guide line 2″ from the edge appears (Figure 4–23). Place guide lines on the other three edges. Note that you can click the Tape Measure a second time and type 2″, and the guide line location will readjust. You must type 2″ before doing any other operation, though.

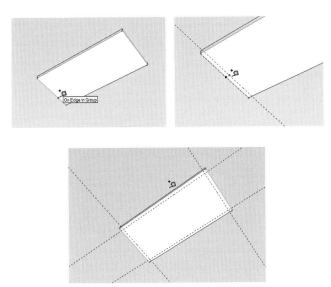

Figure 4–23: Click the Tape Measure on a line, move it in the direction in which the guide line is needed, let go, and type 2″ to create a guide line 2″ from the edge.

Draw the top of one leg. Click the Rectangle tool on the intersection shown in Figure 4–24, and then click a second point. Immediately type *4,4*. The rectangle adjusts to a square 4″ on each side. Again, don't do anything between making the rectangle and typing, or it won't work. To change the rectangle's size later, the Scale tool (discussed later in this chapter) is needed.

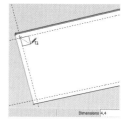

Components

Like a group, a component is a collection of geometry that moves together and doesn't stick to anything. Unlike a group, a change to the *definition* (original) component applies to all *instances* (copies) of it. This makes components a very powerful modeling tool. When multiple copies are needed, make them components. Not only can you update each by updating one, components take up less file space than groups, which becomes an issue as the model is developed.

Figure 4–24: Draw a 4″ × 4″ square to serve as the top of the leg.

Most components are 3D, but there are also 2D ones. These take up less space than 3D, so are suited for entourage items (e.g., trees and people). The human scale figure is a 2D component.

Edit a Component and Make It Unique

As with a group, changes to a component must be made within its editing box; double-click to open. And like a group, loose geometry and components can occupy the same space, so it's easy to think you're editing the component when you're really just drawing outside its shell.

Earlier we learned that changes made to the definition component affect all instances of it. However, you may want to change one component and leave the rest intact. There are two ways to do this.

▶ Select (highlight) the component and apply changes outside the editing box. A common example is using the Scale tool to make it bigger or smaller than other components.

▶ Select one or more components, right-click on one, and choose *Make Unique* from the context menu. Subsequent edits will affect only the one(s) made unique. Change those components' names while you're at it, so you can later tell them apart when viewing a list in a tool called the Outliner (which we'll discuss in Chapter 6).

Make a Component Table Leg

Let's make the square a component, copy it once, and then turn it into a leg.

Make a component. Highlight the square and click the Component tool. Alternatively, right-click the highlighted square and choose *Make Component* from the context menu (Figure 4–25). A dialog box appears. Overtype the default "Component 1" in the *Name* screen with *table leg*.

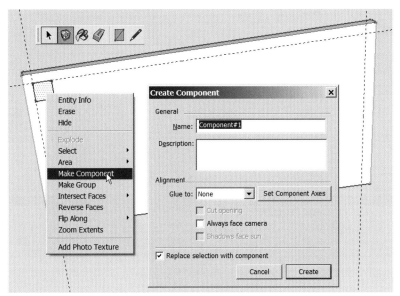

Figure 4–25: To make a component, select the geometry, and then click the Component tool. Alternatively, select the geometry, right-click, and choose *Make Component*. The Component dialog box will appear.

Component Options

Now we're offered options. They are:

▶ *Set the component (local) axis.* Every component has its own axis. It sets orientation upon insert and is the "handle" when moved. The default alignment is with the global axes, and the origin is in the corner of the bounding box closest to the global origin.

▶ *Set the alignment.* This applies to components to be attached to faces, not stand-alone components. The alignment option determines which face the component "glues" or snaps to. If your component is a window, door, or wall art, choose *vertical* to make it snap to walls. A vertical orientation will also make the component automatically rotate when moved to a perpendicular wall.

▶ *Cut opening.* This appears when any alignment setting besides *none* is chosen. It's relevant to door and window components, to make them cut holes in the walls they're placed on.

▶ *Set the component to always face the camera.* This is how the scale figure operates. Have you noticed that no matter which way you orbit, he always faces you?

▶ *Replace selection with component.* Click this box. Otherwise, what you've selected will not be made a component.

▶ *Always face camera box.* This is relevant when making 2D components. Check it; otherwise, you'll see the unfinished backside when orbiting.

The only option relevant to our current project is *Replace selection with component*. So check that box, name the component, and click *Create*.

Copy the component. Select it, activate the Move tool, and then press the **Ctrl** key (**Command** key on the Mac). **Ctrl** serves as a modifier to make the tool copy instead of move. Grab a corner, slide the copy to the other side, and align to a guide line (Figure 4–26).

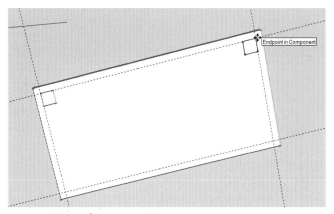

Figure 4–26: Use the Move tool plus the Ctrl key to copy the leg component.

Make the square a block. Activate the Select tool and double-click the component to open its editing box. Click the Push/Pull tool on the square, extrude it down a random distance, and type 6. The leg will adjust to a 6″ length (Figure 4–27). Note that this affected the copied component, too.

Add the leg's lower part. Place guide lines 1″ from each of the block's edges and inscribe a 2″ × 2″ square inside the larger square, using either the Pencil or Rectangle tool. Then push/pull that square down 26″ (Figure 4–28).

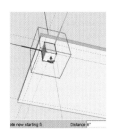

Figure 4–27: Double-click on the component to open its editing box, and push/pull the square down to make it a 6″ block.

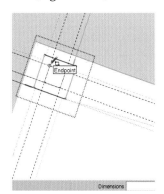

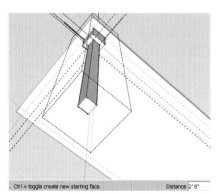

Figure 4–28: Draw guide lines 1″ from each edge of the square for inscribing a smaller square. Then push/pull it down 26″.

Edit the Table Leg's Length

If you later want to add inches to the leg's length, open the editing box, select the bottom of the leg, and stretch it out a random length with Push/Pull. Then type a specific number and hit **Enter**. That number will get *added* to the existing length. To make the leg shorter, push/pull the leg closer to the tabletop, type a number, and hit **Enter**. That number will be *subtracted* from the existing length. When finished, right-click the Select tool anywhere on the screen to close the editing box. To taper the leg, we need the Scale tool.

The Scale Tool

The Scale tool (Figure 4–29) can resize a whole model or just part of it.

Figure 4–30 shows the process for tapering the rectangular leg. Select its bottom surface by clicking twice to activate both the face and its four edges. Then activate the Scale tool. The selected part is automatically highlighted with green cubes called

Figure 4–29: The Scale tool.

grips. Hover the mouse over a corner grip. It will turn red to show that it's activated. Grab that red grip and press the **Ctrl** key, which will force scaling around the center of the selection. Then move the grip inward to taper the leg. Click the Select tool outside the editing box to close. Note how the leg edges are now black, because they're not parallel to any axis.

Different grips create different scaling effects. Corner grips scale proportionally (as does holding down the **Shift** key while holding any grip). Edge and side grips distort geometry.

You can "eyeball" proportions or type numbers for precision. For example, to adjust the table leg to 24″ long, triple-click on it with the Select tool to highlight it all. Then activate Scale. The grips will appear on all sides. Grab one grip, drag it a random length in any direction, then immediately type *24,24,24*. The leg will adjust to that size. Typing *0.5* will scale it down to half its size.

To change the tabletop's size, select it (include its thickness), and activate Scale. Grab a grip, randomly move it, and type two numbers separated by a comma. Remember that the first number scales along the red axis, and the second number scales along the green. Basically, you're scaling a thick rectangle.

The Scale tool can resize whole interior spaces. For instance, if you have a 10′ × 15′ room that is 9′ tall, and you want it to be 15′ × 20′ without changing the ceiling height, select everything and type *15,20*. The floor area will change, but the height won't.

The Tape Measure can also scale a model based on one known dimension. We'll do that in Chapter 5.

Create an apron (Figure 4–31). Draw a 1″ × 4″ rectangle at the top of one of the table legs, and then push/pull that rectangle. Make sure to click on an *Edge* inference at the opposite end.

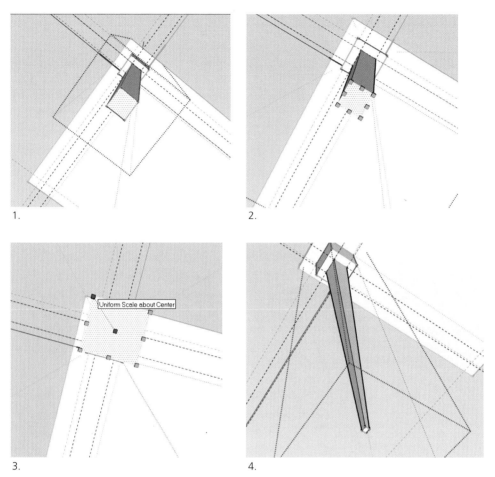

Figure 4–30: 1. Select the leg bottom. 2. Activate the Scale tool. 3. Grab a corner grip and press the **Ctrl** key to scale the leg about the center. 4. The leg is tapered.

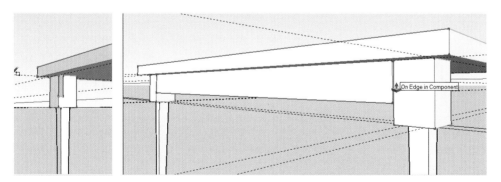

Figure 4–31: 1. Draw a 1″ × 4″ rectangle. 2. Push/pull it to the opposite leg.

Make a second apron and copy/flip it (Figure 4–32). Triple-click on the apron to select all its edges and faces. Then hold the **Shift** key down and click on the two leg components to add them to the selection. Group all three for easier manipulating. Copy the group off to the side with Move and **Ctrl.** Select it (don't open the editing box, just highlight it), right-click, and choose *Flip Along>Group's Green.* This mirrors it. Then move it back into place.

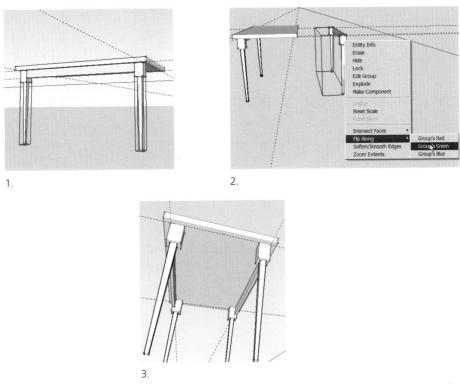

1.

2.

3.

Figure 4–32: Make a group out of the apron and table legs, then copy and flip it. Move the copied apron into place, aligning it with the guide line.

Make an apron for the table's short end (Figure 4–33). Push/pull a 1″ × 4″ rectangle, group it (just the apron, not the legs), copy it, and place the copy at the other end, aligning with the guide line. Flipping isn't needed.

Delete all guides, because a bunch will affect inference engine accuracy. Erase them individually with the Eraser tool. If they were created inside a group or component, they must be erased within the editing box. Or erase them all at once via **Edit>Delete Guide lines**, which will include ones inside groups and components. If you think you'll need the guides later, hide them at **Edit>Hide**, and bring them back at **Edit>Unhide**.

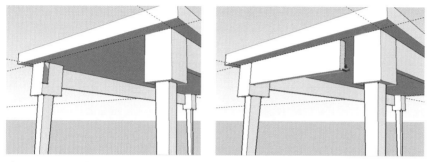

Figure 4–33: Make an apron for the table's short end by push/pulling a 1′ × 4″ rectangle.

Return all edges to black by going to **Window>Styles>Edit**, clicking on the *Edge Settings* icon, and scrolling to *all same* in the Color box. As a final touch, click **View>Shadows** to throw down a shadow (Figure 4–34). Voila! The finished table.

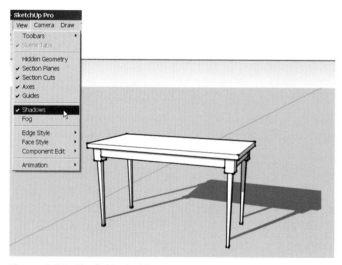

Figure 4–34: The finished table.

Model a Bookcase

Let's model the bookcase in Figure 4–35. Open a new file, ensure the template is set to *Architectural Design -feet and inches* (it should be the default if you haven't changed it since the Table file), and delete the scale figure.

Make a block (Figure 4–36). Draw a rectangle 48″ × 24″ on or near the origin, and push/pull it 72″ (6′) high. To turn the block into a shell, we'll need the Offset tool.

Figure 4–35: Bookcase with glass doors and four shelves.

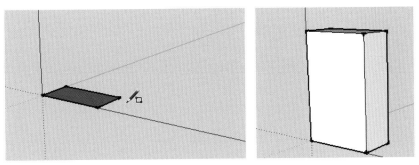

Figure 4–36: Model a 48″ × 24″ × 72″ block.

The Offset Tool

The Offset tool (Figure 4–37) creates copies of faces and edges at a specified distance from the originals. It also works on two or more connected, coplanar lines. Offset is auto-selecting, so just hover it over a face to select. Grab one of the face's edges, move it in or out, then type a specific distance to offset, or just click somewhere. Offsetting a face creates a new face.

Figure 4–37: The Offset tool.

Make a shell (Figure 4–38). Click Offset on one of the block's edges. Drag it toward the center of the block and release. Immediately type 4; it will adjust to a 4″ offset. Next, click Move on the bottom edge. The edge will self-select; move it straight up along the blue axis, release, and type 1′ (or 12). Finally, push/pull the face inward, release, and type 1′10″ (or 22).

Turn the shell into a group (Figure 4–39). Select the entire shell with a selection window or by clicking three times anywhere on it (remember, a triple-click selects all connected faces and edges). Right-click and choose *Make Group.* Now we can place shelves inside it that won't stick.

Make a shelf component (Figure 4–40). Click the Rectangle on the lower-left and upper-right corners of the shell's bottom. Double-click to select the rectangle face and edges, then right-click and choose *Make Component.*

Now let's *array*, or make multiple copies of that shelf.

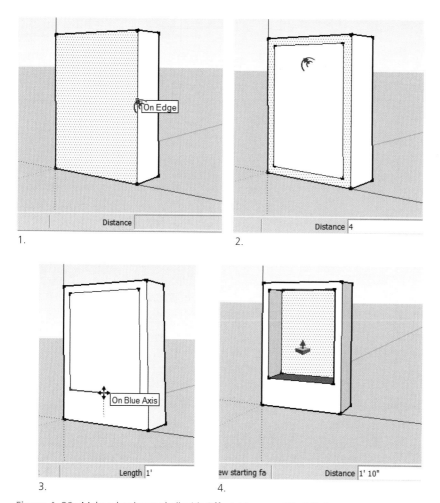

Figure 4–38: Make a bookcase shell with Offset, Move, and Push/Pull.

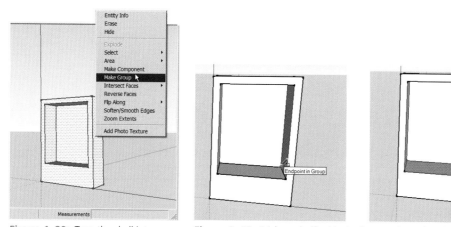

Figure 4–39: Turn the shell into a group.

Figure 4–40: Make a shelf with the Rectangle tool, and then turn it into a component.

Linear Array: Make Multiple, Equally Spaced Copies

A *linear array* is equally spaced copies along a straight line. You can array copies between two endpoints (think shelves inside a bookcase) or array copies with a specific distance between them (think a row of trees in a park).

To array equally spaced copies between two endpoints, make the original, select it, copy it with Move plus **Ctrl**, and place the copy the distance you want from the original. The original and the copy define the endpoints. Next, type / and the number of total copies wanted—for example, /5. This will net four copies equally spaced between the original and first copy (so five copies total). You must type /5 immediately after placing the first copy; don't perform any other action.

To array multiple copies with a specific distance between them, make the original, select it, make one copy with Move plus **Ctrl**, and then place the copy the distance you want from the original. Type x followed by the number of copies wanted—for example, x5. This will net four more copies (so five copies total), each separated by the same distance as between the original and first copy.

Array the shelf component (Figure 4–41). Copy the shelf and move the copy to the top of the bookcase shell. Type /4. This nets three shelves between them. Remember not to do anything else between placing the first copy and typing. If you inadvertently do an intermediate action, go to **Edit>Undo**, recopy the shelf, and type /4 again.

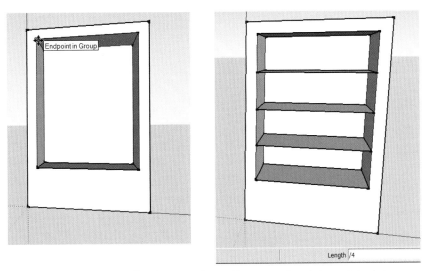

Figure 4–41: Copy the shelf to the top and type *l4* to create three intermediate shelves.

Erase both the original shelf and the first copy (Figure 4–42). We only needed them to define the endpoints, that is, the array distance. Select them, right-click, and choose *Erase*.

Change the shelves' height and depth. Click on one shelf to open its component editing box. Push/pull it 2″ up and 2″ back (Figure 4–43). Activate the Select tool and click it anywhere on the screen to close the editing box.

First copy

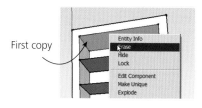

Original shelf

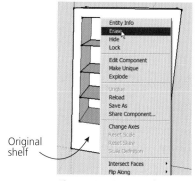

Figure 4–42: Erase the original shelf and first copy.

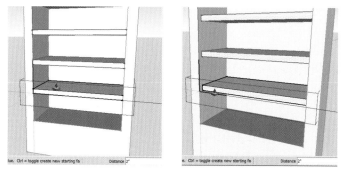

Figure 4–43: Edit one component shelf's height and depth.

Add the curved apron. Double-click on the bookcase to activate the group editing box. We want to draw a line 12″ above the bottom. Make a guide point as a reference mark by clicking the Tape Measure on the bottom-right corner, moving it up, and typing *12*. The guide point will appear 12″ from the bottom.

Starting at the guide point, draw a line with the Pencil across the bookcase, parallel to the red axis. Make sure the *On Face* inference appears, confirming that you are indeed drawing on the bookcase's face (Figure 4–44).

To draw the apron's curve we need the Arc tool.

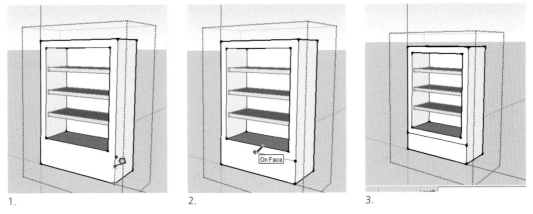

1.   2.   3.

Figure 4–44: Place a guide point 12″ above the bookcase's bottom edge, and draw a horizontal line there.

The Arc Tool

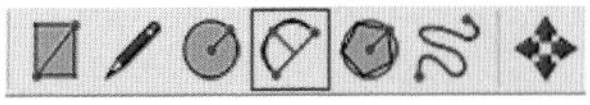

The Arc tool (Figure 4–45) makes circular arcs—which, in SketchUp, are actually 12 straight, connected lines edited as a single arc. If you want more than 12 segments to make the arc look smoother, type that number right after activating the Arc tool, and hit **Enter**.

Figure 4–45: The Arc tool.

    Click Arc twice to define the endpoints, and then lift the bulge. Alternatively, type numbers for the arc's length, radius, and bulge.

    The arc's shape can be somewhat manipulated by clicking the Scale tool on it and pulling the grips. However, you can't make French curves with it. You might try the Freehand tool for that, or better yet, a Bezier curves plugin (a plugin is add-on software).

    After an arc is made, its size can be modified through the Entity Info box.

The Entity Info Box

Entity Info is a dialog box that shows a piece of geometry's *attributes* (properties and characteristics). Select, right-click, and choose *Entity info*. Different options will appear based on what's selected. The Entity Info boxes for circles, polygons, arcs, and lines have fields to change size and length, and to add line segments (Figure 4–46).

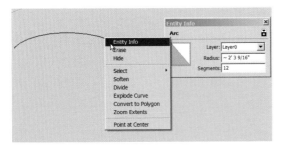

Figure 4–46: Change an arc's size via its Entity Info box.

Now click the Arc on the bookcase bottom's endpoints, and lift the bulge up (Figure 4–47). You can eyeball a distance or type a specific radius. I typed 9″. Note the *On Face* inference. It's so important to pay attention to inference pop-ups, because they tell you if you're placing your entities where you think you are. If you don't see *On Face*, you may be tilting the arc back instead of pulling it straight up. Finally, push/pull the arc through the bookcase shell (click on the shell's back edge to finish the push/pull operation).

Make a component door (Figure 4–48). We'll place it outside the group, so don't open the editing box. Draw a rectangle on the shell, using corner and midpoint inferences. Make the rectangle a component called *Door.* Then double-click to open the editing box, and push/pull it 1″ thick.

Add 4″-wide rails and stiles to the component door (Figures 4–49, 4–50). Click the Tape Measure on the top and bottom door edges, and then click it 4″ away to make guide points; draw vertical lines from those guide points down, to make stiles. Do the same thing at the top and bottom to make rails. For the center stile, draw a line down the middle of the door, copy it 1″ on both sides, and then erase the original line (Figure 4–51).

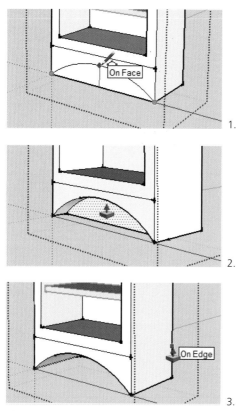

Figure 4–47: Using the Arc tool to make a curved apron.

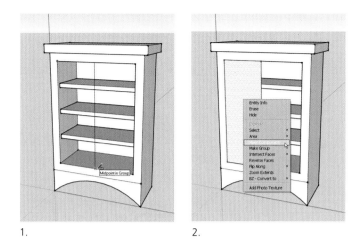

1.

2.

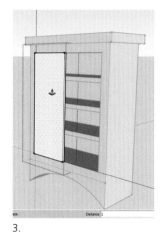

3.

Figure 4–48: Make a component door.

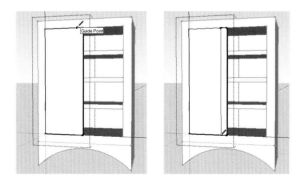

Figure 4–49: Draw the stiles.

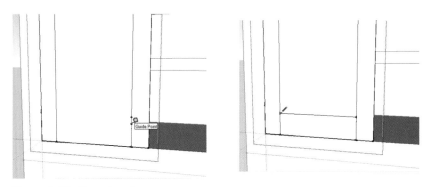

Figure 4–50: Draw the rails.

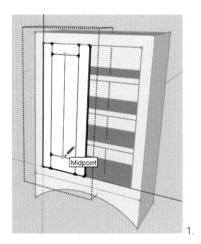

1.

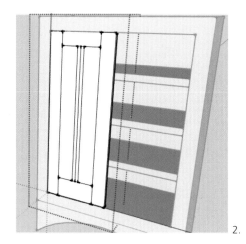

2.

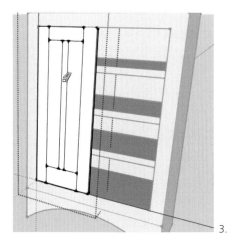

3.

Figure 4–51: Draw the center stile.

Make a second component door and mirror it (Figure 4–52). Copy the door and slide the copy along the red axis off to the side. Select it, right-click, and choose *Flip Along Component's Red.* Now that it's a mirror of the first door, editing applied to one will appear in reverse on the other. Grab it by a corner and move it into place.

Make the top trim piece (Figure 4–53). Orbit to the top of the bookcase, open its editing box, and select the bookcase's edges (click Select on each edge while holding down the **Shift** key). Selecting the edges instead of the face means the bookcase's height won't be affected. Offset the edges 2″ and then push/pull it up 2″.

If you want to later change the top to a solid slab, just draw a line between two corners. This will create a new face. Then erase the remaining lines (Figure 4–54).

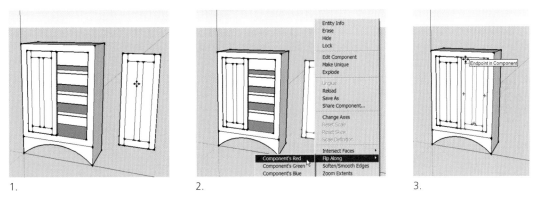

Figure 4–52: Copy the component door and flip it along the red axis.

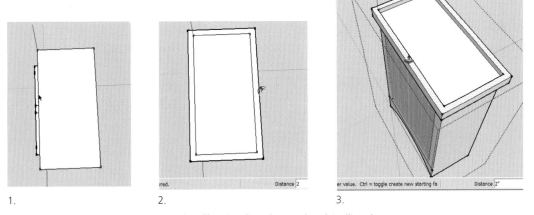

Figure 4–53: Make the top trim piece by offsetting the edges and push/pulling them up.

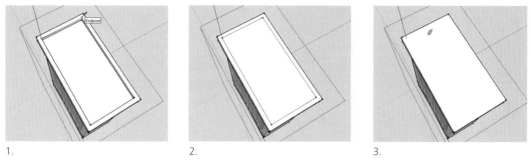

1.   2.   3.

Figure 4–54: Turn the top trim piece into a solid slab by drawing a line between two corners.

The doors would look nice with some glass in them. For that we need the *Materials browser*.

Put Glass in the Doors with the Materials Browser

At **Windows>Materials** is a submenu called the Materials browser. It contains folders of color and texture swatches to paint onto the model. Painting is the entire subject of Chapter 7, but here's a glimpse of it.

Put glass in the doors (Figures 4–55 to 4–57). Open one component door's editing box. Then go to **Window>Materials**. On the PC, a browser with collections (folders) of different materials appears. If *Materials* isn't in the text field, scroll to it. Click on *translucent* for choices of translucent materials, and then on *translucent glass blue*. Mac users, click on the brick. A text field appears; scroll through materials choices to the *translucent* collection.

Next, click on the glass portion of one component door to paint it blue translucent. Close the editing box.

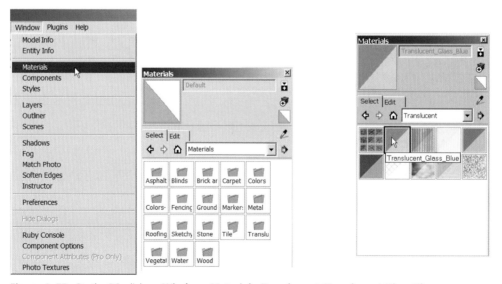

Figure 4–55: On the PC, click on **Window>Materials>Translucent>Translucent Glass Blue**.

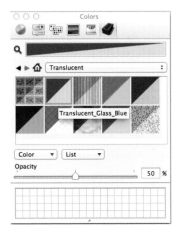

Figure 4–56: On the Mac, click on the brick, then scroll to the *Translucent* folder.

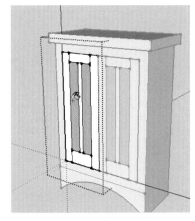

Figure 4–57: Paint the material on one component door. The other will automatically update.

A Translucence Workaround

Okay, the glass is blue, but not translucent. Why?

SketchUp is designed for single-face modeling. When we made the component door, we push/pulled it 1″ thick. That made it double-faced. Double faces present modeling problems, one of which is translucent materials not appearing translucent. A workaround to make the glass in this door appear translucent is to hide the back face. To access that back face, we'll rotate the doors open.

The Rotate Tool

The Rotate tool (Figure 4–58) spins geometry around an axis. It can be tricky to use, because it tries to align itself to the viewer's current position. For instance, if the mouse is above the model, Rotate will align with the blue axis. If the mouse is in front of the model, Rotate will align with the green axis; if the mouse is on the side of the model, Rotate will align with the red (Figure 4–59) axis. The cursor color-coordinates with the axis that it's spinning an object around. A black rotator means the object isn't aligned with any axis.

Figure 4–58: The Rotate tool.

Select the Rotate tool, and move the cursor around the screen. If you orbit so that some sky is visible, it tends to work better. Once the color you want appears, lock it in place with the **Shift** key. If you can't get a certain color to appear, hold the left mouse button down, and drag the cursor around. That makes the tool cycle through all the colors. When the one you want appears, quickly lock it. Alternatively, use the keyboard arrows: The left forces movement along the green axis, the up forces movement along the blue, and the right forces movement along the red. Another tip is to make a rectangle on the axis you want and then lock Rotate onto it.

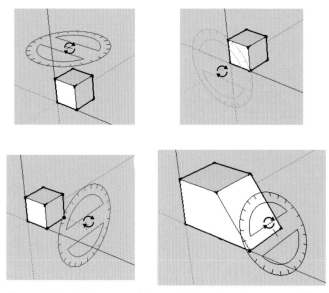

Figure 4–59: The Rotate tool aligns with the viewer's current position.

Beginners often mistakenly click on the Protractor (six icons to the right of Rotate) instead of Rotate, because their screen cursors—a round protractor—are identical. However, the Protractor only measures angles and creates angled guide lines. It doesn't rotate anything.

Rotate the component doors (Figure 4–60). Open one door's editing box, and select the whole door by triple-clicking. Click the blue rotator on the door's top hinge. Then click at the opposite endpoint. Swing the door open with the mouse. Both doors will open.

Note that just opening the editing box isn't enough; you must select the entire door, too. If the door warps when you try to rotate it, you didn't select it all (Figure 4–61).

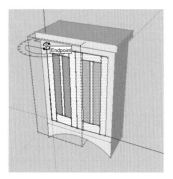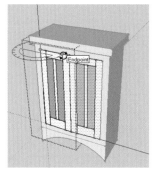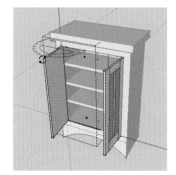

Figure 4–60: Open one component door's editing box, select the whole door by triple-clicking, and rotate it open.

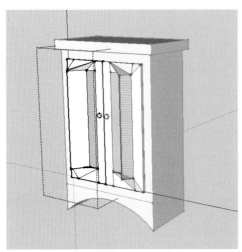

Figure 4–61: Open the component box *and* select the entire door before rotating, or it will warp, as in this image.

Hide Geometry

Hide the back face of the door. Select the back face of the door, and click on **Edit>Hide**. It disappears, making the front face's translucency settings apparent (Figure 4–62).

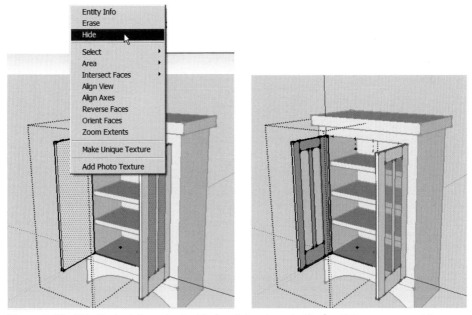

Figure 4–62: Hide the back face of a double-faced door to make the front's transparency settings apparent.

Unhide the face anytime at **Edit>Unhide**. Options there are *hide everything hidden; unhide the last item hid; unhide specific selected items.* If you're wondering how to select hidden items, click on **View>Hidden Geometry**. They'll appear with a light grid (Figure 4–63).

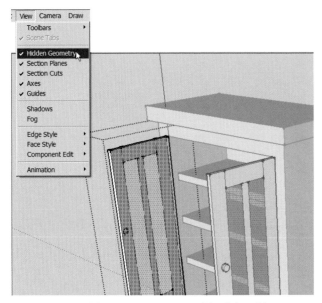

Figure 4–63: Hidden geometry appears with a light grid.

Finally, click the Rotate tool on the hinge, then onto the opposite corner, and move the mouse to swing the doors shut (Figure 4–64).

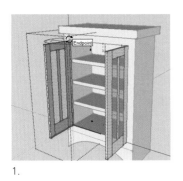
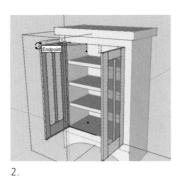
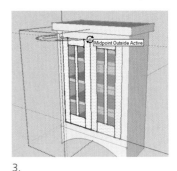

1.   2.   3.

Figure 4–64: Rotate the doors closed after hiding the back face.

All we need now are handles and the Circle tool.

The Circle Tool

The Circle tool (Figure 4–65) does just that: draws circles. When you activate it, the number 24 appears in the Measurements box. Like an arc, a circle is a collection of straight lines, with a default of 24. If you want more lines to make it look smoother, type a larger number. That will become the new default.

Figure 4–65: The Circle tool.

Click to place the center of the circle. You're asked for a radius. Type a number or just click anywhere. The circle becomes a face (Figure 4–66). To change the radius, type a new number before doing anything else. Afterward, the circle's size must be changed through its *Entity Info* box, discussed next.

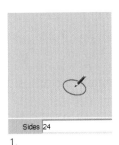
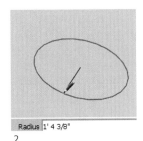
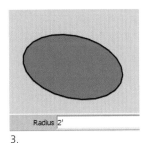

1. 2. 3.

Figure 4–66: Using the Circle tool.

Like the Rotate tool, the Circle tool can be tricky to use because it wants to align with the mouse location. Unlike the Rotate tool, different orientations can't be forced by holding the cursor down. All orientations are most likely to appear if you model near the origin. Or make a rectangle with the orientation needed, draw the circle inside it, and move the circle to the desired location.

▶ To make an ellipse or oval, click the Scale tool on a circle and pull on the middle grips.

Change a Circle's Size

To alter the circle's size later, select the perimeter (don't include the face), right-click, and choose Entity Info. Type a new size in the appropriate field (Figure 4–67).

Add the knobs (Figure 4–68). Click Circle on one of the lock stiles. Click again to define the radius. Then push/pull out. The knobs in the model are about 1¾" diameter and 1" long.

And we're done! See Figure 4–69.

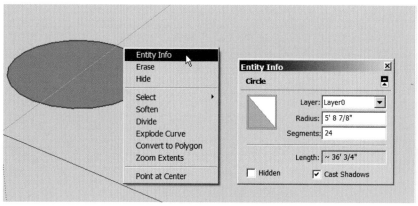

Figure 4–67: To change a circle's size, right-click on its perimeter, choose Entity Info, and type a new number.

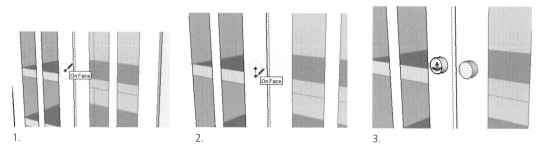

1.   2.   3.

Figure 4–68: Adding the knobs.

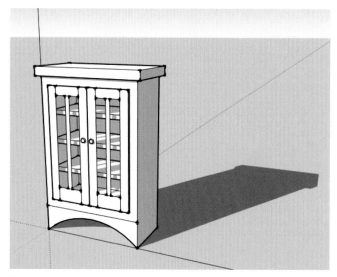

Figure 4–69: The complete bookcase.

Model a Clock with Radial Array

Let's model an accessory now, specifically a clock (Figure 4–70). In the process we'll see how Rotate makes multiple copies while simultaneously arranging them in a circle. This is called a *radial array*. Activate the front view of the Views toolbar to make modeling this project easier

Make a 3'-diameter circle. Use the Circle tool, and put guide lines through its center with the Tape Measure (Figure 4–71).

Make an hour mark with the Rectangle tool. Model it off the circle and turn it into a component. Then move it to the 12:00 position (Figure 4–72).

Figure 4–70: Clock.

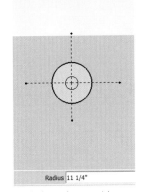

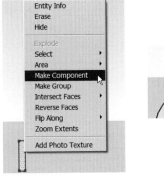

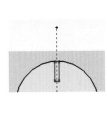

Figure 4–71: Make a 3'-diameter circle and put guide lines through its center.

Figure 4–72: Make an hour mark component off the clock, and then move it to the 12:00 position.

Array 12 hour marks around the clock face (Figures 4–73 and 4–74).

a. Select the component, and click Rotate on the circle center.

b. Click Rotate on the top of the hour mark.

c. Press and release **Ctrl**. A plus sign appears over the Rotate cursor, indicating that multiple copies will be made. Move the cursor a bit to the right (but don't click).

d Type *360* and **Enter**.

e. Type */12* and **Enter**.

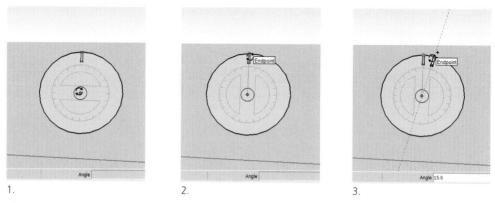

1.   2.   3.

Figure 4–73: The first three steps for arraying 12: hour marks around the clock face.

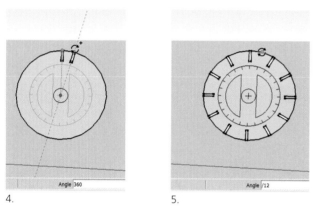

4.   5.

Figure 4–74: The last two steps for arraying the hour marks.

Model clock hands off the clock face, using the Rectangle tool. Group, and then rotate them (Figure 4–75).

Give thickness to the clock face by push/pulling it straight back (Figure 4–76).

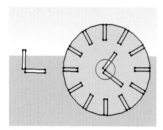 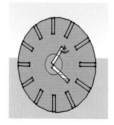 

Figure 4–75: Make clock hands, and then group and rotate them.

Figure 4–76: Push/pull the clock face back.

Offset the clock face and give it thickness with Push/Pull (Figure 4–77).

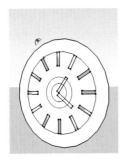

Figure 4–77: Offset the clock face and give it volume.

Give thickness to one clock hand. Open the editing box and push/pull one forward.

Inference-Match the Clock Hand Thickness

You have two items. The first is the thickness that you want. The second needs to match it. Click Push/Pull on the face of the second item, and hover it over the face of the first. The second item will snap to that thickness. Release the cursor. Done. Yes, it's that simple. You can also inference-match line length, which we'll do in Chapter 5.

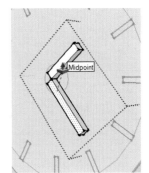

Push/pull the second clock hand forward, but don't click. Move the cursor over the first clock hand. The second clock hand's thickness will adjust to the same thickness (Figure 4–78). Release the cursor, and close the editing box.

Optional: Adjust the size and proportion of the hour marks and hands with the Scale tool (Figure 4–79). Remember that since the hour marks are components, a change to one will affect all. More specifically, scaling one component outside its editing box will affect just that component; scaling inside the editing box will affect all instances of it.

Figure 4–78: Push/pull the first clock hand forward for thickness, and then inference-match the thickness on the second clock hand.

Done! (Figure 4–80.)

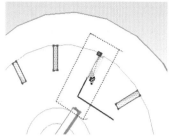  

Figure 4–79: Adjust the hands and hour marks, if needed.

Figure 4–80: The finished clock.

This is the extent of furniture and accessories modeling we'll do. Why? Because there are sources from which you can download just about any ready-made, editable component you need (Figure 4–81). Editing is generally more time-efficient than making from scratch. Let's head over to Chapter 5 now, where we'll model a floor plan and download some components from one of those sources, the Trimble 3D Warehouse.

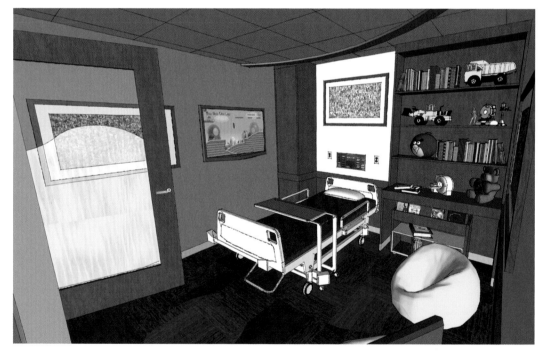

Figure 4–81: Accessories in this model were downloaded from the Trimble 3D Warehouse, scaled to size, and edited as needed. Note the translucent paint on the door.

Summary

In this chapter we used SketchUp's fundamental drawing and editing tools to model a table, bookcase, and clock. In the process, we learned what stickiness is and how to manage it with groups, discussed non-filling faces, made and edited components, mirrored geometry, applied translucent paint, scaled and arrayed geometry, changed a style setting, and inference-matched. We also discussed some best practices and tips for good modeling.

Further Resources

Advice on modeling accurately: www.youtube.com/watch?v=DVO1cpDLbrs

The Arc tool: www.youtube.com/watch?v=o2pgjs3ao9U

Edges and faces: www.youtube.com/watch?v=D3amXjPCtiI

Groups and components: www.youtube.com/watch?v=r1QpoNO-1zMA

The Offset tool: www.youtube.com/watch?v=nIsE6DVJ_lk

The Rotate tool: www.youtube.com/watch?v=09Vd2jj3BGE

The Scale tool: www.youtube.com/watch?v=I_xqUsZnzJA

Exercises

www.wiley.com/go/sketchupforinteriordesign

1. Make a 5′ × 5′ × 5′ cube.
   - ▶ Group it.
   - ▶ Apply the Rotate and Scale tools to it.
   - ▶ Flip it along an axis.
   - ▶ Change the colors of its axes.
   - ▶ Hide and unhide its surfaces.
   - ▶ Click shadows on and off it.
   - ▶ Turn it into a component.
2. Make a window component, utilizing *cut hole* and *glue to* options.
3. Model a piece of furniture from a photo.
4. Model Exercise 4–1 by visually estimating its size.
5. Model Exercise 4–2 using the dimensions given. Estimate any dimensions not given.
6. Model a clock similar to the one in this chapter.

Drafting, Modeling, and Furnishing a Floor Plan

I n Chapter 4 we modeled furniture. Now we're going to draft and model a two-story space. We'll do it three ways: (1) by tracing over a raster file, (2) by drawing it from a paper sketch, and (3) by importing an AutoCAD file (a Pro feature). So, open a new SketchUp file.

Prepare a Raster File for Import

SketchUp Make/PC can import *jpg, png, tif,* and *bmp* raster files. SketchUp Make/Mac imports the same plus *pdf.* The common *gif* format is not supported. SketchUp will resample (downsize) anything larger than 1024 × 1024 pixels. However, that size is much larger than what's usually needed. Since large files slow down the software, crop and resample them yourself before importing.

To further keep file size down, use compressed file types. *Bmps* are not compressed. *Jpgs* and *pngs* are, plus they're smaller than other file types, hence the best choice. *Pngs* in particular preserve transparency layers, an issue when you're importing a file adjusted with digital imaging software. Know that *gif and bmp* files can be converted with Windows' Paint utility or the Mac's *Save As* function.

Once imported, a raster file is permanently part of the model. SketchUp doesn't externally reference files, meaning that it won't search for them on your computer each time the model is opened, and display a red X when it can't find them.

Draft a Plan by Tracing a Raster Image

Import the raster image (Figure 5–1). Click on **File>Import**. A navigation browser opens. In the *Files of Type* field at the bottom, scroll to *All Supported Image Types,* and click the radio button in front of *Use as image.*

Objective: This chapter shows different ways to draft and model a plan, and how to import ready-made components.

Tools: Section, Text, Protractor

Concepts and Functions: camera, prepare and import a raster image and AutoCAD file, view the model orthographically, apply a transparent face style, change line color, inference-match line length, tracing techniques, scale a model, reverse faces, explode, stretch a line, Trimble 3D Warehouse, Components browser, import components, native and local collections, link a local collection to the Components browser, model porch steps, paste in place, purge unused components, move geometry with coordinates, clipping, make a sloped ceiling, measure an angle

Figure 5–1: At **File>Import** bring in the *jpg*. Make sure the bottom settings show *All Supported Image Types* and *Use as image*.

Place the file. Click once to place the jpg's lower-left corner, and then click anywhere else to place the upper-right. Recall from Chapter 4 that it's best to model on/near the origin and in the upper-right quadrant.

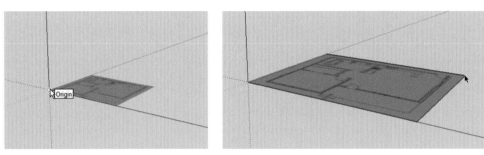

Figure 5–2: Click twice to place the jpg.

Resize Geometry to Make It to Scale

You're probably wondering why we didn't address scale when importing the file. We can scale anything at any time. All geometry and imported files can be resized on the basis of a known dimension. Say you want to make a wall 10′ long. Click the Tape Measure on the wall's endpoints, then immediately type *10′*. The wall resizes, and so does the rest of the model in proportion. Be aware that this affects everything in the open file, including geometry you didn't want to resize. The workaround is to make the item a group or component (if it isn't already), and then resize it inside the editing box.

Resize the Imported Plan with the Tape Measure

Adjust the size (Figure 5–3). We'll adjust the plan by adjusting a doorway. Click the Tape Measure on one side of a door jamb and then on the other (Steps 1. and 2.). A pop-up box displays the distance as about 10″. Since residential interior doors are usually 2′8″ wide, type *2′8* (if you want a fraction after the eight, type a space and then type the fraction). A dialog box appears, asking if we want to resize the model. Click *Yes*. The whole model will resize to a proportion in keeping with the new doorway opening size of 2′-8″.

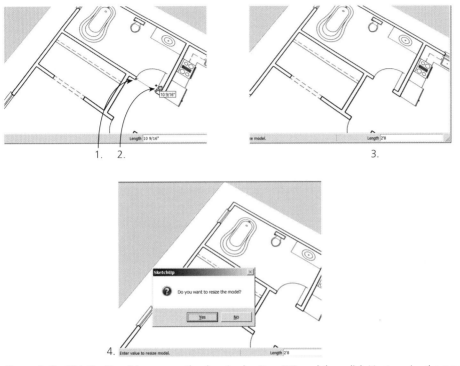

1.   2.   3.

4.

Figure 5–3: Click the Tape Measure on the door jambs. Type *2′8*, and then click *Yes* to resize the model.

Turn the raster file into a group (Figure 5–4). The imported image has some grouplike qualities but isn't a true group. Let's make it one so it will be easier to work with. Select, right-click, and choose *Explode*. Then select it again, right-click, and choose *Make Group*.

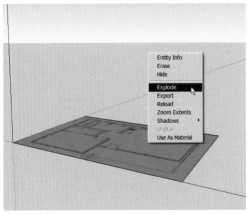 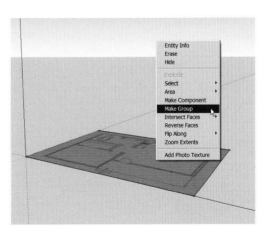

Figure 5–4: Explode and then group the plan.

The Explode Function

Explode reduces a group or component to its individual geometry. Nested groups and components—that is, groups or components that are enclosed in other groups or components—might need to be exploded multiple times to reach what you're trying to reach. Be aware that adjacent nested geometry may become fused upon explosion. Know, too, that exploded circles and arcs cannot have certain editing operations performed on them afterward because the explosion reduces them to individual line segments that don't behave together anymore.

Since it's easier to trace in a plan view, add the Views toolbar to your workspace (we discussed it in Chapter 3). It contains icons that display the model orthographically. Click its plan icon to view the image as a plan (Figure 5–5). Remember that even when you draw in 2D mode, the model is still 3D.

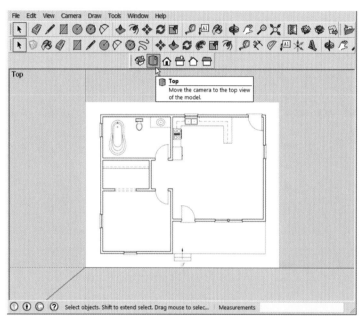

Figure 5–5: Click the *Plan* icon on the **Views** menu to display the plan in 2D.

1. Trace the plan's perimeter (Figures 5–6 a–h). Use the Pencil tool and draw parallel to the axes, clicking on each corner. Match line lengths by inference-matching, as shown in *f.* When finished, a face is created, as evidenced by the opaque fill. If the fill doesn't appear, a face hasn't been created. Something went wrong, resulting in the corner points not being coplanar. Erase and redo (the easiest fix).

2. Trace the perimeter to form a face. On *f,* inference-match the line length. Here's how. Click the green point in the bottom-right corner, and then hover the cursor over the upper-left corner—but don't click. Instead, move the cursor straight down. When the cursor is aligned with both corners, the inference will lock. Click, and the result is a bottom horizontal line the same length as the upper horizontal line.

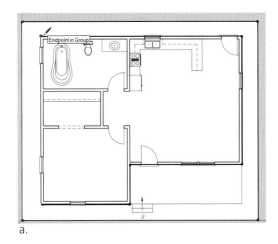

a.

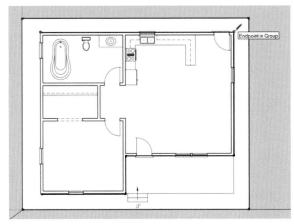

b.

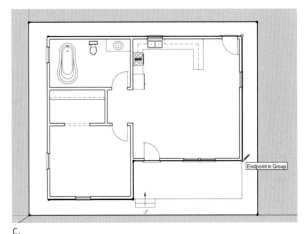

c.

Figure 5–6a–c

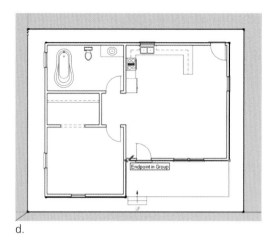

d.

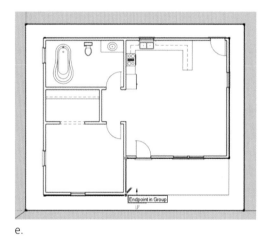

e.

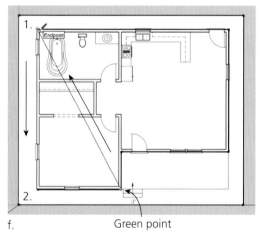

f.

Green point

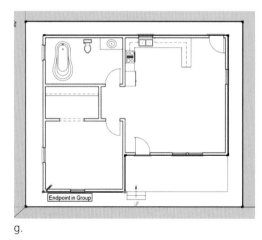

g.

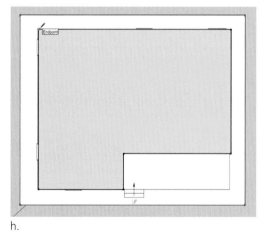

h.

Figure 5–6d–h

SketchUp for Interior Design

Make the face transparent. We can't trace the interior walls through an opaque face, so go to **View>Face Style** and click *X-ray* to make the face transparent (Figure 5–7).

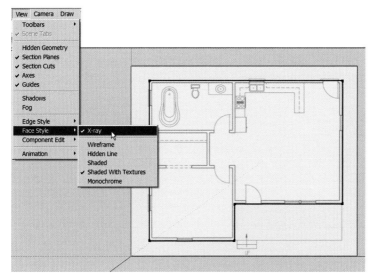

Figure 5–7: Make the face transparent so the walls below can be traced.

Offset the perimeter walls. Use the Offset tool and type *6″*, the wall thickness (Figure 5–8).

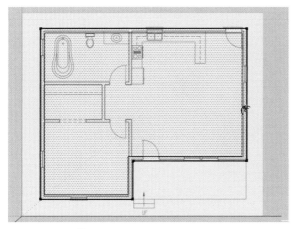

Figure 5–8: Offset the perimeter walls.

Change the Line (Edge) Color

Black lines over a black-and-white drawing are hard to see, so make them red. To do this, go back to the same Styles dialog box used in Chapter 4 to color-coordinate the lines with the axes.

Change the edge color (Figure 5–9). Go to **Window>Styles**. A dialog box appears. Click the *Edit* panel. At the bottom are a Color field and box that shows the current edge color (black). Click that box.

On the PC, a picker wheel and slider appear. Click the color on the wheel that you want, and then move the slider up. The box will change to that color, indicating that the edges are now that color. To return the edges to black, just move the slider back down. On the Mac, clicking the Color field box brings up the color picker. Scroll to *Colors* and pick the one you want (Figure 5-10).

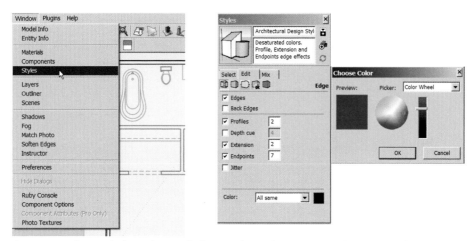

Figure 5–9: Change the line color at **Window>Styles>Edit**. On the PC, click the *Color* field box at the bottom to get a color wheel and slider.

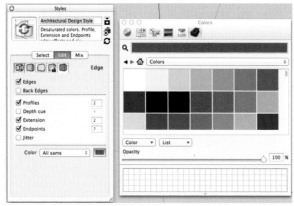

Figure 5–10: On the Mac, click the *Color* field box to get the color picker.

Trace Interior Walls

There are multiple approaches to tracing the interior walls, so rather than go step-by-step, here are some techniques for you to apply.

▶ Trace one line on each interior wall, and then copy it 6" to the left or right (Figure 5–11).

▶ Obtain line lengths by inference-matching. Click the new line's first endpoint. Hover the cursor over the point shown in the top graphic in Figure 5–12, and then move the cursor up (bottom graphic) until it locks in place.

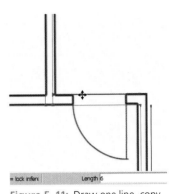

Figure 5–11: Draw one line, copy it, and move it 6" away.

▶ Use the Move tool to stretch lines longer or shorter (Figure 5–13). Select the line, and move its endpoint forward or backward. Do the same with a face edge by selecting it, grabbing it somewhere along its length, and stretching it forward or backward. Of course, this won't work if the line or face are connected to other geometry that stretches with it.

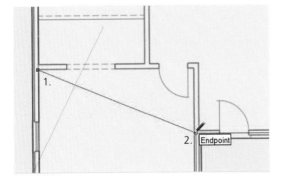

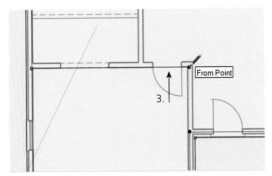

Figure 5–12: Inference-match to obtain line lengths. Click the new line's first endpoint, hover the cursor over a point at the desired distance from the first endpoint, and move the cursor up until it locks in place.

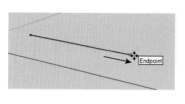
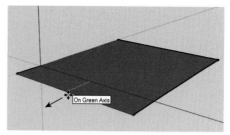

Figure 5–13: Stretch a line by moving its endpoint; stretch a face by moving its edge.

▶ Use the Pencil to add to lines whose endpoints can't be moved because they're attached to other geometry. This will result in two lines: the original and the added (Figure 5–14).

After you finish drawing the interior lines, return to **View>Face Style** and unclick *X-ray*. The face will become opaque again, allowing you to see any missing lines or areas to clean up, such as crossed lines at intersections. If you inadvertently erase a line, just redraw it with the Pencil.

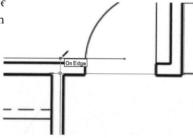

Figure 5–14: Add line length with the Pencil. Then erase any overhang.

Edge Styles Again

Eventually your plan should look like this:

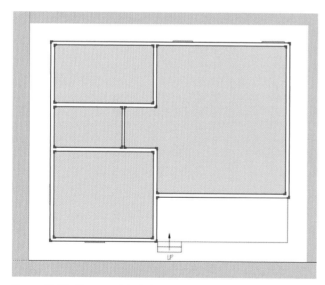

Figure 5–15: The completed plan.

Note that all intersections are "clean," because crossed lines were erased. This makes the walls contiguous, which is necessary to pull them up together. Also note the thickened endpoints; those are a default style. If you don't like them, you can get rid of them. Return to **Window>Styles**. You can change endpoints, line weight (the appearance of thickness), and other characteristics. Unclick the *Endpoints* box, and the endpoints will disappear (Figure 5–16). Experiment with different numbers in the checkbox to see how the endpoints are affected. Increase the number in the *Profiles* checkbox to make the edges thicker (Figure 5–17). Know that technically the edges are still thin; they just appear thicker.

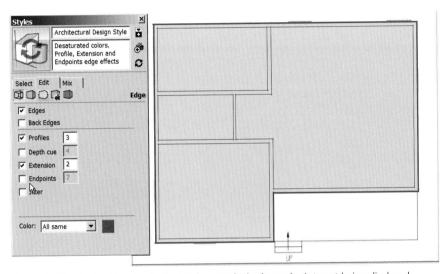

Figure 5–16: Unchecking the *Endpoints* box results in the endpoints not being displayed.

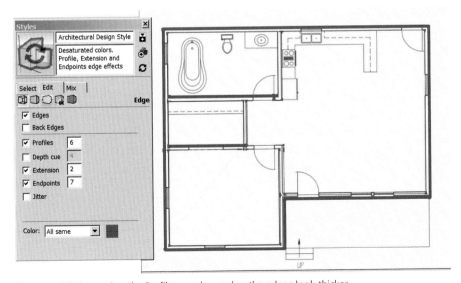

Figure 5–17: Increasing the Profiles number makes the edges look thicker.

Note that the interior lines look thinner than the perimeter lines. The enabled profiles feature causes this. It's indicating that those lines do not enclose a coplanar face; that is, those lines are not connected at both ends to other lines. In the *iso* and perspective views, a thicker appearance is the default, mimicking how designers outline forms with thicker line weights to visually define them. You cannot assign different thicknesses to different edges. If you don't like profiles at all, turn them off by unchecking the *Profiles* box. However, leaving it on helps to see which lines aren't connected, which is useful when you are troubleshooting problems like a non-filling face.

Return the edge style to black by moving the slider down. Click the *iso* icon in the Views toolbar. Your plan should now look like Figure 5–18.

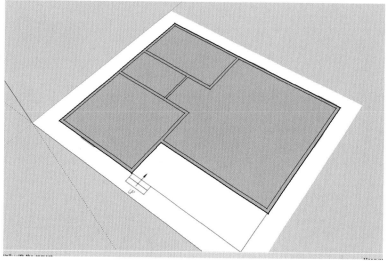

Figure 5–18: The finished plan. X-ray is turned off, the edge color is black, and the *iso* icon in the **Views** toolbar is checked.

From Plan to Model

Hover Push/Pull over a wall. Ideally, all walls should become highlighted. Extrude up 10′ (Figure 5–19). Erase any extraneous vertical lines that appear on the walls.

I say "ideally" because if your walls didn't extrude this smoothly, something went wrong. Did a floor area extrude up with the walls? Push/pull the walls back down and trace the perimeter of that floor area with the Pencil. Sometimes that solves the problem. Erase some faces or walls and redraw them. SketchUp takes playing and practice to get things to go exactly as you want.

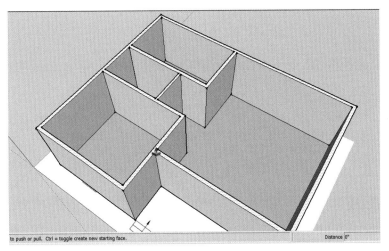

to push or pull. Ctrl = toggle create new starting face.   Distance 0"

Figure 5–19: Push-pull the floor plan up.

Add the Porch, Door, and Window Openings

Put the faces in X-ray mode again (**View>Face style>X-ray**), and we'll add the porch and a couple of openings.

Add the porch (Figures 5–20 a, b, c). Use inferencing to draw the length of the porch, and then push/pull it up 12″ (Figure 5-21).

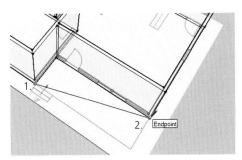

Figure 5-20a: Inference match the line length.

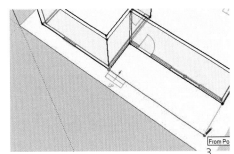

Figure 5-20b: Click the new line into place.

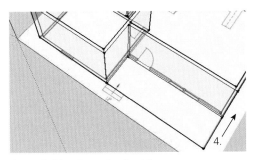

Figure 5-20c: Draw the short line.

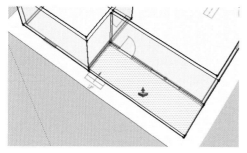

Figure 5–21: Push/pull the porch up 12″.

Add the porch steps (Figure 5–22). Trace them with the Pencil. Push/pull the second step level with the porch. Push/pull the first step to the midpoint of the second (an inference dot and tooltip will appear as the cursor approaches the midpoint).

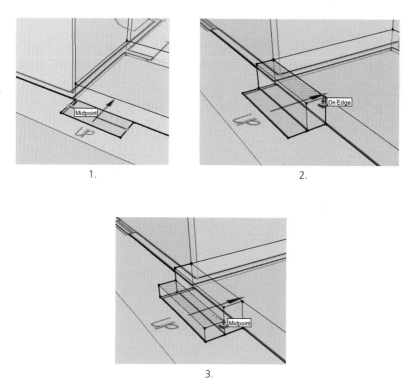

1.   2.

3.

Figure 5–22: Trace the steps with the Pencil, and push/pull them up.

Add the door (Figure 5–23). Click the Rectangle at the bottom of the wall (level with the step) for the door opening's lower-left corner, and then type 2'8,7 and hit **Enter** to make the rectangle 2'-8″ wide and 7'-0″ tall. You could also click anywhere the second time and immediately type the size. The opening will adjust.

Add the window (Figure 5–24). Place its head (top) level with the door head. Hover the Rectangle at the top of the door, move it to the right along the axis (watch for the dotted inference line), and click to place the window's upper-left corner. Click again to place the lower-right corner, or type a specific size. Alternatively, you could place guide lines at the window locations in the plan view and then click the Rectangle on those guide lines (Figure 5–25).

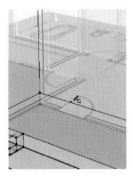
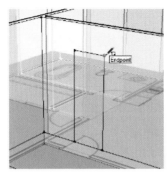

Figure 5–23: Add a door opening with the Rectangle tool.

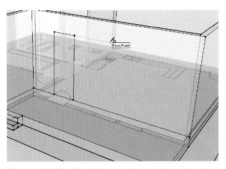
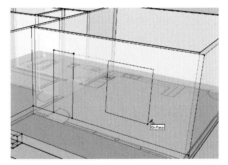

Figure 5–24: Use inferencing to align the door and window heads.

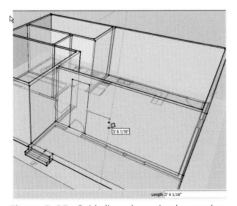

Figure 5–25: Guide lines drawn in plan can be used to place the window opening.

Cut the door and window openings. Push/pull the faces back a bit, type *6* (the width of the wall), and hit **Enter** (Figure 5–26).

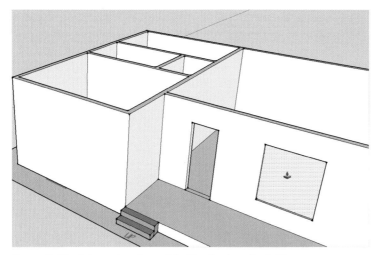

Figure 5–26: Cut openings by push/pulling the faces back 6″.

Raise the interior floor. Orbit inside the model. The doorway is above the floor. Fix by push/pulling the floor up and clicking it on the door sill (Figure 5–27). Raise the floors in the other rooms by inference-matching them to that floor (Figure 5–28).

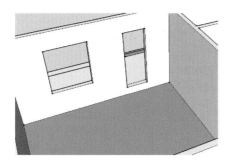 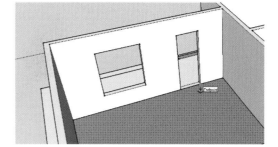

Figure 5–27: Raise the interior floor to the door sill.

Flashing Planes

By now you've probably noticed how the floor planes flash when you orbit around the cottage (Figure 5–29). This is called "z-fighting" and happens when two planes are adjacent. Flashing tells you that the planes are occupying the same space, and SketchUp doesn't know which to display. Here it's happening because the floor planes are on top of the imported floor plan, itself a plane.

A workaround to get rid of the flashing is to raise the floor, effectively making it double-faced. This thickness makes the flashing stop because the new floor plane isn't adjacent to the imported one anymore.

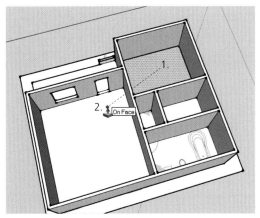

Figure 5–28: Inference-match the other rooms' floors to the new floor height by clicking Push/Pull on those floors, moving the cursor over the new floor, and then letting it go.

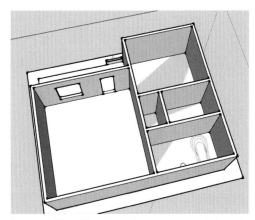

Figure 5–29: When two planes are adjacent to each other, they flash.

Sometimes SketchUp orients a face the wrong way when creating it. The steps on our porch are an example. The back faces are showing, as evidenced by their blue color. Select them, right-click, and choose *Reverse Faces* to fix (Figure 5–30). We'll discuss why correct face orientation is important in Chapter 6.

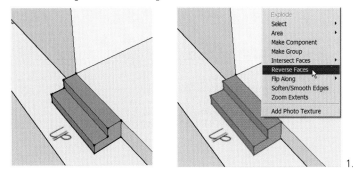

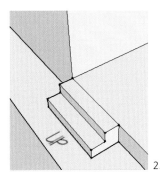

Figure 5–30: Right-click to reverse faces so their white fronts show instead of their blue backs.

Draft a Plan from a Paper Sketch

Designers usually have a sketch of a space's layout and dimensions. In this project we'll draw and model the dorm room in Figure 5–31. Click the View toolbar's plan icon to start.

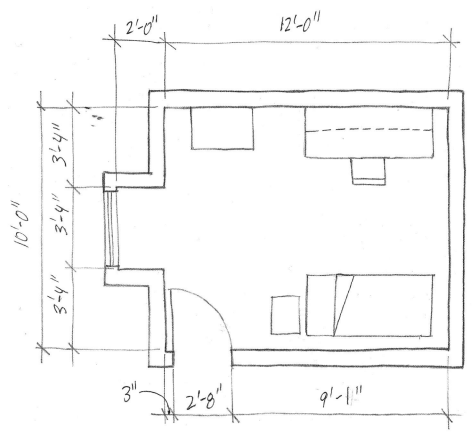

Figure 5–31: A sketch of a dorm room's plan.

Place guide lines at the sketch's dimensions. Use the Tape Measure to create guide lines defining a 14″ × 10″ rectangle, and then place the guide lines at the smaller dimensions (Figure 5–32). Start the first couple of guide lines by clicking on and dragging the axes.

Trace the floor plan over the guide lines (Figure 5–33). Look for inference tooltips each time you click, to ensure coplanarity.

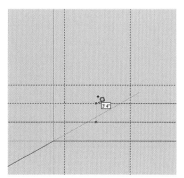

Figure 5–32: Outline the floor plan with guide lines.

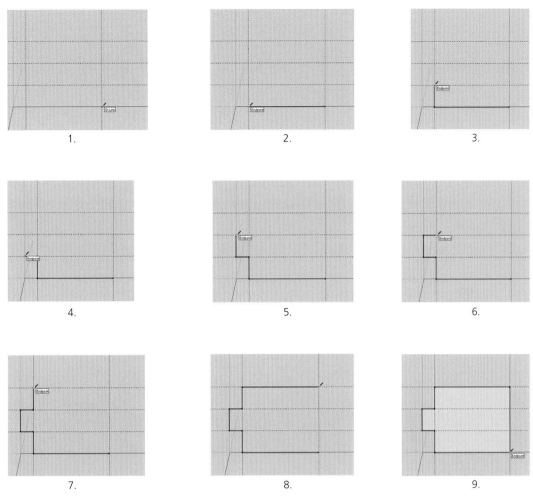

Figure 5–33: Trace the floor plan over the guide lines.

Return the plan to a perspective view (click *iso* on the **Views** toolbar), and delete all guide lines at **Edit>Delete Guides** (Figure 5–34).

Model the plan. Push/pull it up 9′ and erase the ceiling by right-clicking and choosing *Erase* (Figure 5–35). Or choose *Hide* if you think you'll use it later. Make a guide line 3″ from the corner, to place the door.

It's time to get the door now.

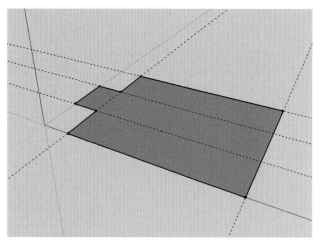

Figure 5–34: Return the model to a perspective view and delete all guide lines.

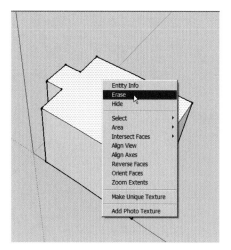
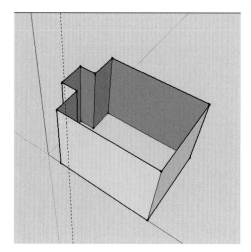

Figure 5–35: Model the plan and remove the ceiling.

The Trimble 3D Warehouse

In Chapter 4 you made several components. The ability to do that is nice, but saving time by using other people's is even better. You can import doors, windows, furniture, flower pots, cake and pizza, video game characters, whatever you want from various websites. The largest source of free components is the Trimble 3D Warehouse, an online repository where millions of people upload and download models. It holds SketchUp (.skp), Google Earth (.kmz), and Collada (.dae) file formats.

The SketchUp team uploads architectural components; companies upload their products; beginners and pros upload their own creations. Anyone with a Google account can contribute. There are replicas of whole buildings and cities, and rooms filled with brand-name furniture, fixtures, and equipment. Excluding branding and logos, all content is free, reusable, editable, and republishable. In that spirit of sharing, this book liberally uses Warehouse components.

A Warehouse component (as well as any component you make) is really a full-fledged model. When you download a model, you're embedding one model into another. You're also bringing in all its layers, files, and anything else it contains.

Access the Warehouse through the *Components browser,* a submenu of component collections. An Internet connection is needed. You can also access it directly at **http://sketchup .google.com/3dwarehouse/,** where its contents are easier to browse.

People use the warehouse for different purposes, such as selling products and advertising their modeling and design services. You can set up a private folder for your own work and securely collaborate with others by specifying who gets to see and download its contents.

Import a Door through the Components Browser

Import a door component (Figure 5–36). Click on **Window>Components**. Then click on the navigation (down-pointing) arrow to see a drop-down menu. Under *Favorites* are eight *collections,* folders with category-specific content. Click on *Architecture.* Thumbnails of architectural components appear in the browser. Scroll to *Doors* and click on it. Door choices appear; double-click on one, and move it into the model. (The Select tool needs to be activated.)

Figure 5–36: Go to **Window>Components>Architecture**, and click on the *Doors* thumbnail.

Place the door (Figure 5–37). The Move tool is attached to the door's local axis, enabling you to place it right away. Note how the door attaches, or "glues," itself to whatever plane it's on. Click it on the floor and guide line.

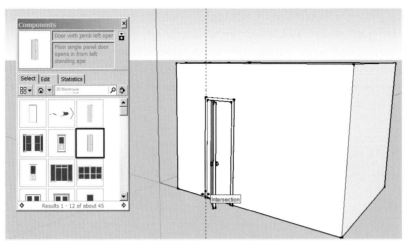

Figure 5–37: Drag the door out of the Components browser and click it on the wall.

Select the door. Four crosses appear, on which you can click Move and then rotate for angle adjustment (Figure 5–38). While you obviously don't want to rotate a door, those crosses appear on all downloaded components to enable any needed rotation right away, instead of as a separate task.

Further adjustments may be needed. In this case, the door needs to be moved forward so its frame protrudes outside the space, not inside it (Figure 5–39). Since the local axis is the grab-handle when moving, relocating it to the door's interior side will save steps over time, if the door is used a lot. Relocating a component axis is discussed in Chapter 6.

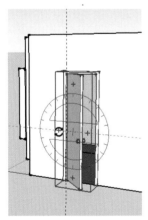

Figure 5–38: The four crosses on an imported component are locations where a Rotator will appear when clicked with the Move tool.

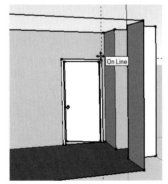

Figure 5–39: The door has been adjusted so its frame protrudes on the exterior. The wall opposite it was hidden to make this move easier.

Import and place the window (Figure 5–40). Draw a guide line 2′-2″ from the ceiling to mark the window head. Then go to **Window>Components** and click on the Windows thumbnail this time. Choose one, bring it into the model, and click to place. If you have multiple windows and doors, it's easiest to import a new instance of each component for each differently oriented wall. Right-click on the component to quickly access options for it, including *Reload*.

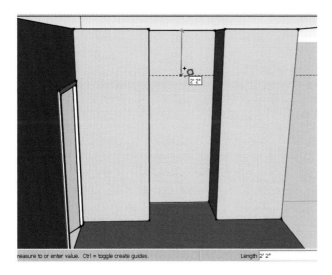

Figure 5–40: Mark a guide line for the window head, and then import and place a window.

Interior vs. Exterior Models

Orbit around to view the room from the outside (Figure 5–41). The door and window protrusions make this a not-so-great exterior model. As a beginning SketchUpper, decide if your model's purpose is to show the interior or exterior, and focus on that. Models that realistically portray both the interior and exterior are possible to make but take longer and require more techniques.

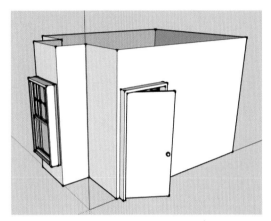

Figure 5–41: The dorm room as viewed from the exterior.

Components in Single- vs. Double-Sided Walls

I'm sure you've noticed that you can see through the component door and window! Recall from Chapter 4 that *Cut opening* was a component option. This is the result. Further greatness comes when you move a door or window component: The goes with it. Erase or hide, and the hole disappears. However, door and window components only cut openings on single-face walls, not the double-face ones we modeled in the cottage. Since interior and architectural designers typically draw walls with thicknesses, a workaround is needed. Sometimes you can draw a rectangle around the door or window component, push the face back, and that cuts a hole. Other times, you might have to do that on both sides of the wall, or cut an opening first and place the component over it. There are also plugins for this purpose (software add-ons are discussed in Chapter 9).

In Chapter 4 we discussed making a component unique (select, right-click, choose *Make unique*), which enables changes to it that don't affect other instances. This is particularly useful for Warehouse components, as you can copy them, make them unique, rename them, and then use them as is or with your own edits.

Import Warehouse Furniture through the Components Browser and with the Get Model Tool

Now import a desk, dresser, and bed, as shown in the sketch. Go back to the Components browser and type *small dresser*, *dorm bed*, and *desk* in the search field. Lots of options will appear in the browser; double-click the thumbnails that interest you to download them, and move them into the model (Figure 5–42).

Or click the Details arrow and choose *View in 3D Warehouse* from the fly-out menu (Figure 5–43). You'll be spirited directly to a Warehouse page with the same search results. Choose a model and download it to your computer. We'll talk about where to store that model in a bit. One more way: Access the Warehouse through the Get Model tool (Figure 5–43a). When downloading, you'll be given the option to download it directly into the open model (Figure 5–43b). There's also a Warehouse toolbar you can activate through the Tools dialog box.

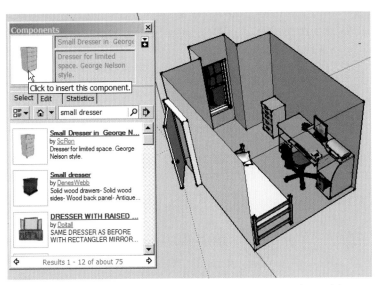

Figure 5–42: Move components from the browser directly into the model.

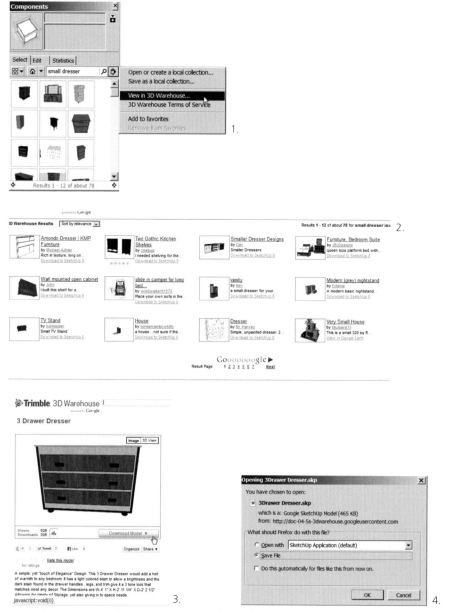

Figure 5–43a Click the fly-out menu, choose *View in 3D Warehouse*, select a model, and download it to your computer.

Copy, Paste, and Paste in Place between SketchUp Files

You can copy and paste components from one SketchUp file to another. Open both files. Remember from Chapter 2 that you must click the second file open from the SketchUp icon to have two instances of the software open. Merely clicking **File>Open** will close the active file.

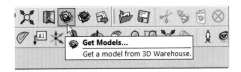

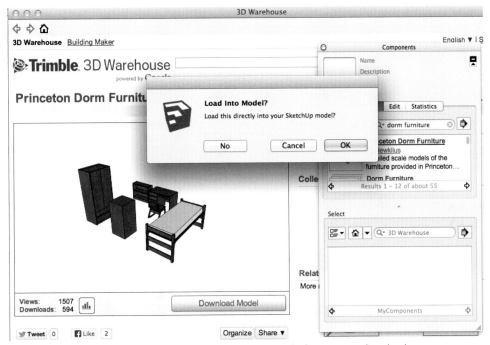

Figure 5–43b Access the Warehouse with the Warehouse tool. Then you can download the model directly into the active file, as seen on this Mac screenshot.

Select the item in the first file and press **Ctrl C** (copy). Click on the second file, activate the Select key, and press **Ctrl V** (paste). On a Mac, press **Command C** and **Command V**. Alternatively, go to the **File** menu and click **Edit>Copy** in the first file and **Edit>Paste** in the second. Cutting and pasting works on geometry *within* a file, too.

Simple pasting puts the content anywhere in the active SketchUp file. The Edit menu has an option called *Paste in Place* that puts an item in the same location it was cut or copied from. This is great for moving items that are outside a group/component into it, while preserving the location. Recall from Chapter 4 that since groups/components and loose geometry can occupy the same spot, a common beginner mistake is inadvertently drawing additions *outside* a group/ component when what you should have done was open the editing box and drawn *inside* it. Relocate geometry to the same place inside the group/component like this: Select it, click **File>Cut**, open the group's editing box, and click **File>Paste in Place**.

Here are a couple more tricks: Go to **File>Import**, set the *Files of Type* field to *skp*, and navigate to the file you want to import. This brings the whole file into the open one. Or drag that file's desktop icon into the open file. Be aware that large files take a while to import.

See All Components Loaded in the Model with the *In Model* Icon

At **Window>Components** we clicked the navigation arrow to see a list of all native (built-in) component collections. To see only components loaded in the model, click the *In Model* icon; it's the house (Figure 5–44). Every component added to the model through any method—downloading, importing, making it yourself, cutting and pasting—shows up here. You'll return to this window often to purge, delete, and retrieve components.

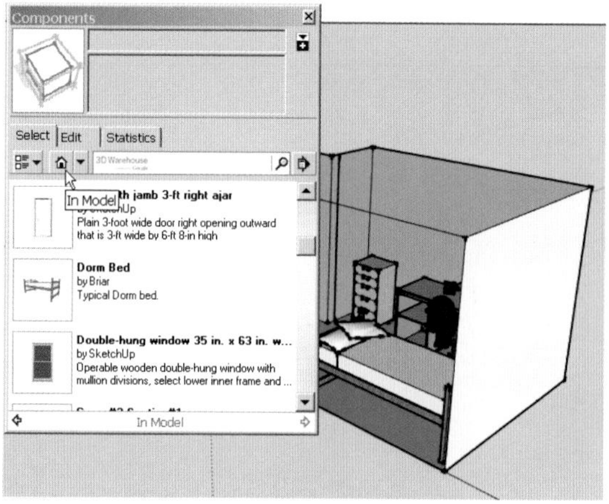

Figure 5–44: Click the house icon to see components loaded into the model.

Purge Unused Components

Every imported component stays in the model, even if erased or never used. This increases the model's size, so purge them occasionally. Click the *Details* arrow on the Components browser, and choose *Purge Unused* from the fly-out menu (Figure 5–45).

Figure 5–45: All components remain in the model, even if never used or erased. Purge unused ones to keep the model's size down.

Purging removes all unused components from the model. However, if you think you might use some of them for a different project, make a local collection for them.

Make a Local Collection and Link It to the Components Browser

A *local collection* is a folder on your computer in which non-native components are kept. It can be linked to the Components browser for easy access to its contents. Figures 5–46 to 5–50 show how.

1. Click the arrow in the upper-right corner of the Components browser to open the bottom pane. It looks just like the top pane. However, you can create your own collection folders in it and then drag components from the top pane down into them. This makes their contents available each time you open a SketchUp file. Click the Details arrow and choose *Open or create a local collection*. (On the Mac, choose *Create a new collection*).

2. A navigation browser opens; locate where you want to place the folder. I navigated to the Desktop, clicked *Make new folder*, and named it *MyComponents*. That collection is now open in the lower pane.

3. Type what you're looking for in the search field and drag some of the resultant thumbnails into the model.

4. The six components I downloaded are visible in the top pane. Drag them into the bottom pane.

5. Right-click on the Details arrow in the lower pane, and choose *Add collection to favorites*. (On the Mac, choose *Save as a local collection*). Clicking on *In Model* now shows *MyComponents* in the submenu.

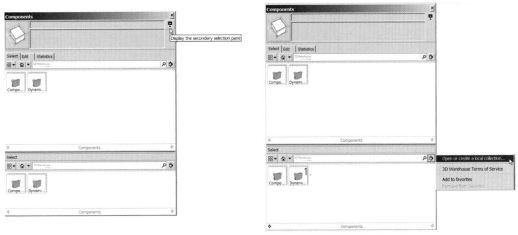

Figure 5–46: Open the bottom pane. Then click the Details arrow on the top pane and choose *Open or Create a local collection* (Mac: *Create a new collection*).

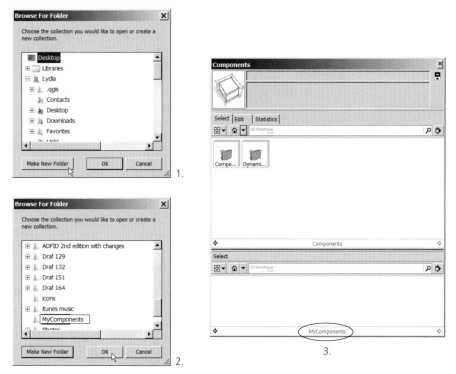

Figure 5–47: Navigate to where you want to place the folder, then create and name it.

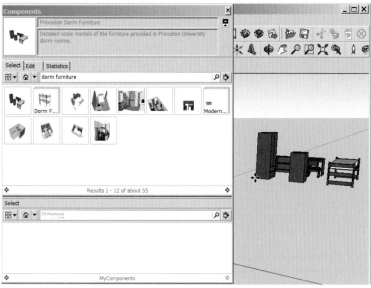

Figure 5–48: Do a Warehouse search, and then download some components into the open model.

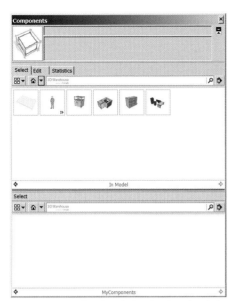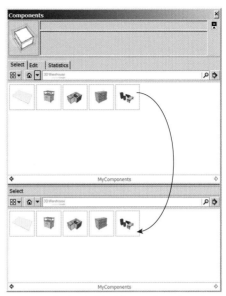

Figure 5-49: Thumbnails for the downloaded components appear in the *In Model* pane. Drag them into the MyCollections folder in the lower pane.

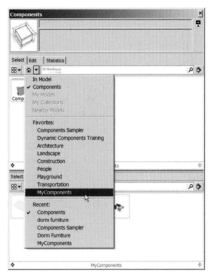

Figure 5-50: Right-click on the Details arrow and choose *Add to favorites* (Mac: *Save as a local collection*). MyComponents is now listed with all the native collections.

Eventually you'll want to make local collections for many different categories, such as rugs, tables, finishes, and lighting fixtures. You can even save searches (Figure 5-51). Enter search terms, hit **Enter**, and after results are returned, click the Details arrow and choose *Add to favorites*. The search will appear with all the collections. To remove it, click the Details arrow again and choose *Remove from favorites*.

Figure 5–51: Searches can be added and removed from the Favorites list.

▶ If you can't drag components from the top to bottom pane or make local collection folders, your permission settings may be locked. On the PC, navigate to the Components folder (**C drive>Program files(x86)>SketchUp>Components**), right-click on it, choose *Properties* and then *Security*. Click *Edit* and change all permissions to *Allow*. On the Mac, navigate to the Components folder through the Finder. Right-click on it, choose *More Info*, and *Edit*. Grant *Read and Write* permissions for everyone.

Purge vs. Delete

Get rid of components you don't want anymore by right-clicking on their thumbnails and choosing *Delete*. This is different from Purge in that it removes the components from both the model and the software. Deleting components is an efficient way to remove unneeded blocks that were part of an imported AutoCAD file, discussed later in this chapter.

Create Plan and Elevation Views

If you prefer to study or present furniture arrangements in orthographic views, you can. When we imported the *jpg* plan of the cottage, one click on the Views toolbar's Plan icon made the *jpg* a plan view. However, clicking the plan view of a model yields an aerial perspective (Figure 5–52).

Figure 5–52: A model's plan view is actually an aerial perspective.

Make an orthographic top view of the model by clicking **Camera>Parallel Projection** (Figure 5–53).

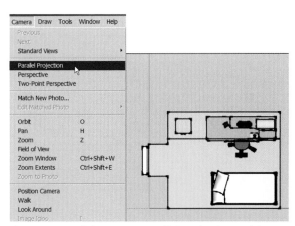

Figure 5–53: Click **Camera>Parallel Projection** and the View toolbar's plan icon to create an orthographic top view of the model.

The other **Views** toolbar's icons yield exterior elevation views, so a workaround is needed for an interior elevation view. One way is to hide the wall opposite the one for which you want an interior elevation (Figure 5–54). To finesse the exact location of the elevation view is made, the Section tool is needed.

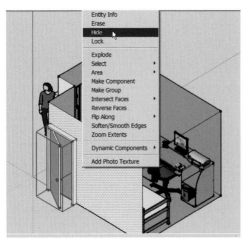

Figure 5–54: Hide the wall opposite the one you want an interior elevation of, and click the Front icon on the **Views** toolbar.

The Section Tool

The Section tool (Figure 5–55) is on its own toolbar and needs to be activated at **View>Toolbars>Section**. There are two section icons: one toggles the display of the section plane on and off; the other toggles the display of the cut view. It creates cut-through views of the model. Be aware that the plane isn't actually cutting the model, just providing a view of a cut.

Figure 5–55: The Section toolbar. Its icons toggle the plane and cut displays on and off.

When activated, a plane appears that flits around like the Rotator tool. When the correct orientation appears, hold the **Shift** key down to lock it in place. Then move the plane to the desired location and click in place (Figure 5–56). To change its location or direction, select it and activate Move or Rotate (Figure 5–57). To remove a section plane, just erase it.

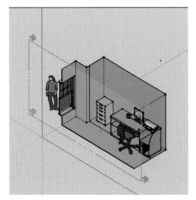
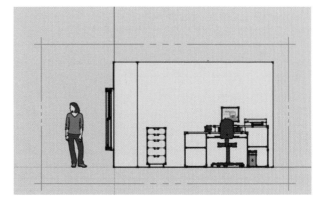

Figure 5–56: Click the Section tool on the model, and then click the **Views** toolbar's Front icon to generate an interior elevation.

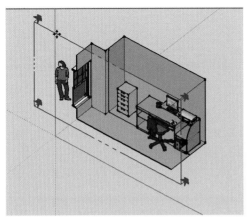 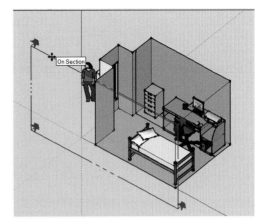

Figure 5–57: Finesse the elevation view by moving the section plane back and forth.

Make a Section Cut with *Create Group from Slice*

The section plane can create cuts as well as views. Right-click on an active (highlighted) plane, and choose *Create Group from Slice*. This makes a cut at the insertion location. The cut is a grouped orthographic section. It can be removed as is or exploded in place. Removing enables developing the section further. Exploding severs the model in two, enabling editing of each part.

You can create multiple section planes, but only one will be active at a time. A workaround for making simultaneously active planes is to group the model with a section plane and then create another section plane outside the group.

Edit a Long Couch into a Short Couch with a Section Cut

The following shows how to use the Section tool to make a section through a couch, and then edit the couch at that section (Figures 5–58, 5–59).

1. Activate the Section tool and orient it on the side you want a section of. Click.

2. Select the section plane (if it isn't selected already), and locate where desired with Move. Click. Right-click on the plane, and choose *Create Group from Slice*.

3. Erase the section plane. The hidden part of the couch—that is, the portion in front of the section plane—becomes visible again, and the cut appears as a line.

4. Slide the plane off to the side with the Move tool.

In Figure 5–58 the cut is left in place. Right-click on it and choose *Explode*. This severs the couch on either side of the cut, and those sides can now be selected and edited separately. A possible edit here would be to erase the selected portion shown, and then slide the right arm over to make the couch shorter.

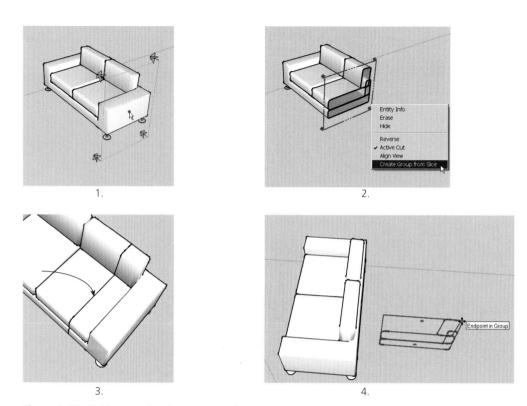

1.

2.

3.

4.

Figure 5–58: Cutting a section through a couch.

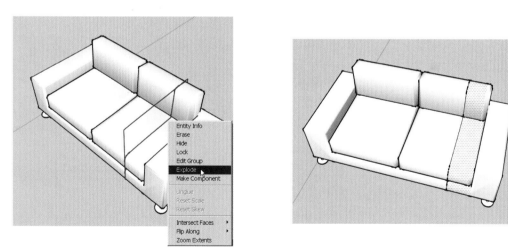

Figure 5–59: Explode the slice to sever the model at the section location.

Model a Building from an AutoCAD Plan

So far we've drafted a floor plan from an imported jpg and from a sketch. Pro can import an AutoCAD file, which you can model right over (Figure 5–60). This is a great time-saver. The *dwg* file becomes SketchUp geometry upon import. Know that the educational (free) version of AutoCAD does not import into SketchUp Pro.

AutoCAD software doesn't need to be installed on your computer, but for best results, a *dwg* file needs some preparation before import, optimally done within AutoCAD. Simpler files need less preparation than data-rich ones with lots of layers and line weights, and you probably don't need to do everything on the following list, but they are things that can make a difference. You might want to import the *dwg* into a new SketchUp file before bringing it into an active file you're modeling, just to make sure there are no problems with it.

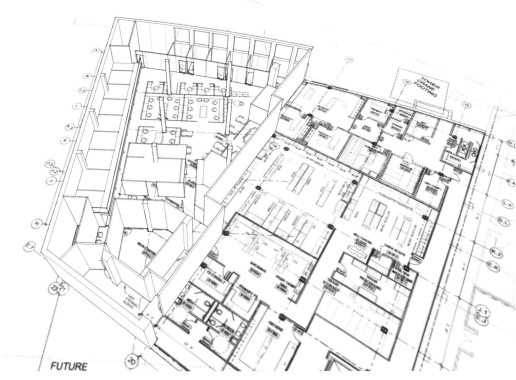

Courtesy Matthew Kerr, IIDA, ASAI, Zimmerman Architectural Studios, Milwaukee, WI

Figure 5–60: A hospital modeled in SketchUp from an imported AutoCAD plan.

Prepare a *dwg* File for Import

Copy and paste the plan into a new AutoCAD file. This helps keep stale metadata from getting imported into SketchUp. Locate the plan at the origin.

Run the PURGE and AUDIT commands to clean up any old data that did enter the new file.

Delete unused layers. SketchUp automatically discards anything in the imported *dwg* file that has no 3D relevance, such as text, dimensions, hatch lines, and title blocks. However, it doesn't discard the layers they're on. Get rid of 2D data or put it on its own layer. That way the layer can be turned off after import, meaning that its data won't slow the model down. Layer creation in SketchUp is discussed in Chapter 6.

Explode all polylines, arcs, and filleted lines. Also erase any construction entities, such as points created where lines were divided. These often import as artifacts (bits and pieces of geometry).

Remove all textures, x-referenced and imported files, colors, and dynamic blocks. These often cause problems upon import.

Ensure that lines connected at endpoints are connected. This applies to lines that define surfaces you plan to model.

Run the Units command so you know what the units are. Scale the file to 1:1, if it isn't already.

Ensure the file is smaller than 15MB, as larger ones might not import.

Import a *dwg* File of the Cottage

Click **File>Import** and then locate the *dwg* file. Make sure that *AutoCAD Files* is visible in the Files of type field at the bottom (Figure 5–61).

Click *Options* and check the boxes in Figure 5–62. The top two tell SketchUp to treat the AutoCAD file like a SketchUp file. Set the units field to the AutoCAD plan's units. That is, if the plan's units are feet, set it to feet. This is important! If the AutoCAD plan's scale and this box's scale are different, scaling the plan after import will be difficult. It's also best to uncheck the *Preserve drawing origin* box. This enables SketchUp to place the imported Auto-CAD plan at the origin. If it's placed elsewhere, "clipping" may occur, a glitch that causes part of the plan to disappear.

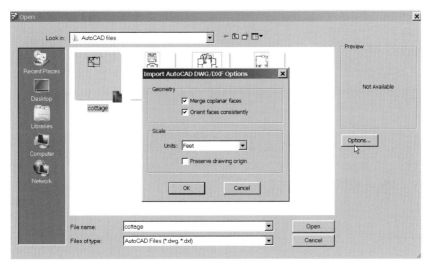

Figure 5–61: Scroll to *AutoCAD Files* in the *Files of type* field, and then locate the file.

Figure 5–62: Click *Options* and check the boxes shown.

Click *Open* to import the *dwg* file into SketchUp. A box appears showing the specific data imported. Click again and ta-da! The imported AutoCAD file (Figure 5–63) is now SketchUp geometry.

If the plan imported as a group, explode it (select, right-click, choose *Explode*). One explosion shouldn't affect imported blocks, which enter SketchUp as components. However, you might find that some blocks (now components) behave oddly when panning and orbiting. Fix by exploding and remaking them as components again. Finally, scale the plan to its correct dimensions with the Tape Measure.

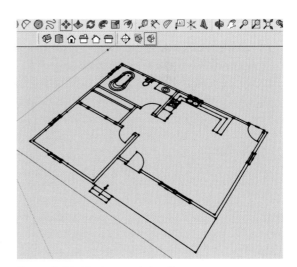

Figure 5–63: The imported *dwg* file.

Some cleanup tasks can be done on the AutoCAD file after import. Delete unneeded layers by clicking on **Window>Layers**, and choose *Purge* on the fly-out menu (Figure 5–64). Get rid of all unused data at **Window>Model>Statistics** by clicking the *Purge Unused* button at the bottom. Delete unneeded AutoCAD entities individually by selecting and erasing.

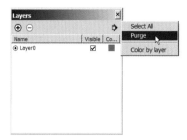

Figure 5–64: Some cleanup of the *dwg* file can be done after import, such as deleting layers.

Trace and model the walls. Turn walls into faces by tracing over them with the Pencil. It will snap to endpoints (Figure 5–65), and just one line is usually enough to form a face. Erase any portion covering the windows. Then push/pull the walls up.

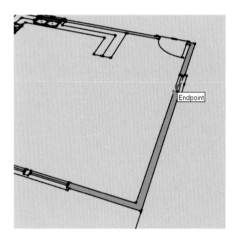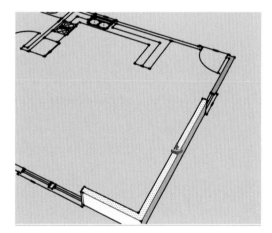

Figure 5–65: Trace walls to create faces and push/pull them up.

SketchUp Pro can also export *skp* files into AutoCAD. All exported plans, elevations, and sections keep their true scale, and components and layers stay intact. Units default to inches.

Interact with Revit, 20–20, and Other Programs

Import a Revit model into SketchUp by exporting the *rvt* file to a *dxf* or *dwg* file (within Revit) first, and then importing that file into SketchUp. Import 20–20 models into SketchUp by exporting the *kit* file to a *dfx* file (within 20–20) first, and then importing the *dfx* into SketchUp. A lot of cleanup will be needed, since you're importing a solid model into a surface modeler. SketchUp models can be imported into both Revit and 20–20.

SketchUp Make can import and export files with some other 3D programs, notably Maya, Poser, 3ds Max, and Blender. A free program called COLLADA must be downloaded as an intermediary. COLLADA converts *skp* and those other programs' files into a generic format with an *xml* extension.

"Clipping" (Disappearing Geometry)

Clipping is a glitch that causes faces to partially disappear when orbiting and zooming. It occurs when geometry is very small or very large or when it's located far from the origin. The latter is common after a *dwg* import. Fix by clicking *Zoom Extents*, and then move the geometry to the origin.

Move Geometry by Typing Coordinates

To move a faraway piece of geometry to the origin, select it, activate Move, and grab a ground-plane corner. Then type *[0,0,0]* (include the square brackets), and **Enter** (Figure 5–66). The selected geometry will snap there.

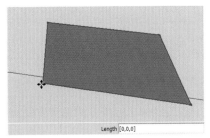

Figure 5–66: To move a faraway piece of geometry to the origin, select it, click Move on a ground-plane corner, move it a bit, immediately type [0,0,0] (include the square brackets) and **Enter**.

This technique also moves distant pieces of geometry together. By now you've probably experienced the difficulty of moving two items together that are far apart and not aligned. It can take a frustrating number of attempts. Instead, click the Text tool (Figure 5–67) on a corner of one item to see its coordinates. Select the other item, activate Move, grab a bottom corner, type those coordinates in square brackets, and **Enter**. The item will snap to, or near, the coordinate location. The Text tool is discussed more in Chapter 8.

Figure 5–67: The Text tool.

Model a Sloped Ceiling with the Protractor Tool

Let's end this chapter with one more modeling trick: a sloped ceiling. To draw it we need the Protractor tool.

The Protractor (Figure 5–68) measures angles and creates angled guide lines. It looks like the Rotate tool, but doesn't rotate anything; it just measures.

Figure 5–68: The Protractor tool.

Like Rotate, it aligns with whatever edge it touches. Hold the left mouse key down and drag to make it cycle through all axis colors. Hold the **Shift** key down to lock the correct axis, and then move the Protractor to the desired location. The Protractor has lines spaced in 15° increments. When the cursor is close to the Protractor, it snaps to those increments. When the cursor is farther away, it moves more precisely.

Let's make a space with a 6:12 ceiling slope (for every 12 units horizontal, it goes 6 units up), and then measure some angles on it.

Draw two 6:12 sloped guidelines. The Protractor requires three clicks. First click it on the right corner, as shown in Figure 5–69. Then click again in the same spot to mark the guide line's first endpoint. You can now rotate the guide line with the cursor and click the second endpoint anywhere, or type a precise slope expressed as a ratio or angle. Type *6:12* and click a third time. The sloped guide line is finished. Then click the Protractor on the opposite corner. Click again to set the guideline. Type *-6:12* to make the guide line go the opposite way. Click a third time to set. If, for whatever reason, the guide line doesn't appear on the corner you wanted, use Move to put it there.

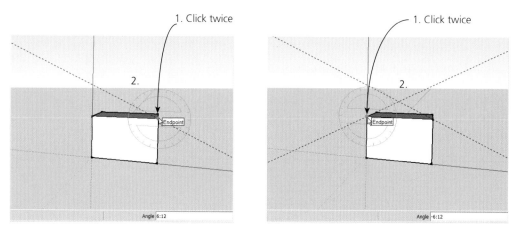

Figure 5–69: Click the Protractor twice on a corner, type an angle, and click a third time to set.

Model the ceiling. Trace the guide lines with the Pencil and push/pull the length of the space (Figure 5–70).

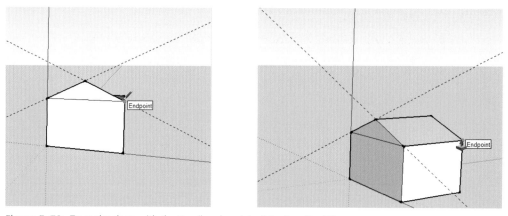

Figure 5–70: Trace the slope with the Pencil and push/pull the length of the room.

Delete the front face . Now you can see the interior space (Figure 5–71).

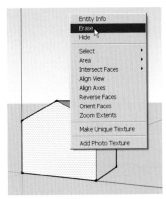

Figure 5–71: Delete the front face to expose the interior and its sloped ceiling.

Measure an Angle with the Protractor Tool

If you need to measure an angle, the Protractor can do that, too. Even though we know the ceiling's slope already, let's apply the Protractor to it as if we didn't.

1. Click the Protractor on the corner.
2. Move it left until it's under the ridge. Click.
3. Move it straight up to the ridge. Click. The Measurements box shows the angle as about 26.6° (Figure 5–72).

Let's measure one more angle, the one between the wall and floor (Figure 5–73).

1. Click on the corner.
2. Click on the floor edge.
3. Click on the wall edge. The Measurements box shows the angle as 90°.

Up for more challenges? They're right ahead. In Chapter 6 we'll model a two-story space and stairs.

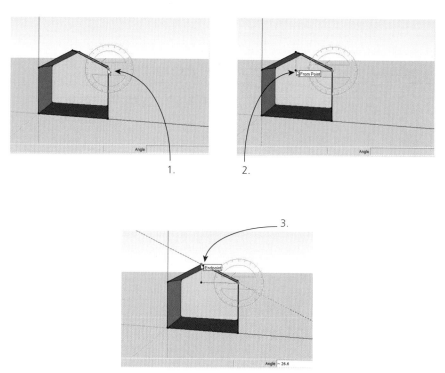

Figure 5–72: Measuring the ceiling angle.

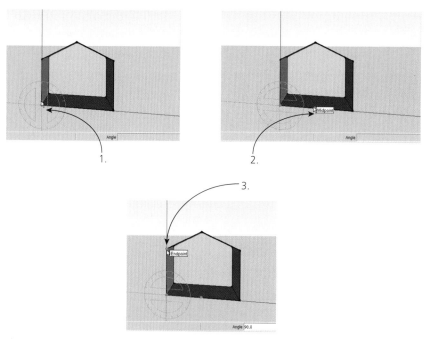

Figure 5–73: Measuring the angle between the wall and floor.

SketchUp for Interior Design

Summary

We drafted a floor plan by tracing over an imported file, using a paper sketch, and importing a *dwg* file. During the modeling process we applied different face and edge styles, inference-matched line lengths, resized the model based on one part's known dimension, and imported components from the Warehouse. We made a component collection and linked it to the Components browser. We generated floor plans and interior elevations from the model with the Section tool, and modeled a sloped ceiling.

Further Resources

Download COLLADA, an intermediary program that facilitates the import/export of SketchUp Make with other modeling programs. http://collada.org/mediawiki/index.php/ OpenCOLLADA

Download free SketchUp and Revit models from the Herman Miller furniture company. www.hermanmiller.com/content/hermanmiller/english/design-resources/3d-models-revit/ 3d-models-by-product/seating.html

Download Irfanview, a free digital imaging program. http://www.irfanview.com/

Online Photoshop clone. www.gimp.org/

Source for models and textures that are free, low cost, and by subscription. http://sketchucation.com/shop

Source for SketchUp, Revit, and 3ds Max models via paid subscription. www.formfonts.com/

The Trimble 3D Warehouse. http://sketchup.google.com/3dwarehouse/

The Warehouse terms of service. http://sketchup.google.com/3dwarehouse/preview_tos.html

Exercises

www.wiley.com/go/sketchupforinteriordesign

1. Model Exercise 5–1 (3D of a house), estimating room sizes.
2. Trace and model Exercise 5–2 (cottage floor plan).
3. Do a Google image search for floor plans. Right-click and save one to your computer. Import and scale to a known dimension (e.g., 24″-deep cabinets or a 3′0″ door).
4. Trace and model Exercise 5–3 (apartment floor plan). Import a Warehouse fireplace component for it.
5. Import an AutoCAD plan that you've done for work or school, and then model it.
6. Download some Warehouse models from the Components browser. Edit them and save them under different names. Make one unique.
7. Make a collections folder, and link it to the Materials browser.

Modeling a Two-Story House Interior

I n Chapter 5 we modeled simple spaces. Here, we'll build on the tools and techniques learned there to make an interior model of a two-story home. Our approach will be: (1) Import and model a raster first-floor plan, (2) make a shell to enclose the floors, and (3) import and model an AutoCAD second-floor plan.

Objective: This chapter models a two-story home interior, stairs, and cabinets, and utilizes layers and the Outliner.

Tools: Follow Me, Axis, Intersect Faces, Paint Bucket, Outliner

Concepts and Functions: layers, edit an AutoCAD plan inside SketchUp, model a staircase, guard, cabinets, beveled cabinet doors, crown molding, and mansard roof; change endpoint appearance, divide a line, auto-fold, Components dialog box, components in model, smooth/soften curves, mirror with the scale tool, apply the default paint color, reverse faces, orient faces, relocate a component axis, monochrome face style, field of view, definition name, instance name

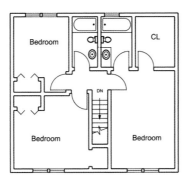 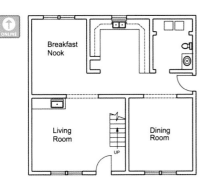

Figure 6–1: Floor plans of a two-story house.

Model the Shell and First Floor

Import a jpg of the first floor (Figure 6–2). Explode and group it. Resize it based on a 3'0"-wide exterior door, using the Tape Measure. Outline the perimeter with the Rectangle to make a face. Then change the face style to transparent at **View>Face Style>X-ray**.

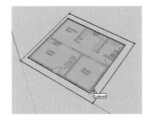

Figure 6–2: Trace a face over an imported floor plan jpg.

Push/pull the face up 20'. Then select the top and erase (Figure 6–3). This creates the exterior walls.

Group the walls (Figure 6–4). This creates a shell inside which modeling can be done without sticking to the walls.

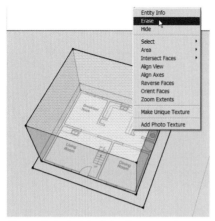

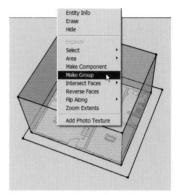

Figure 6–3: Push/pull the face up and erase the top to make the exterior walls.

Figure 6–4: Group the walls to create a shell.

Trace the interior walls (Figure 6–5). Switch to a plan view (**Views** menu/plan icon, click on **Camera>Parallel projection**, and change the edge settings color to red. Draw single-line walls for simplicity. As discussed in Chapter 5, double-sided walls present problems when inserting door and window components, and aren't essential for interior models. Instead, draw a single line in the center of the plan walls.

Model the interior walls. Place a 10'-high guide line on the shell, and draw a line around its perimeter (Figure 6–6) to serve as a height guide. Then model interior walls along the plan lines (Figure 6–7). When you're done, the model should look like Figure 6–8.

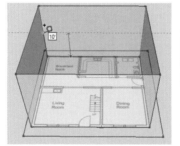

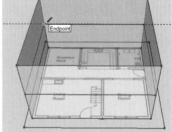

Figure 6–5: Trace the walls.

Figure 6–6: Place a guide line 10' high and draw lines around the shell's perimeter.

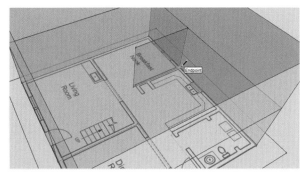

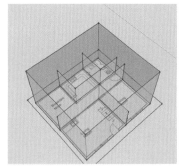

Figure 6–7: Model the walls along the axes and look for inferences.

Figure 6–8: The first-floor interior walls.

Group the interior walls (Figure 6–9). Double-click the faces to select them plus their edges. *Group the floors.* Again, double-click to select faces and edges (Figure 6–10).

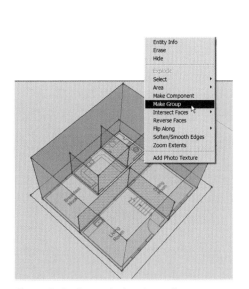

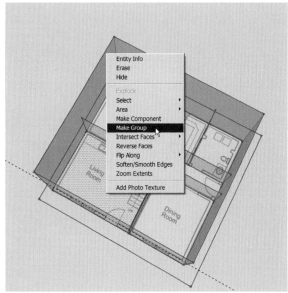

Figure 6–9: Group the interior walls.

Figure 6–10: Group the floors.

A building's major components—floors, exterior walls, interior walls, ceiling—should all be grouped separately. Once a building reaches this level of complexity, it also needs organization. This is achieved with layers.

What Is a Layer?

A layer is a visibility property. You can turn it on and off, making it visible or invisible. This enables you to do things such as view and work in areas obscured by other areas, present different design options for the same space, speed up regeneration time, and organize the model.

When a layer is turned off, only visibility is affected. The geometry on that layer is still attached to the geometry on other layers and will move with it. You can easily deform a model by forgetting about geometry on invisible layers. Therefore, it is critical that only groups and components be placed on any new layer you create. This will also make it harder to "lose" pieces of geometry. All loose geometry belongs on Layer 0, and that's the layer you should always model on. Group what you want to move to another layer, and then move it there. Don't put loose geometry, ever, on any layer but 0.

Add Layers and Move Parts of the House to Them

To make a new layer, click **Window>Layers** (Figure 6–11). A dialog box opens showing the default Layer 0. The checked radio button means it's the active layer; everything you model goes on the active layer. The checked *Visible* box means you can see this layer. Create a new one by clicking the plus sign. A text field will appear to name it. Layer 0 cannot be renamed or deleted.

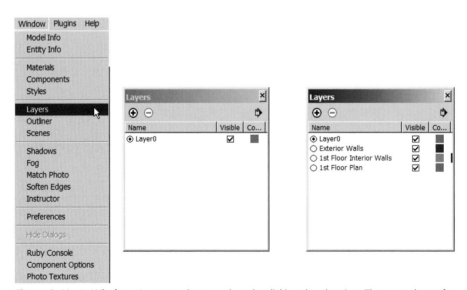

Figure 6–11: At **Window>Layers** make a new layer by clicking the plus sign. Three new layers for the house are shown in the dialog box on the far right.

All geometry remains on the layer it was created on, which, again, should be Layer 0. Physically moving geometry to another layer doesn't "change" it to that layer. To move geometry—which, again, should be only a group or component—to a different layer, select and right-click to bring up the Entity Info box (Figure 6–12). Scroll through the *Layers* field and select one. That action moves the group/component to that layer. Close, and then verify the layer change by reselecting the group/component and viewing its Entity Info box again.

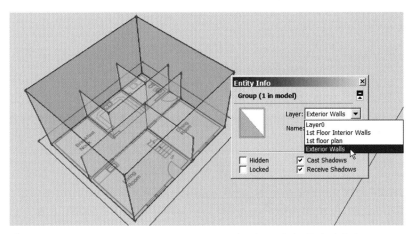

Figure 6–12: Move a group or component to another layer via its Entity Info box.

To muddy the waters a bit, the group/component moves to another layer, but the loose geometry inside it remains on Layer 0. You just move the "shell." But this is okay. Leave the loose geometry on Layer 0, because layers are just for visibility, and moving the shell achieves that. However, if you ever do need to move some interior pieces (there are times when this is appropriate, mostly related to third-party rendering applications), open the editing box, select those pieces (Figure 6–13), right-click to access Entity Info, and scroll to the appropriate layer. Be aware that when a group/component is on one layer and its geometry is (correctly) on Layer 0, exploding it moves the geometry to the same layer as the group/component! It will all be selected, however, so immediately move it back to Layer 0.

Put the other groups in the house on their appropriate layers. Figures 6–14 and 6–15 show the grouped interior walls and floor plan selected for moving to their respective layers. The jpg was given its own layer so it can be turned off instead

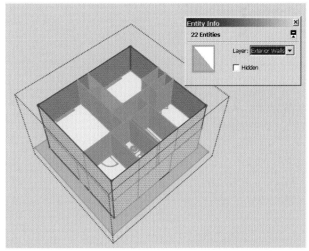

Figure 6–13: When a group is moved to another layer, its geometry remains on 0. Exploding the group moves the geometry to that layer. Open the editing box and move it back to 0.

of erased, in case it's needed later. When a layer is turned off, SketchUp doesn't calculate it in the zoom, pan, and orbit functions, which makes it run faster. Merely hiding an entity does keep it in the calculations.

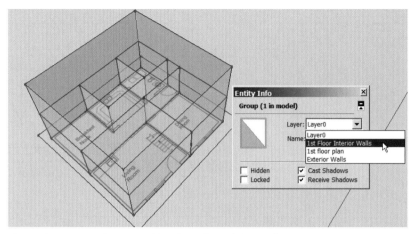

Figure 6–14: Move the grouped interior walls to their own layer.

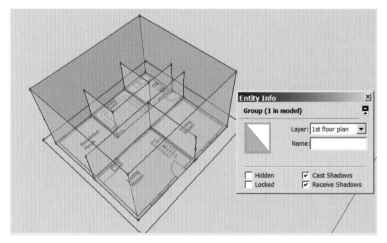

Figure 6–15: Move the floor plan jpg to its own layer.

Make sure Layer 0 is checked before you resume modeling. If you inadvertently draw on another layer, select what you drew and move it to Layer 0 via its Entity Info box.

Delete a layer by highlighting it in the Layer dialog box and clicking the minus symbol. If the layer contains geometry, SketchUp asks if you want to delete or move it to another layer. Click the desired option and *ok*.

Model the Second Floor

Model the second floor by tracing the perimeter of the first floor. Move it off the house and group it (Figure 6–16).

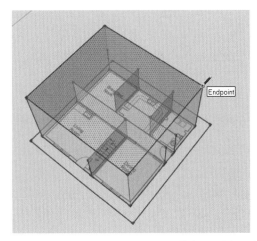
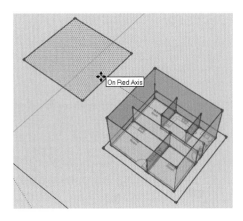

Figure 6–16: Make a face, move it off the model, and group. That will be the second floor.

Now we need an image of the second floor plan to model the walls. And this is where we hit a wall with Make. Importing a *jpg* isn't a good solution because we can't precisely match its size to the first floor; there are no endpoints to click on. We need to import an AutoCAD file, a Pro feature discussed in Chapter 5.

Import the AutoCAD file. It will enter at the origin. Overlay it on the second floor face (Figure 6–17). We can see that the face is larger than the plan.

Scale the AutoCAD file to match the floor plan. Highlight the AutoCAD file, click the Scale tool, and adjust the middle grips (Figure 6–18).

The AutoCAD plan may need to be exploded to be editable. Portions of it may need to be exploded again. You'll find this out when you start editing it.

Erase the stairs, because they'll be modeled on the first floor (Figure 6–19).

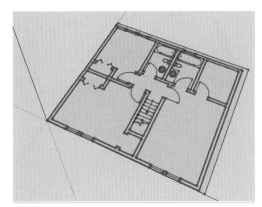

Figure 6–17: The imported AutoCAD plan overlaid on the second floor face.

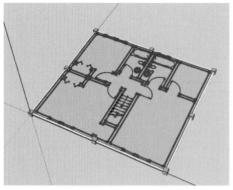

Figure 6–18: Adjust the AutoCAD plan to the face below it with the Scale tool's middle grips.

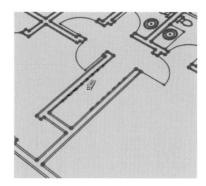

Figure 6–19: Erase the stairs.

There are multiple approaches to modeling the second floor. Here are some techniques:

▶ CAD plans represent walls as double lines. You can use the plan as is and model the walls with double faces, or you can erase one set of lines, leaving the other to model single-face walls on (Figure 6–20). The latter is what we'll do.

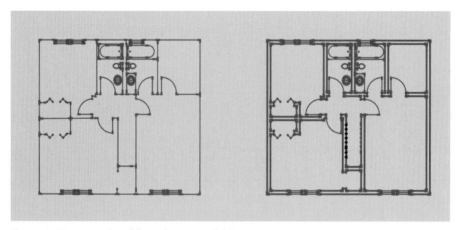

Figure 6–20: Two styles of floor plans to model from.

▶ Reconstruct a broken floor face by tracing the perimeter (Figure 6–21). If a face won't fill, review the discussion in Chapter 4 for possible causes.

▶ Trace the stairwell opening to create a separate face from the rest of the floor. Then right-click and erase it (Figure 6–22).

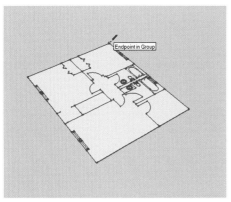

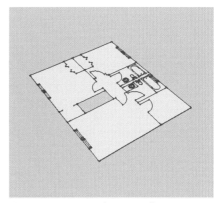

Figure 6–21: Trace the perimeter to reconstruct a broken floor face.

Figure 6–22: Trace the stairwell opening to create a separate face, then erase it.

▶ Mark the middle of the shell with a guide line. Group the floor, then grab it by a corner and click into place (Figure 6–23).

▶ Model the walls using the shell as a height guide (Figure 6–24).

▶ Model the walls outside the shell, if you find that easier. Use a guide line for height references (Figure 6–25). If you don't get the wall height right, adjust it after moving the floor into the shell. For instance, if a wall protrudes above the shell, just draw a horizontal line the correct height across the wall's face and erase everything above that line.

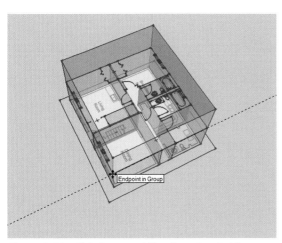

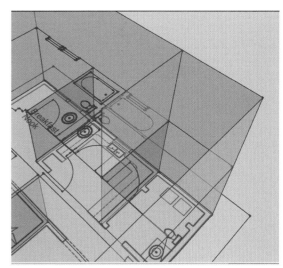

Figure 6–23: Click the second floor into place inside the shell.

Figure 6–24: Model the walls using the top of the shell as a guide. Use inferencing to match the upper walls' lengths to the lower walls' lengths.

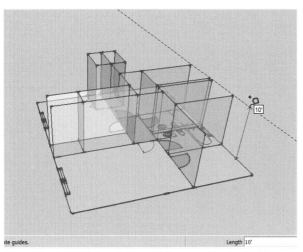

Figure 6–25: Modeling the second floor outside the shell is an alternative.

When the second floor is finished, group all the walls and put them on their own layer.

Tips for Efficient Modeling

You've probably found by now that modeling an interior isn't easy. Most walls probably took multiple attempts just to make them coplanar. Here are some general tips for efficient modeling:

- ▶ Inference-match to obtain line lengths, watch for inference tooltips when connecting the lines, and draw along the axes. Hold the **Shift** key down to lock the Pencil and Move tools along the axes.

- ▶ If geometry is in an awkward location to modify, cut and paste it somewhere else on the screen, work on it there, and then move it back.

- ▶ Make a copy of the work, and try different techniques on it. For instance, if drawing multiple parallel lines or walls is problematic, select one already drawn and copy it to other locations. That's quicker than drawing each separately, and if something goes wrong, *undo* is your friend.

- ▶ Nested groups and components require opening multiple editing boxes to reach the geometry that needs editing. When you are editing a group or component, if a piece of geometry you want to select is grayed out, it means the geometry isn't in that group. If it's currently in the same spot outside the group, relocate it in the same spot inside the group by clicking **File>Edit>Cut**, opening the group editing box, and clicking **File>Edit>Paste in Place**. Otherwise, close the editing box, erase that piece, and redraw it inside the group.

- It's easy to inadvertently put a group's geometry on multiple layers, or to group walls and leave their edges out. When grouping, be mindful of what's on hidden layers, and double-click faces to select them plus their edges. Orbit before grouping to ensure that everything you want to group is selected.

- Create separate layers for groups, components, and different kinds of components. Name all layers recognizably.

- Change the face style to hidden line or wireframe to find hidden lines or other issues causing problems.

Keep your model clean and organized to make working on it easier, both for you and for any other people on the project. Commercial designers often send their SketchUp models to professional renderers, who import them into their own programs. If the file is sloppy and bloated, they'll have to edit or rebuild parts of it. If it's too large, they may not even be able to import it.

Model a Staircase

The plan shows a straight-run staircase with 10 risers and 9 treads. The first floor's total rise (height) is 10′-0″, and its total run (length) is 9′-0″. We'll make each step's riser 12″ tall and each tread 12″ deep. Not quite architectural standards (typical riser height is 7″, and tread depth 10″), but simpler to demonstrate. Turn off layers that obscure the stairs area by unchecking their visibility boxes (Figure 6–26). Draw a vertical construction line where the stairs start. The risers will be marked on this line by splitting it into 10 parts using the *Divide* function.

Figure 6–26: Hide layers obscuring the stairs area.

Mark the Risers by Dividing a Line into Segments

SketchUp automatically divides a line into two segments when a second line touches it. It can be divided into multiple, equal segments by selecting it, right-clicking, and choosing *Divide* (Figure 6–27). Dots appear along the line. Drag the cursor up and down the line to increase or decrease the number of divisions. A tooltip appears, describing the current number length of each line segment. Click to set that number. To see how many segments a divided line has, select the whole line, right click, and choose *Entity Info*.

Each line segment has endpoints. If you can't see them, increase the *Endpoints* number at **Window>Styles>Edit** (Figure 6–28). As an aside, adjusting endpoint appearance is something you might do if you don't like their default appearance. Put a *0* in the *Endpoints* box to make them invisible.

Draw two steps, inferencing their riser heights from the riser markers (Figure 6–29).

Copy the steps with Move and **Ctrl** to the top of the wall (Figure 6–30).

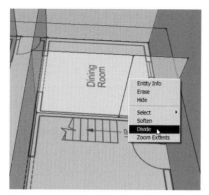 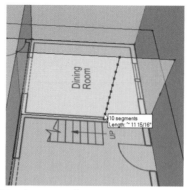

Figure 6–27: Select the line to be divided, right-click, choose *Divide*, and move the cursor up and down until the tooltip shows 10: segments.

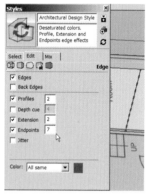

Figure 6–28: Adjust end-points size in the Style box, and their appearance will automatically update.

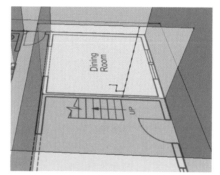

Figure 6–29: Draw two steps, inferencing their riser heights from the riser markers.

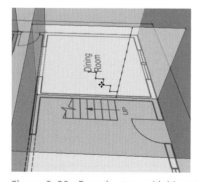 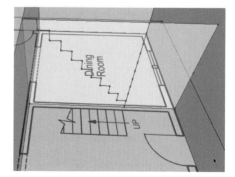

Figure 6–30: Copy the steps with Move and **Ctrl** to the top of the wall.

Complete the face. Draw the staircase's vertical and horizontal edges to form a face (Figure 6–31).

Push/pull the staircase to a width that lines up with the plan (Figure 6–32). Press and release the **Ctrl** key first (look for the plus sign), to keep the wall behind the staircase intact. Otherwise, it will get extruded with the stairs.

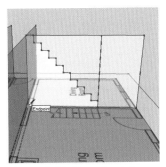

Figure 6–31: Draw the staircase's vertical and horizontal edges to form a face.

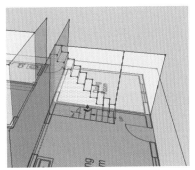

Figure 6–32: Push/pull the staircase to a width that lines up with the plan.

Erase the construction line. Drag the Eraser over the construction line to quickly delete it (Figure 6–33). You may first need to orbit to a position to avoid erasing other geometry.

Group the staircase, turn on all the layers, and here it is (Figure 6–34)!

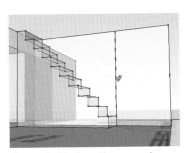

Figure 6–33: Drag the eraser down the line to delete it.

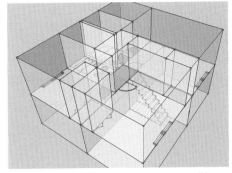

Figure 6–34: The two-story model with all layers visible.

This model enables the study of applied colors and textures as well as the study of space, proportion, and scale. In Chapter 8 we'll learn camera tools that will let you walk inside this model to view its spaces from a consistent eye-level.

Let's finish it off with a mansard roof. Uncheck the X-ray view at **View>Face Style** to make it easier to see.

Draw a roof face. Trace the perimeter of the roof with the Pencil tool. Push/pull it up a little bit, and then offset it 6′ (Figure 6–35). To create the mansard form, we'll do an operation called *autofold*.

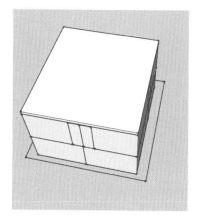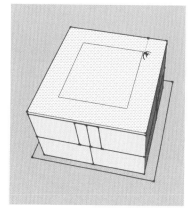

Figure 6–35: Make a roof face, push/pull it up, and then offset it.

Model a Mansard Roof with Autofold

SketchUp only lets you move planes horizontally or vertically, as this keeps them coplanar. But you can override this restriction by holding the **Alt** key down (**Command** on the Mac) while using the Move tool. The plane will then freely move in any direction. However, to create a nonplanar face, SketchUp must create additional edges and faces. That creation of additional edges and faces is called autofolding.

Autofold the roof. Activate the Move tool and press **Alt**. Then lift the roof straight up along the blue axis. The perimeter of the roof will fold, or bevel in (Figure 6–36).

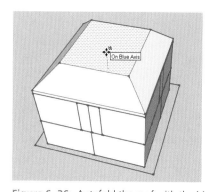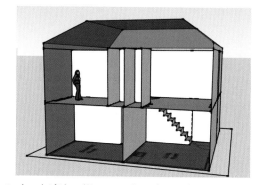

Figure 6–36: Autofold the roof with the Move tool and **Alt** key (**Command** on the Mac).

Model the Living Room

We're going to model the living room by adding a wet bar and crown molding. We'll also import a nicer staircase and edit it to fit.

Field of View

The *field of view* (FOV) is how much of the model you can see at one time; in perspective drawing, it's called the *cone of vision*. The wider the field of view, the more of the model you see. You may find it easier to work with a wider view of the space than Make's default of 35° and Pro's default of 30°. Both of these are quite narrow, as the human eye sees the world through a 60° cone of vision.

Go to **Camera>Field of View**. The default FOV will appear in the measurements box. Type *60*. This results in a wider view of the space, at the price of some distortion (Figure 6–37). The FOV can be set up to 120°, but when it's very wide, clipping (disappearing faces) may occur. The FOV can also be changed by pressing **Shift** while zooming in or out.

The FOV can be set in inches or millimeters as well as degrees; type the number and include the inch sign (″) or *mm*. A 60° view is equivalent to 2.2″ or 57 mm. Return to degrees by typing the number and *deg* after it (no space).

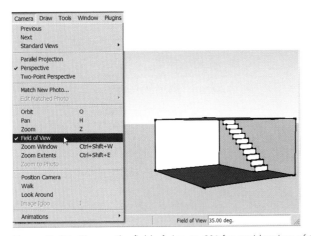

Figure 6–37: Change the field of view to 60° for a wider view of the space.

Model the Wet Bar Cabinets

The plan shows cabinetry on the back wall. Place a guide line along the cabinetry edge (Figure 6–38).

Choose an approach for modeling the cabinets. Do you need to show a specific brand, or will a generic that resembles it suffice? Should you model it yourself, or import it?

If you need a specific brand, search the Warehouse, manufacturer's website, or sweets.com (an

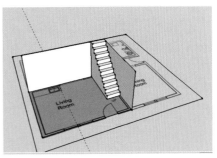

Figure 6–38: Place a guide line along the cabinetry edge.

online database of building product literature and CAD drawings), for downloadable models. If approximating a brand's appearance will suffice, download generic cabinets from the Warehouse and edit as needed.

Find Warehouse Collections

Find product catalogs at the Warehouse by scrolling to *Collections* in the search field at the top of the page and typing a keyword, such as *furniture*, *finishes*, *appliances*, *fixtures*, *cabinets*, or *countertops* (Figure 6–39a). You can also enter generic keywords, brand names, product lines and models, even SKU codes. Returns will include company and user-generated models.

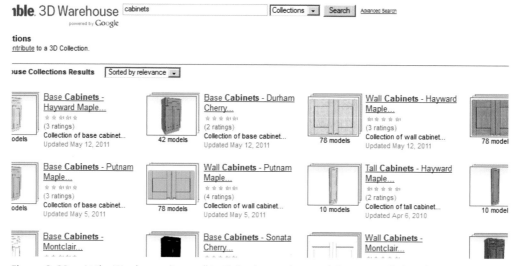

Figure 6–39a: At the Warehouse site, scroll to *Collections* at the top of the page to find product catalogs.

Save as a Local Collection: Download Multiple Models at Once

In Chapter 5 we downloaded models one at a time from the Warehouse and saved them in a local collection (a folder on your computer in which components are stored). You can also download every model returned from a Warehouse search at the same time, instead of one at a time, and save them in their own collection (Figure 6–39b).

Open the Components browser discussed in Chapter 5 and type a search in the text field. I searched for stairs. Click the Details arrow and choose *Save as a local collection*. A browser appears; choose a location to place the new folder, and then name it. I made a folder called Warehouse Components on the desktop. The models displayed in the browser quickly downloaded to it. Delete unwanted models by right-clicking and choosing *Delete*. Then go back to the Details arrow and choose *Add to favorites* for this collection to appear in the Favorites submenu.

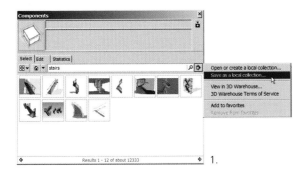
1.

2.

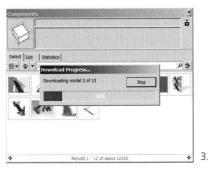
3.

4.

Figure 6–39b: Download multiple models at once into a local collection.

Model a Cabinet

Using ready-made components saves time only if extensive editing isn't needed. Our floor plan shows cabinetry that isn't the exact length of any Warehouse model. We could edit, but constructing generic cabinets from scratch won't take much longer. Watch.

Draw the cabinet profile (Figure 6–40) using product literature as a guide; there's often a cross section you can trace. Alternatively, explode a Warehouse cabinet component and erase everything except its profile.

▶ Typical cabinet dimensions: Base (bottom) cabinets are 24″ wide and 34½″ high. The countertop adds another 1½″ in height, and has a 1″ overhang. The toe kick is 3″ deep × 4″ high. There is 18″ between the countertop and bottom of the wall (upper) cabinets. Wall cabinets are 12″–18″ deep and 12″–36″ tall.

Model the cabinets by orbiting around and push/pulling the profile to the guide line (Figure 6–41). Or type the numerical length. Voila—instant cabinets with toe kick and countertop.

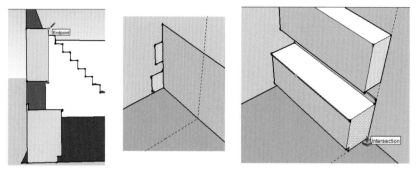

Figure 6–40: Draw the cabinet profile.

Figure 6–41: Push/pull the profile the length of the cabinets.

Add the doors (Figure 6–42). Divide the wall cabinet into five parts, draw lines at the endpoints, and copy those lines to the base cabinets.

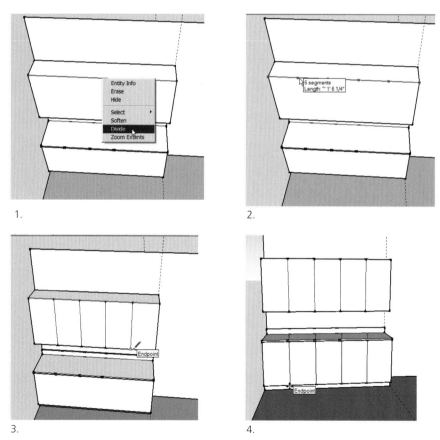

1.

2.

3.

4.

Figure 6–42: Add doors by dividing the length, drawing lines at the endpoints, and copying the lines to the base cabinets.

Download a sink. Back to the Warehouse. The *Bar Sink* by Grill-rite looks good. It imports backward, so rotate it (Figure 6–43).

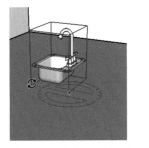

Figure 6–43: Rotate the sink to position it in the cabinet.

Make the rotated sink a new component (Figure 6–44). Explode, select it, right-click, choose *Make Component*, and name it *Bar Sink 2.* Its thumbnail will appear in *In Model* next to the downloaded one; click on the house icon in the Components browser to verify (Figure 6–45). Incidentally, you can view the models in different ways by clicking the *List* icon left of the house. Copy both sinks to the local collection made in Chapter 5, if you want them available to all SketchUp files. Finally, copy *Bar Sink 2* once more and make it unique (right-click, choose *Make unique*) so you can make further changes to it without affecting the definition instance. Use that one going forward.

 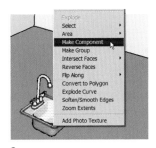

1.   2.

3.

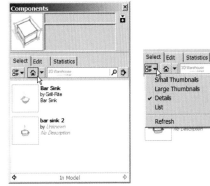

Figure 6–44: Rotate the downloaded sink and make it a new component.

Figure 6–45: View both sinks *In Model* (click the *List* icon for a different display).

Install the sink (Figure 6–46). Relocate the unique copy of *Bar Sink 2* into the cabinet, watching for the *on face* inference. Explode. The bowl is now visible.

In this case, exposing the bowl was a simple matter of exploding the sink. It's not always that simple. A component's construction might require multiple explosions. Eventually it should explode down to a face over the sink, which, when erased, exposes the bowl (Figure 6–47). Again—depending on the exact construction—you might also have to apply a tool called *Intersect Faces* (discussed later in this chapter) after the sink is inserted into the cabinet, but *before* it's exploded. What is exactly needed is determined by trial and error.

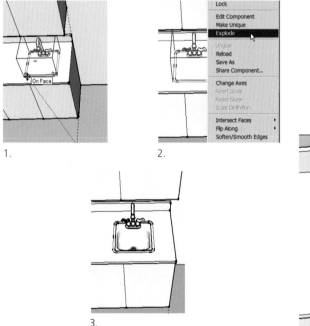

Figure 6–46: Relocate the sink into the cabinet and explode it to make the bowl visible.

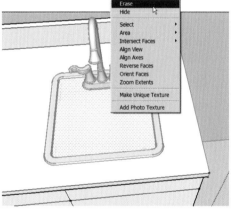

Figure 6–47: Erase the face over the exploded *Bar Sink 2* to expose the bowl beneath.

Let's make the cabinet doors a little less plain.

Add a raised panel (Figure 6–48). Offset the door edge twice: once for the reveal (the space between the cabinet frame and door), and once for the panel. Autofold the inner rectangle by pulling it out, using Move plus **Alt**. Then make the panel a component.

Use components for multiple copies because they take up less space than groups. And if a change is needed, changing one will change all.

Copy the component panel to the rest of the doors (Figure 6–49), and the wet bar is done.

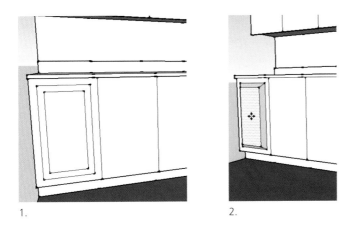

1.

2.

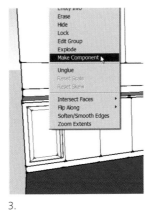

Entity Info
Erase
Hide
Lock
Edit Group
Explode
Make Component

Unglue
Reset Scale
Reset Skew

Intersect Faces ▸
Flip Along ▸
Soften/Smooth Edges
Zoom Extents

3.

Figure 6–48: Make a beveled panel with the Offset tool and autofolding.

Figure 6–49: Copy the component panel to the rest of the doors.

Model Crown Molding with the Follow Me Tool

Crown molding, the trim at the top of the wall, is easily made with a tool called *Follow Me* (Figure 6–50). This tool extrudes (stretches) a face along a perpendicular path. Draw a face at one end and stretch it to the other.

Figure 6–50: The Follow Me tool.

Follow Me won't stretch along grouped geometry. But it's dangerous to use within a group because it may adversely affect surrounding geometry. A workaround is to open the group: Use **Edit>Copy** on the geometry chosen as the path, close the editing box, and **Edit>Paste in Place** that geometry in the same place outside the group. Then apply Follow Me on that copy.

Draw a molding profile with the Pencil and Arc. If the profile is elaborate, trace an imported file. Scale to size when finished (4″ height is typical), and move the profile onto the wall. Don't group it.

There are two ways to use Follow Me:

1. *Manually drag it* (Figure 6–51). Orbit to the profile's back face, click Follow Me on it, press the cursor down and drag the profile across the wall. Click into place against the stairs.

2. *Click on a path* (Figure 6–52). Rotate along the red axis and copy the profile along the other wall. Select the wall's top edge. Click Follow Me on the profile. The profile will be selected, and the wall edge will appear to be deselected, but it really isn't. Click the profile. It will extrude down the path.

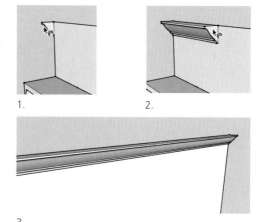

1.   2.

3.

Figure 6–51: Create crown molding by dragging the profile with Follow Me across the wall.

The second way is usually the easiest, especially if the path isn't straight. It also yields a continuous result, whereas stopping along the path while manually dragging creates an edge at each stop. Of course, that may be what you want (to show the molding in pieces).

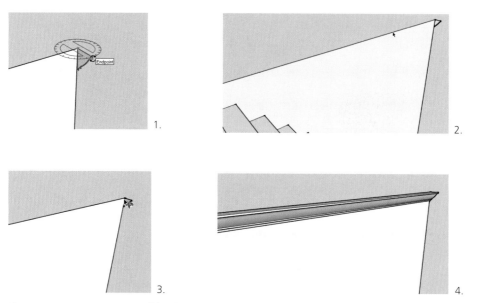

1.   2.

3.   4.

Figure 6–52: Create crown molding by selecting a path and then clicking Follow Me on the molding's profile.

Follow Me extrudes the face behind it. Looking behind the walls, we see that the face is now hollowed out (Figure 6–53). To avoid this, press and release the **Ctrl** key (look for the + sign) right before extruding. That leaves the original face in place.

Smooth/Soften Curves

If the second piece of molding has an inexplicable bunch of lines that the first one didn't have, you probably copied its profile *after* that profile was extruded. Here's what happened. Circles and arcs are made of a bunch of short lines, and SketchUp automatically smooths them for a better appearance. However, after they're stretched with

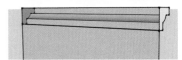

Figure 6–53: Follow Me extrudes the face behind it. Click **Ctrl** immediately before extruding to keep the face intact.

Follow Me or exploded, they lose that smoothing, and their appearance reverts back to what it is: a bunch of lines. This happens frequently when modeling curved items such as columns, handrails, the bonnet on a highboy, or a headboard.

To fix, select the curved area, right-click, and choose *Soften/Smooth Edges*. The default smoothing returns, and even offers up a settings adjustment box (Figure 6–54). Smoothing is also how you can round the sharp edges of a couch cushion. Perform small, detailed smoothing with the Eraser plus the **Ctrl** key.

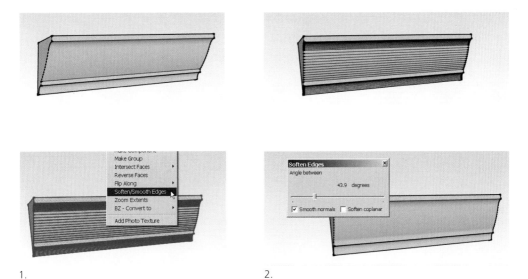

1.   2.

Figure 6–54: A curve is actually a bunch of short lines and loses its smoothness when stretched or exploded. Restore by selecting, right-clicking, and choosing *Soften/Smooth Edges*.

Smoothing has another use. Some lines can't be deleted, such as the lines that connect an arc to a straight line (Figure 6–55). Deleting them will delete the face. Smooth the line to make it invisible. This is different from hiding it, because smoothing enables the adjacent faces to be selected as one. If the line is simply hidden, the straight and curved parts will be selected separately. Smoothing works best on aligned surfaces. On perpendicular surfaces, results may be uneven.

The Intersect Faces Tool

Look at the other end of the molding (Figure 6–54). It touches the stairs but doesn't create an edge. Adjacent geometry doesn't always intersect. In such cases, use the Intersect Faces tool to force an intersection. Select the stairs or the molding and right-click or go to **Edit>Intersect Faces**, and choose *With Model*. An edge will appear (Figure 6–56).

Groups and components can be intersected with this tool, but their editing boxes must be open. The resultant edges will become a part of that group or component.

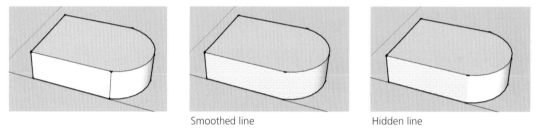

Smoothed line   Hidden line

Figure 6–55: Smooth a line that you can't delete to make it invisible and enable selecting the adjacent surfaces together. In the second graphic, the line has been smoothed; in the third graphic, the line has been hidden.

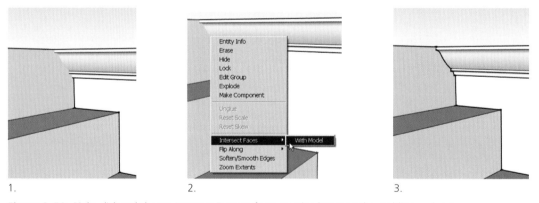

1.   2.   3.

Figure 6–56: Right-click and choose *Intersect Faces* to force an edge between the molding and stairs.

Model a Stairs Guard

Let's put a guard on the stairs and utilize the *parallel inference* in the process.

Draw the two stiles and upper rail in Figure 6–57's first graphic. Add the bottom rail by clicking its first endpoint and then touching the Pencil to the top rail. This lets the inference engine know you want the second line to be parallel to the first. Slowly move the Pencil back down. The line turns magenta when it's parallel to the top rail. Continue drawing, and click the second endpoint.

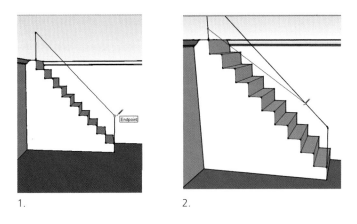

1.   2.

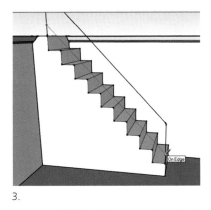

3.

Figure 6–57: Use a parallel line inference to draw the bottom rail.

Add width to the stiles (Figure 6–58). You'll need to extend the rail horizontally a little at the top in the process, as per the first graphic. The guard is now a face.

Add thickness to the face with Push/Pull (Figure 6–59).

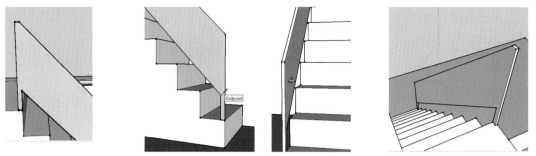

Figure 6–58: Add width to the stiles to turn the guard into a face.

Figure 6–59: Add thickness to the face with Push/Pull.

Edit a Downloaded Staircase

Earlier in this chapter, we downloaded a bunch of staircases to a local collection. We're going to edit one of them now (Figure 6–60) and replace our blocky staircase with it.

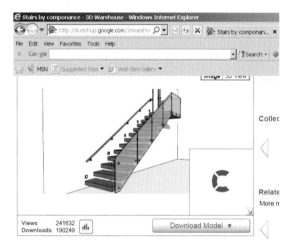

Figure 6–60: A staircase downloaded from the Warehouse.

It's best to download a component into its own file and edit it there before importing it into the active file, since everything it holds—layers, raster files, components, and more—will also be imported. Editing it in a separate file will avoid potentially messing up the active file. Erase and purge everything not needed.

> ▶ Tip: Before purging, you might browse the *In Model* components to see what unused ones the modeler left. Some might be useful, depending on your editing goals or for other projects.

Erase everything except the stairs and handrails (Figure 6–61). Open its editing box to do so.

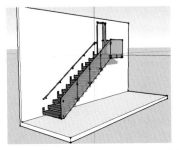

Figure 6–61: The downloaded model on the left, and after erasures on the right.

Mirror the stairs (Figure 6–62). This can be done outside the editing box. Select it and then activate the Scale tool. Grab the red grip shown and push it left until it's on the other side. Stop when the numbers in the measurements box read *-1,1*; that means the stairs are now mirrored. Alternatively, push the grip a little, release the mouse and type *-1,1*. The stairs will adjust.

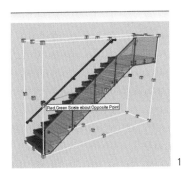

1.

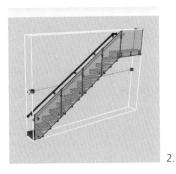

2.

3.

Figure 6–62: Mirror the stairs with the Scale tool by pushing the stairs through itself and typing *-1,1*.

Scale the stairs horizontally (Figure 6–63). This can also be done outside the editing box. Draw a line the stairs' length because two aligned endpoints are needed. Click on the endpoints. A tooltip shows the length as 18'-6". That length needs to be 10'-0", to match the existing stairs. Type 10', and click "yes" when asked if you want to resize the model. The staircase is now 10'-0" long.

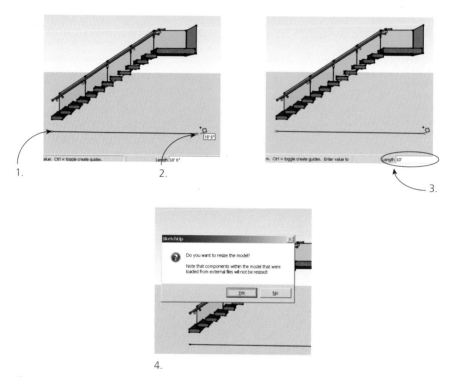

Figure 6–63: To scale the staircase, click on the endpoints of a line whose length is the staircase's length. Type the new length and then click "Yes."

Copy and paste the staircase into the living room model. Select it and click on **Edit>Copy**. Make the living room model active by clicking Select, then click on **Edit>Paste.**

Scale the stairs vertically (Figure 6–64). Line the stairs up with the existing stairs and scale the staircase vertically until it matches the other stairs' height.

Erase the back guard (open the editing box), and verify the stairs are aligned with the top of the wall (Figure 6–65).

Erase the original stairs and move the component stairs over. Inside the editing box, add a piece to the guard to lengthen it (Figure 6-6). Erase the line between the new piece and the old. Note that the new piece automatically adopts the color properties of the old. Perform an *Intersect Faces* operation between it and the top of the wall.

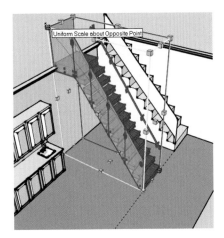

Figure 6–64: Scale the stairs vertically to match the existing stairs' height.

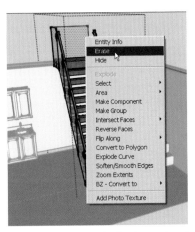
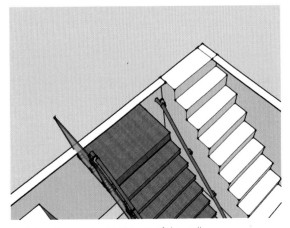

Figure 6–65: Erase the back guard and check the stairs' alignment with the top of the wall.

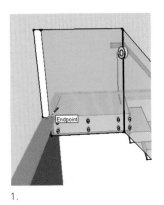
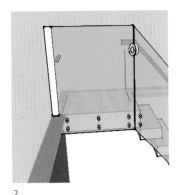

1.   2.   3.

Figure 6–66: Lengthen the guard by adding a piece to it.

Scale the handrail inside its editing box (Figure 6–67). Done!

Troublesome Components

The stairs component edited fairly easily, but not all editing goes so smoothly. Anyone can upload to the Warehouse, and nothing is vetted. Hence, its models are of uneven quality. The best ones are usually done by the SketchUp team and companies who professionally model their products.

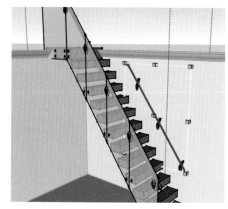

Figure 6–67: Scale the handrail.

If a downloaded model isn't working, don't spend hours trying to fix it. Just abandon it and find another. If it has a piece you really want, cut it out and paste it into another component. Some troublesome components work after minor edits. Cutting and pasting into a brand-new file may fix them, as this removes stale metadata.

Two common problems and fixes are:

▶ You've imported the model but can't see it. This may be because the model is far from the origin, causing it to import out of camera view. Click *Zoom Extents* to find it, and then move it to the origin. Recall from Chapter 5 that a quick way to do this is to select it and type *[0,0,0]* (include the square brackets).

▶ A window or door component isn't gluing to a wall or cutting a hole. Open its Entity Info box to see if the Glue to Vertical, Glue to Any, and Cut opening boxes are checked. Is its axis aligned to the wall in your model? If not, right-click and select *Change axis* to adjust—which brings us to the Axis tool.

Relocate a Component Axis with the Axis Tool

Just as each model has a global axis, each component has one, too, called the *component* or *local axis*. A local axis misaligned with the global axis will cause problems when you try to paint, scale, place, or dimension it, and won't display well with the standard views in the Views menu.

The local axis is also the "handle" grabbed when a component is imported into another model. It's typically in the lower-left corner, but can be changed for easier import.

The Axis tool (Figure 6–68) relocates the component axis or changes its alignment. Select the component (don't open its editing box) and click the Axis tool on one of the component's back corners. That sets the new local origin. Now set the axes themselves. Move the cursor along the red axis (look for the *along red axis* inference). Click to place. Do the same with the green axis. The blue axis should remain right-side up.

Figure 6–68: The Axis tool.

If that doesn't work, here's another method. Draw guidelines parallel to the axes, with their intersection at the local origin. Right-click on the component and choose *Change axes*. Click the origin on the guidelines' intersection. Drag the red axis along the red-parallel guideline and click to set. Drag the green axis along the green-parallel guide and click to set.

SketchUp automatically aligns the local axis with the global axis on components imported through the Components browser. Otherwise, you have to align any nonaligned axis with the Axis tool. Know that this adjustment will also affect the axis of any similar, already-loaded components. If that's not your intent, make the adjusted component unique first.

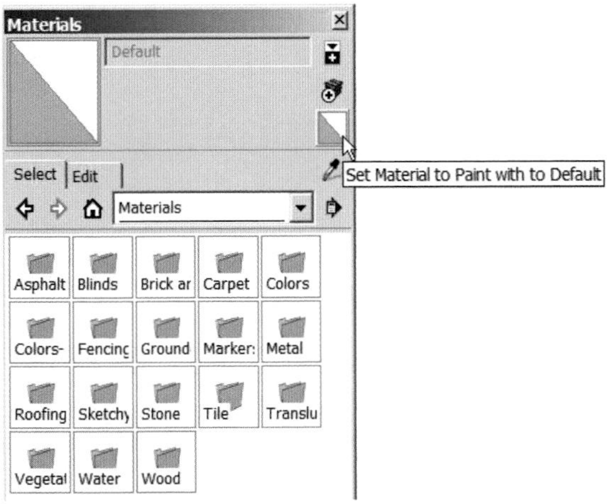

Figure 6–69: The Materials browser on the PC. The large white/blue square means the default paint is active.

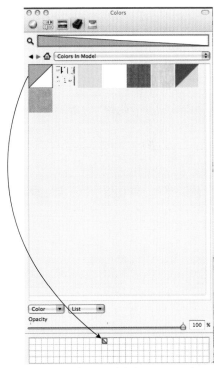

Figure 6–70: The Paint Bucket tool.

Remove Colors

The original staircase is painted brown and semitransparent blue. Let's remove that paint for a blank slate to enter Chapter 7 with. Open the Materials browser at **Window>Materials**. The large window in the upper left of the top pane (Figure 6–69) shows the active paint; right now it's SketchUp's default color (white front face/blue back face). Click on the small, similar window opposite it to activate the Paint Bucket (Figure 6–70), a tool that covers faces with color and texture.

On the Mac, the default paint icon is somewhat hidden; click on **Window>Materials**, then on the brick, then scroll to *Colors In Model* (Figure 6–71). Drag that icon down into a color well square at the bottom. That makes it accessible on every model and color palette open.

You can paint a component outside its editing box, if it hasn't already been painted. But this staircase is painted, so click its editing box open. Click the Paint Bucket on a component stair, the handrails, and the guard to replace their paint with the default paint

Figure 6–71: The Materials browser on the Mac. The default paint has been dragged to a color well at the bottom for easy access.

(Figures 6–72, 6–73). Since the stairs are nested components themselves, multiple clicks are needed to reach them.

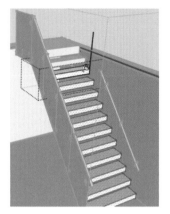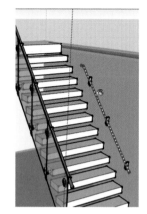

Figure 6–72: Replace the component stairs and handrail colors with SketchUp's default paint color.

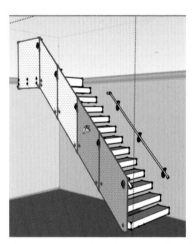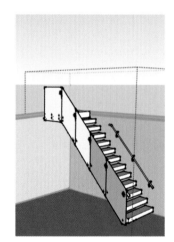

Figure 6–73: Replace the guard color with SketchUp's default color.

Face Orientation

Note in Figure 6–73 that the unpainted guard panels have two shades. As discussed in Chapter 4, every face has a white front (the *normal*) and a blue back. The guard shows three panels facing front and two facing back. Maybe the face was inadvertently reversed during construction, or maybe SketchUp just created it reversed; that often happens. To fix, select the latter two panels, right-click, and choose *Reverse Faces* (Figure 6–74). If multiple reversed faces are scattered around a large model, select one oriented correctly, right-click, and choose *Orient Faces*. All faces will usually flip to the orientation of the selected one. This doesn't always work when an edge of a face bounds three or more other faces. In that case, hold the **Shift** key down to select multiple faces, right-click, and choose *Reverse Faces*.

Why bother fixing the orientation? It's good modeling practice to keep the front side out for two reasons:

1. *To export correctly.* Some file formats, such as *dwg* and *dxf,* recognize only one face. If the front face isn't out, the resulting export will not look the way you wanted it to.

2. *To tell third-party software the correct face to render.* Some, like the popular plugin Podium or the digital imaging program Photoshop, can render only the front face.

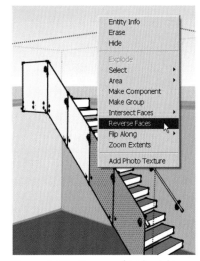

Since SketchUp shades the faces as you orbit around the model, it can be difficult to tell which side is front or back. Go to **View>Face Style>Monochrome** (Figure 6–75). This setting shows the model without textures; they're still there, just not displayed. The white and blue sides will be obvious.

Figure 6–74: Reverse a face by right-clicking and choosing *Reverse Faces*.

If telling faces apart becomes difficult, you can change the default white front/blue back colors. Go to **Window>Styles,** click on the **Edit** tab, and then click on the second box (Figure 6–76). Then click on the *Front color* and *Back color* boxes to bring up a color wheel. Assigning a bright color to the back face makes it easier to tell it from the front.

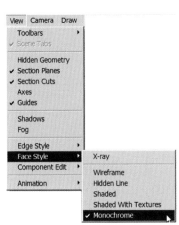

Figure 6–75: Change the face style to Monochrome to see the faces' orientation.

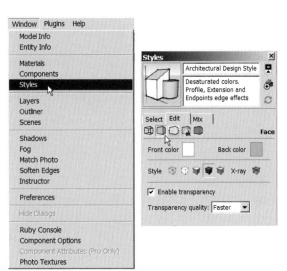

Figure 6–76: Change the default front and back face colors in the Styles box.

Behold the modeled living room (Figure 6–77)! You can continue with this project by making the opposite walls visible and adding window and door components.

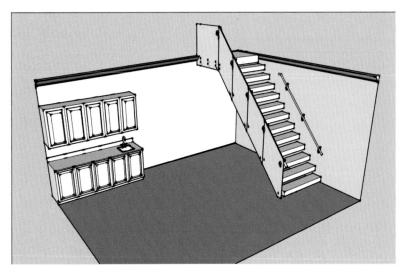

Figure 6–77: The modeled living room.

The Outliner

Earlier in this chapter, we discussed layers as a means to keep the model organized. Another organizational tool is the *Outliner*. This is a window that shows groups and components in a hierarchical order (Figure 6–78). Go to **Window>Outliner**. A dialog box with a collapsed list appears. Click the Details arrow, choose *Expand All*, and the entire nested hierarchy of groups and components appears. Four black squares in front of an entry mean component; one solid square means group. Clicking on one of those components selects the component in the model.

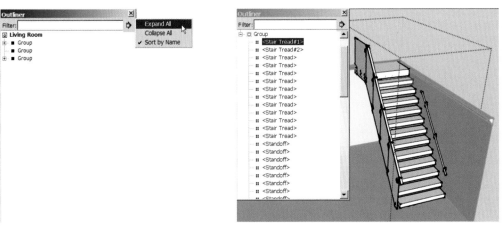

Figure 6–78: The expanded Outliner for the component stairs. Click on an Outliner entry to select it in the model. Here, one step is selected.

Through the Outliner you can name, rename, hide, and edit parts of the model. You can also reorganize it by dragging the names to different nested locations. Editing and hiding parts of a model are often easier to do through the Outliner than on the model itself. Here's how:

1. Highlight the part's name; that part will be selected on the model. Double-click on the part's name to make the editing box open.

2. Right-click on the part's name to bring up the context menu (Figure 6–79). This menu is identical to the one you'd get by clicking on the model, with one additional entry: a *Rename* function at the bottom.

Typing a name in the Filter field on top makes every group or component with that name appear (Figure 6–80). Delete the name to restore the hierarchy list.

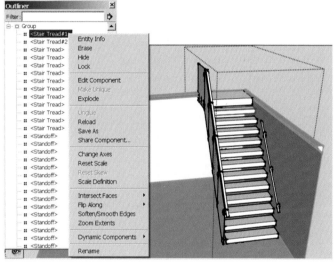

Figure 6–79: Right-click on the part's name in the Outliner to bring up the context menu. Choose the operation wanted, and then edit the model.

Figure 6–80: Type a name in the Filter field to find all groups and components with that name.

Components have a *definition name* and an *instance name*. Recall that when you created components you named them. That's the definition name, and the Outliner puts it in brackets. Each of its instances can be separately named through their Entity Info boxes or the Outliner. At the bottom of Figure 6–81 see the instance that I named "Third Tread." Its parent component is "Stair Tread." Naming instances is useful when multiple instances have different functions, or when some are unique.

When you create a model, consider its organization as you work. Make decisions early in the process. Which parts

Figure 6–81: The component definition name is shown in brackets. Each instance can be separately named.

should be separate? Which parts should be nested? Which should be moved together? Which will need to be frequently copied? What should be a component, rather than a group? Ultimately, this will make the modeling process easier and more productive, especially as the model becomes more complicated (Figure 6–82).

So, are you ready to apply color and material textures to the living room now? That's coming right up in Chapter 7.

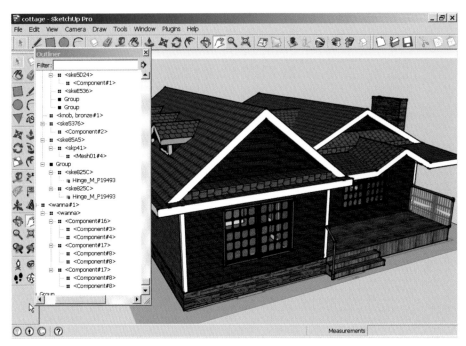

COURTESY ALI MAZEN, AIA

Figure 6–82: Real-world projects have many layers, components, and groups. Keeping them organized helps maintain an efficient workflow.

Summary

In this chapter we modeled a two-story house complete with stairs and a wet bar. We imported raster and AutoCAD plans, edited the AutoCAD plan, imported sink and staircase components from the Warehouse, and edited them. We applied some more **Styles** menu options, used the Scale tool to mirror a component, divided a line, and learned why faces should have their front side out. We discussed why lines may appear on curved objects and how to fix that by softening. We also made layers, moved geometry to them, and examined the Outliner.

Further Resources

Information and video about layers: http://help.sketchup.com/en/article/38572

SketchUp Blog entry about the Outliner function: http://sketchupdate.blogspot.com/2010/02/layers-vs-outliner.html

(Sweets) Source for free SketchUp, AutoCAD, and BIM components and building product information: http://products.construction.com/

Video about adding molding to a bookcase and using the Outliner: http://sketchupforwoodworkers.com/tutorials/2009/02/02/curves-moulding-and-the-outliner/

Video about Autofold: www.youtube.com/watch?v=bZrzUrqQ61U

Video about the Axis tool: www.youtube.com/watch?v=LPqJovjd-sM

Exercises

www.wiley.com/go/sketchupforinteriordesign

1. Import the house floor plan files (Exercises 6–1 and 6–2). Scale them to a known dimension (e.g., 24″-deep cabinets), and then trace and model them as shown in this chapter.

2. Open the staircase component (Exercise 6–3), and edit it as shown in this chapter (erase the surrounding elements, remove color, mirror, scale to a different size).

3. Model a staircase from a photo.

4. Draw a profile of base and wall cabinets, and then model it.

5. Import the crown molding file (Exercise 6–4), and trace and model it using Follow Me.

Painting with Colors, Textures, and Photo-Matching

In Chapter 6 we modeled a house and living room. Here, we'll apply color and textures to that living room. First we'll use native file swatches (thumbnail files of color and pattern) to learn the process. Then we'll import and edit swatches to represent a real-world design scheme.

What Is Painting?

Painting, also called *filling*, is the application of color and texture files to a model. Colors are files of solid pigment. Textures are files that have color and pattern, the pattern being a photo of a material that *tiles*, or repeats itself, to cover a face. These files are kept in product-specific collections at **Window>Materials**.

Paint with Native SketchUp Materials

At **Window>Materials**, scroll to Colors (Figure 7–1) in the search field. There are actually two color collections: *Colors* and *Named Colors*. The latter has descriptive names that appear in a tooltip when the mouse hovers over a swatch. The former are just described with a letter and number. Clicking the Details arrow on the PC offers a list view option of those names, which is helpful when multiple colors and materials are applied. The Mac does not offer a list option.

Clicking on the Colors collection makes a color palette—a bunch of swatches—appear. On the Mac, this palette is called the *Color Picker*. The Mac additionally has an icon of crayons to the left of the brick. Clicking on it accesses a separate, smaller palette of standard Apple colors.

Click on a color from the *Colors* collection. This activates the Paint Bucket tool. Then click on a face to apply that color (Figure 7–2). Clicking on the Paint Bucket tool icon activates the Materials browser.

Objective: This chapter discusses how to apply and edit color and texture paints.

Tools: Paint Bucket, Eyedropper (Sampler), Fixed Pins, Free Pins

Concepts and Functions: painting, texturing, tiles, tiling, collection, Materials browser, Palette/Color Picker, create materials, adjust a material, color wheel/slider, colors in model, sample, tile square, tiling, import colors and textures, Mac color wells, check face orientation, face style, RGB number, import as texture, import as image, purge unused material, seamless pattern, open a digital imaging program within SketchUp, model a picture frame, straighten a skewed raster image, link a local textures collection, project a texture on a curved face, photo-match

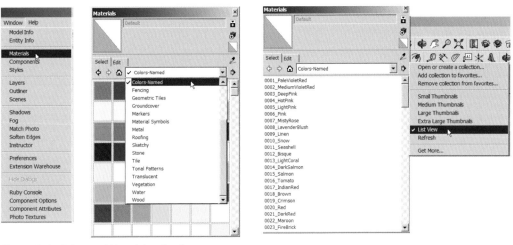

Figure 7–1: Colors and Materials collections.

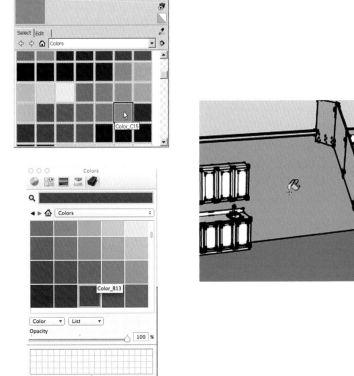

Figure 7–2: The Colors Palette on a PC (top) and Color Picker on a Mac (bottom).
Click on a color swatch, and then click on the wall to apply.

The Paint Bucket Tool

The Paint Bucket (Figure 7–3) assigns materials and colors to geometry. It paints single faces and multiple connected faces, and replaces one material with another. Be aware that it only paints faces; it cannot fill an outline.

Figure 7–3: The Paint Bucket tool.

To paint a group or component, just select it; you don't have to open the editing box. The paint will cover all unpainted surfaces with one click. However, any surfaces in that group or component that have already been painted won't be affected. For that, the editing box must be opened and paint applied inside it.

SketchUp often presents painting challenges. For instance, in Chapter 6 we inserted a component sink into a cabinet and grouped everything together. Selecting and then painting that group with one click results in the sink getting painted, too. Therefore, the group must be opened and painting carefully applied on the countertop around the sink. The cabinets can be selected and painted with one click each (Figure 7–4). Later in this chapter, we'll paint with textures, and you can overpaint the countertop with a more appropriate material such as granite.

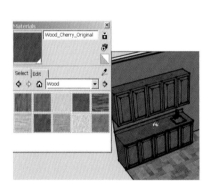
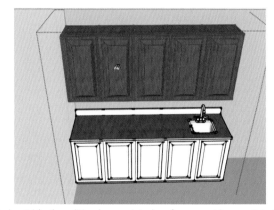

Figure 7–4: Unpainted surfaces can be painted outside the editing box; painted surfaces must be repainted inside the editing box.

Both sides of a face can be painted independently. Some painting tips:

▶ To quickly paint multiple faces, hold the **Shift** key down; all connected faces will get painted.

▶ To quickly paint one side of multiple faces, select all those faces. Paint the front of one; the fronts of all will get painted. Paint the back of one; all back faces will get painted.

▶ On the Mac, a swatch from the Color Picker can be dragged and dropped onto a face.

▶ Select a face plus its edges, paint the front side (not the back), and the edges will get painted, too. To see the paint on the edges, display the edge color by material (**Window>Styles>Edit**, click the *Edge Settings* button, and choose *By Material* in the Color menu).

Adjust a Color

All colors can be value-adjusted, meaning made lighter or darker. Make sure you're in *In Model* and select a color. However, don't make changes to the original color; make duplicates and change those.

On the PC, click the box with the plus sign. This opens the *Create Material* dialog box and duplicates the active swatch. Move the slider next to the color wheel up or down (Figure 7–5). The swatch adjusts accordingly. Then click *ok* on the PC, and click the new color on the wall.

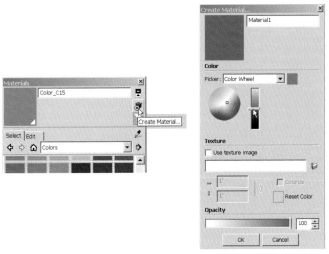

Figure 7–5: Click the *Create Material* box (PC) to copy the active swatch, and adjust its color with the slider.

On the Mac, right-click on the color swatch, choose *Duplicate*, and name it (Figure 7–6a). This duplicates the active swatch. Click the small color wheel in the upper-left corner to open a large color wheel (Figure 7–6b). Move the slider next to it to adjust the duplicate swatch, and click the new color on the wall.

You can also change the color of the whole swatch, not just its value, by clicking somewhere on the color wheel and then clicking *ok*. PC users, you can always change an adjusted color back to the original by clicking *Reset Color* at the bottom of the Edit panel. This works even after closing the file and reopening.

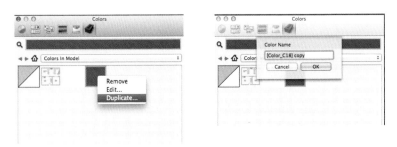

Figure 7–6a: On the Mac, duplicate a swatch, name it, and then adjust it.

At the bottom of both the PC's and the Mac's editing boxes is an opacity (translucence) slider. In Chapter 4 we clicked a material from the *Translucent* folder on a bookcase door to make it glass. Materials in that folder have translucency built in and their thumbnails show two colors; one represents paint, the other translucency. However, any paint or texture can be made translucent. Select its thumbnail, set the level with the slider, and then click the Paint Bucket on a face. If only the paint color, not the translucency, appears, fix by clicking the face's other side, too.

Setting the opacity level to zero makes a face invisible. And since both sides of a face can be painted independently, it's possible to make one side translucent and the other opaque.

Colors *In Model*

Whenever you create a new color, SketchUp creates a palette thumbnail for it. Scroll to *In Model* or click on the house icon to see it (Figure 7–7). Mac users, click on the brick to find the house icon. *In Model* is a window that displays only the colors loaded into the model. New colors are assigned names such as "Material 1" and "Material 2," which you can overwrite. On the PC, palette thumbnails in active use have a small triangle. Be aware that every color you click on the model remains in it, even when replaced with another color.

Sample a Color

To *sample*, or match, a paint color on the PC, click the eyedropper onto the color you want, and then click it on the face to match. The crown molding in Figure 7–8 was matched to the wall this way. On the Mac, there's no eyedropper icon; instead, hold the **Command** key down, click the Paint Bucket on the color wanted, release the **Command** key, and click the Paint Bucket on the face to match.

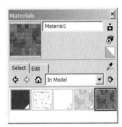

Figure 7–6b: Move the slider up or down to change a color's value.

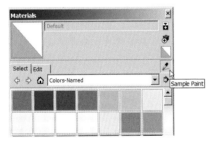

Figure 7–7: The *In Model* window shows thumbnails of all materials applied to the model, whether currently in use or not. On the PC, thumbnails of materials in use have a small triangle.

Figure 7–8: Click the eyedropper icon (PC) or Command key (Mac) to match the crown molding to the walls.

Paint with Textures

Textures are applied the same way as paint. Scroll to the *Tile* folder (Mac users, click the brick first) and apply a pattern to the floor (Figure 7–9). Adjust a pattern color the same way as a solid color.

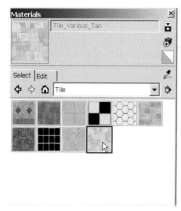

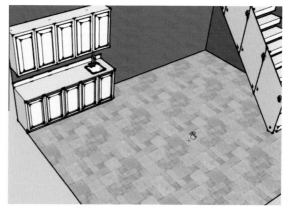

Figure 7–9: Apply a texture by clicking on its palette swatch and then clicking on the model.

The *In Model* box now shows two thumbnails for that texture, the original and the adjusted one (Figure 7–10).

Adjust a Texture

Textures have more adjustment options than solid colors do. On the PC, click the *Edit* tab on the Materials browser to see the options in the bottom pane.

Figure 7–11 shows 4′ as the default number in the width and height adjustment boxes, which is the size of a *tile square* (the square area the pattern covers). It's not the size of the stones in the pattern. This tile will repeat when applied to areas larger than 4′ square. To change the tile size, type a different number in the top field. The same number will appear in the bottom field, to maintain height/width proportions. To alter those proportions, click on the link symbol to break

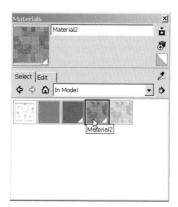

Figure 7–10: The original and adjusted textures both have thumbnails in *In Model*.

it. You can then type different numbers in the boxes. Type *8'*, click *ok*, and click on the floor (Figure 7–12). A swatch for that tile size appears in the palette. You haven't altered the texture itself, just the tile size.

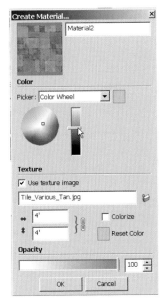

Figure 7–11: The default number (*4'*) in the width and height boxes refers to the size of a square the pattern completely covers.

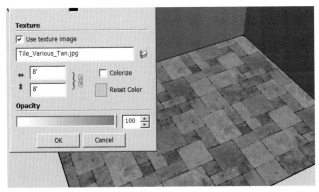

Figure 7–12: Type larger numbers in the adjustment boxes to make the tile larger.

On the Mac, right-click on the texture and choose *Edit* to make an options pane appear (Figure 7–13). Adjust the tile size by typing new values; adjust the color by clicking on the small color wheel to make the large one appear. Click *Close* when finished.

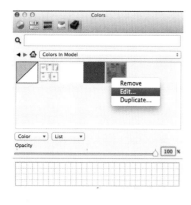

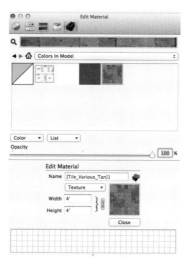

Figure 7–13: On a Mac, right-click on a texture and choose *Edit* to make an options pane appear.

Figure 7–14 shows additional adjustment options. The PC has eyedroppers that match the color of any object in the model or on the screen. The Mac has a magnifying glass that lets you match a color on the screen; click it on the screen (Figure 7–15) and then on whatever you want to paint with that color.

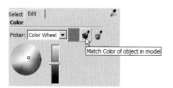

Figure 7–14: Eyedroppers on the PC offer more adjustment options.

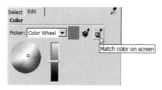

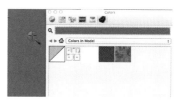

Figure 7–15: On the Mac, click the magnifying glass on the screen and then on whatever you want to paint with that color.

Paint the Stairs

As we saw from the Outliner in Chapter 6, almost every stair on the downloaded staircase is a component instance. Open the editing box on one, apply paint, and close (Figure 7–16).

Next, open the *Translucent* folder and paint the guard. Each guard panel was modeled separately, requiring separate Paint Bucket clicks. An unexpected challenge is presented: Only the top panel is visibly translucent after painting (Figure 7–17). The others show the color but not translucence. There are several possible causes for this, but just fix it by orbiting around and applying the Paint Bucket to the back faces, too. Turn off the back walls' layer first, to make working in that small space easier (Figure 7–18). Finally, paint the handrails (Figure 7–19).

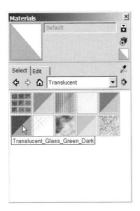

Figure 7–16: Open the editing box of one stairs component and apply paint.

Figure 7–17: If a face doesn't appear translucent after you paint its front side, paint its back side, too.

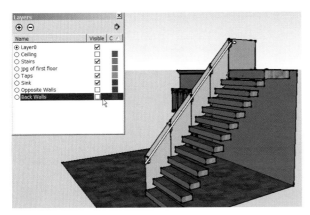

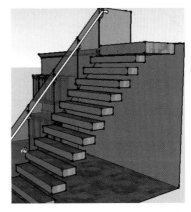

Figure 7–18: Turn off the back walls' layer, to make working in a tight space easier.

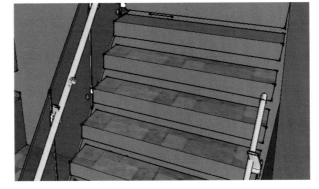

Figure 7–19: Paint the handrails.

Import Swatches from Other Models

If another model has a color or texture you want, three ways to get it are:

▶ Copy and paste a face painted with that swatch into your current model (select it, and then **Edit>Copy**, **Edit>Paste** or **CTRL C, CTRL V**).

▶ Open both files, make the other model active, and drag the swatch from its Materials browser onto a face in your model.

▶ Copy and paste the whole other model into your model. When a file is large, there may be some lag time between copying and pasting. However, very large files may just freeze the software. In that case, go to **File>Import**, set *Files of type* to SketchUp, and try importing it that way. All its model's layers and files will be pasted into yours.

Put New Colors and Textures into the Software

Adjusted and imported materials only live in the models they were created in. To make them available to all models, you can: (1) make a local collection and link it to the collections menu or (2) add them to a native collection. We'll discuss making a local collection later in this chapter, because the process differs a bit from the components collection we made in Chapter 5. Right now, let's discuss adding them to a native collection.

On the PC, open the bottom pane and scroll it to the native collection where you want to store the new swatch, and drag the swatch from the top pane down into it (Figure 7–20). It's now part of that collection, available each time you open the software.

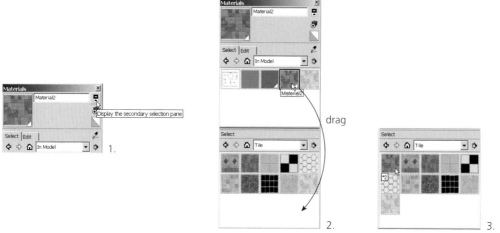

Figure 7–20: On the PC, drag new swatches from the top pane to an existing collection in the bottom pane. This makes them available to all SketchUp models.

On the Mac, the process is different (Figure 7–21). We're going to make a new collection and drag the new swatches into it.

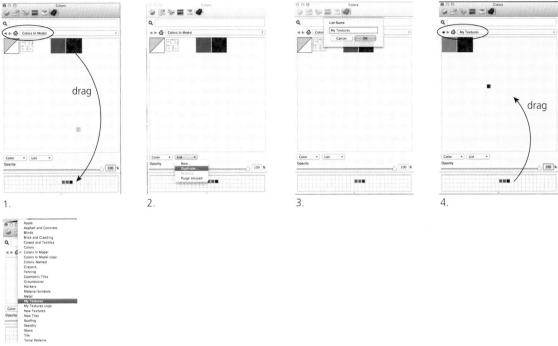

Figure 7–21: On the Mac, drag new swatches down to the color well, and then back up into the folder where you want to store them. This makes them available to all SketchUp models. Here, a new collection called My Textures was made and appears in the menu with all the collections.

Scroll to *In Model*. Drag the swatches you want into the color wells at the bottom. In the *List* field, scroll to *Duplicate*. Type a name for the collection—I called it *My Textures*. That collection is now listed with all the others in the menu and is open. Drag the swatches from the color wells up into it. If you want to eventually delete that collection, select it, go back to the *List* field, and scroll to *Remove*. Alternatively, you could just open an existing collection in the top pane and drag the swatches from the color wells into it.

Use the Mac's color wells to park often-used swatches. No matter which collection is open, the swatches will remain accessible there. When you don't need a swatch anymore, drag a blank well over it to erase.

Check Face Orientation on Painted Surfaces with *Entity Info* and *Face Style*

In Chapter 6, we discussed the importance of correct face orientation. After painting, it's impossible to visually tell front from back. Here are two ways to check:

▶ Select the face and open its Entity Info box. At the top are two panels. The left is the front face; the right is the back face. In Figure 7–22, we see that the front face is painted. If it showed the back face as painted, we'd fix it by reversing the face, painting the back with the default paint, and painting the color on the front.

▶ Go to **View>Face Style>Monochrome** (Figure 7–23). This displays the model with the default front and back face colors. The paint is still there, just not displayed.

▶ Tip: If you paint the model but the paint doesn't appear, check the face style setting. *Shaded with Textures* must be set for paint to be visible

Figure 7–22: To discern the orientation of a painted face, look at its Entity Info box. The left panel is the front face; the right panel is the back face.

Figure 7–23: The Monochrome display option shows the model with default front and back colors, even though it may be painted.

Apply a Real-Life Design Scheme to the Model

Interior designers typically choose finishes from physical samples such as paint chips, tiles, and fabric. They may also choose from digital swatches found on manufacturers' websites (some collections are in the Warehouse). All can be imported and painted onto the model. Let's do that now.

Import Paint Colors

Two ways to apply the color from a physical chip are:

▶ Scan. Open the scanned image on the desktop, and sample it with the *Match Color on Screen* eye-dropper (PC) or magnifying glass (Mac). Then click it on the wall.

▶ Enter the paint's RGB (red, blue, green) numbers into the Materials browser. These numbers are available from the manufacturer; some have charts on their websites (Figure 7–24). On the PC, scroll the Picker window to RGB and enter the numbers in the field (Figure 7–25). Click *ok*; its swatch will

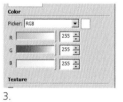

COLOR NO.	COLOR NAME	RED	GREEN	BLUE
0001	Mulberry Silk	149	120	108
0002	Chelsea Mauve	189	172	158
0003	Cabbage Rose	199	163	148
0004	Rose Brocade	155	109	110
0005	Deepest Mauve	108	88	88
0006	Toile Red	140	85	78
0007	Decorous Amber	173	119	87
0008	Cajun Red	142	77	56
0009	Eastlake Gold	192	146	94
0010	Wickerwork	192	162	128
0011	Crewel Tan	204	191	158
0012	Empire Gold	193	162	109
0013	Majolica Green	173	181	145
0014	Sheraton Sage	142	139	103
0015	Gallery Green	109	135	115
0016	Billiard Green	70	89	79
0017	Calico	138	163	156
0018	Teal Stencil	98	128	125
0019	Festoon Aqua	160	186	185
0020	Peacock Plume	117	150	150
0021	Queen Anne Lilac	105	183	183

Figure 7–24: RGB paint chart on the Sherwin-Williams website.

appear in *In Model,* and you can click it on the wall. On the Mac, click the sliders icon on the Materials browser, and scroll to RGB in the field below it. There is no *ok* button; instead, click on the new color in the bar at the top, and then click it on the wall (Figure 7–26).

1.

3.

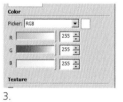

2.

Figure 7–25: The RGB fields on the PC.

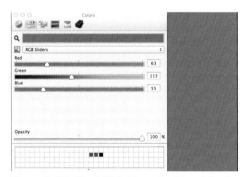

Figure 7–26: The RGB fields on the Mac. After the numbers are entered, click on the color bar at the top, and then on the wall.

The new paint thumbnails will appear in *In Model* (Figure 7–27). To make them a permanent part of SketchUp, drag them into a collection folder, as described earlier.

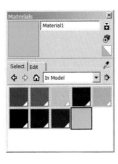 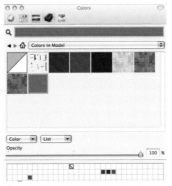

Figure 7–27: New paint thumbnails generated by inputting RGB numbers automatically appear in *In Model*.

Importing textures is more complicated because the pattern's scale usually has to be adjusted upon import. But before we do that, let's sidetrack to discuss how the interior space should be set up to make applying imported textures easier.

The Modeling Workflow

If you plan to apply patterned textures to a room that has a lot of built-in casework (e.g., cabinets, bookcases), a different workflow than what was shown in Chapter 6 and earlier in this chapter is needed. The following steps are suggested:

1. Model the walls and floor.
2. Apply the floor texture, and then group the floor (Figure 7–28).
3. Apply the wall textures, and then group the walls.
4. Model all built-ins off to the side, group, and then move into the space.

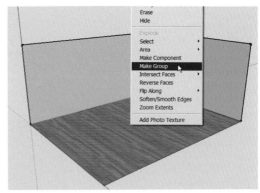

Figure 7–28: Model an empty space, apply flooring, and group the floor before applying wall textures and built-ins.

This sequence is recommended because modeling all built-ins first and applying textures afterward will result in blank spots on the floor and walls when the built-ins are moved. Those spots are difficult to repair. Textures can also be difficult to apply to a wall that already has geometry attached to it.

Import a Texture

Turn physical samples into files by scanning or photographing them. Flat items such as wallpaper can be scanned. Photograph all others by holding a camera directly above them, looking straight down; ensure that the sample is well-lit with no shadows. Avoid photographing materials with irregular features such as wood knots, because they will be visually distracting when tiled.

In Chapter 5 we discussed the raster file types SketchUp can import and how to prepare them. Be aware that multiple textures slow down a model, and large-size files slow it down even more. Unless close, high-resolution views are needed, use the smallest size possible that will show the texture, in both resolution (number of pixels) and file size. As little as 15 KB or 512×512 pixels may be enough.

Click on **File>Import**. A browser window appears; set the *Files of type* field at the bottom to *All Supported Image Types*. Locate the file, click once to select it, select *Use as texture* and *ok* (Figure 7–29). Then click the texture on a face (Figure 7–30). Textures must be applied to faces; they cannot be randomly placed anywhere on the screen.

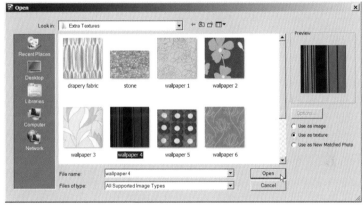

Figure 7–29: When importing a texture, make sure *Use as texture* is selected.

The pattern covers the wall, but is not to scale. Find its swatch in *In Model*, double-click to access the editing box, and adjust the tile numbers, preferably with the pattern's actual sizes. I clicked the link icon first to break the default proportion ratio, then typed *1'* for the horizontal and *9'* for the vertical (ceiling height). Once new numbers are entered, the pattern's scale automatically adjusts (Figure 7–31).

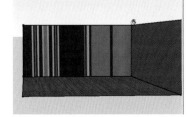

Figure 7–30: Click the texture on a face. Textures can only be applied to faces, not to blank space.

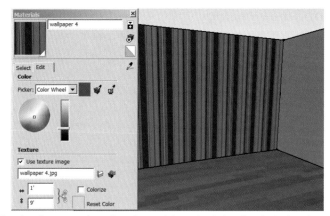

Figure 7–31: Click on the *In Model* thumbnail to open the editing box. Click on the link to break the height/width proportion, and then enter 1′ and 9′. The scale automatically adjusts.

Textures can also be imported directly from the *Edit* panel on the Materials browser. On the PC, click the *Browse* icon (Figure 7–32, left graphic). On the Mac, scroll to *Colors in Model*, and in the *Color* field, scroll to *New Texture* (Figure 7–32, right graphic).

A navigation browser appears; locate the file. Upon import, enter sizes in the tile fields. Then click on the resultant *In Model* thumbnail with the Paint Bucket and on the wall (Figure 7–33). Entering different tile sizes makes the pattern adjust automatically, which is useful for experimenting with scale.

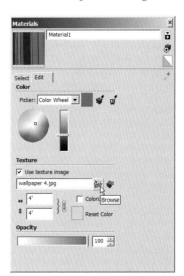

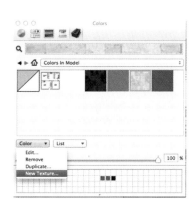

Figure 7–32: Import new textures from the *Edit* panel on the Materials browser (PC) or at **Color>New Texture** (Mac).

On the PC, click on the Details arrow and choose *Get More* for an entry on the SketchUp blog that links to lots of textures you can download and practice on (Figure 7–34). Mac users, see Further Resources, at the end of the chapter, for the website address.

As mentioned in Chapter 5, when files are imported they are a permanent part of the model. SketchUp doesn't search for them on the computer each time the model loads.

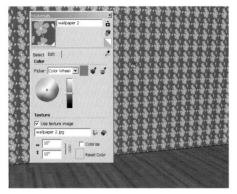

Figure 7–33: Experiment with different pattern scales by changing the tile numbers.

Figure 7–34: PC users can find lots of textures to download and practice on by clicking the Details arrow and selecting *Get More*.

Purge Unused Materials

Every color and texture painted on the model remains in it even after being erased or replaced, which increases the model's size. Purge unused files (Figure 7–35) on the PC by opening the Materials browser, clicking the *Details* arrow, and choosing *Purge Unused*. This removes them from the model. On the Mac, open the Materials browser, click on the house, and scroll in the *List* text field to *Purge Unused*.

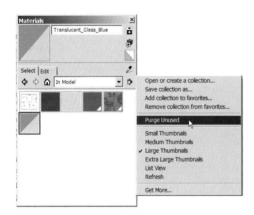

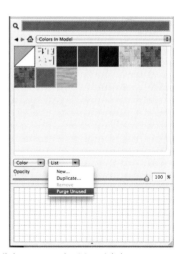

Figure 7–35: To remove unused files on the PC, click the *Details* button on the Materials browser and choose *Purge Unused*. On the Mac, open the Materials browser, click on the house, and scroll in the List text field to *Purge Unused*.

Purge vs. Delete

Purging removes unused files from the model. Those files remain in the SketchUp software, available for later use. Deleting a file (right-click on its thumbnail, choose *Delete*) removes the file from the SketchUp software entirely. This makes it unavailable to the model it's in and to other models. If it's currently used in other models, it will be replaced with the default paint.

Delete components through the Components browser the same way. This removes all copies of them from both the model and the software. Deleting components is a useful way to get rid of unneeded blocks that were part of an AutoCAD import.

Repeating and Seamless Textures

Wallpaper patterns have *repeats*, the vertical distance between tiles where the pattern is identical ("repeats"). When glued onto a physical wall, pattern repeats are matched across sheets. This action ranges from easy to impossible to replicate in SketchUp. A *seamless*, or

random, pattern has edges that blend when tiled; it is easy to apply because it requires no matching. The stripes in Figure 7–31 are an example; other examples are brick, stone, and carpet. A *straight-across* pattern just repeats at the ceiling line, so it can be easily positioned (we'll discuss positioning later in this chapter). A *drop* pattern, however, needs to be aligned both horizontally and vertically (Figure 7–36). For that, digital imaging software is needed.

Figure 7–36: A drop pattern must be aligned with digital imaging software.

Access a Digital Imaging Program inside SketchUp

There are three ways to access a digital imaging program that's installed on your computer (Figure 7–37): Click the *Edit texture image in external editor* icon in the Edit dialog box, right-click its *In Model* thumbnail, or right-click the face it's painted on. Then choose *Texture>Edit Texture Image*. This opens the swatch inside a digital imaging program. After editing, flatten and save. The file saves to a temporary folder in SketchUp and automatically updates within the model, saving you the trouble of deleting and re-importing the new file.

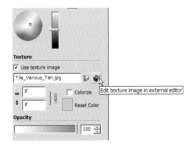

Figure 7–37: Three ways to access a digital imaging program within SketchUp.

If the texture is painted on multiple faces and you only want to change its look on one, right-click on that face and choose *Make Unique Texture*. This creates a separate swatch that can be edited without affecting the other faces. Then edit it in digital imaging software or by right-clicking on it to bring up the material editing box.

Map Digital Imaging Software to SketchUp

Digital imaging software has to be mapped to SketchUp in order to open when *Edit Texture Image* is chosen. Go to **Window>Preferences>Applications**. Figures 7–38 and 7–39 show how to map Photoshop to SketchUp on the PC.

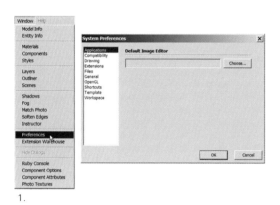

1.

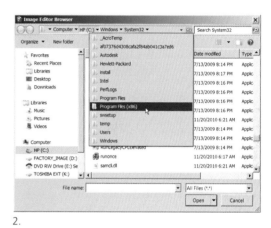

2.

3.

Figures 7–38 and 7–39: Steps 1-3 to link Photoshop to SketchUp on the PC.

Navigate to the software's files folder. It will be in the Program Files area on the hard drive. Inside that folder, select the *.exe* file. Double-click to load.

▶ Good, free digital imaging programs are IrfanView (**www.irfanview.com/**) and GIMP (**www.gimp .org/**); the latter is an online Photoshop clone. Or Google "portable gimp" for websites to download a GIMP app from.

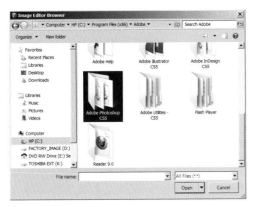

4.

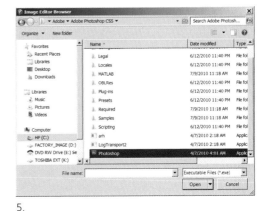

5.

6.

Figure 7–39: Steps 4-6 to link Photoshop to SketchUp on the PC.

Import an Image

When you imported the texture files, you clicked *Use as texture*. Another import option is *Use as image*. This is used when only one instance of that file is needed, such as for wall art, a landscape photo behind a window, or a drawing to trace. Images don't tile and can be clicked on blank space. Figure 7–40 shows how images can really make a model pop. Images don't appear in the Materials browser because they're not materials until exploded. Then their thumbnail appears.

Figure 7–40: The photo of books painted on the back wall lends realism to this library space, as do the jewelry photos inserted into a woodworking project model.

Make Wall Art with an Image

In Figure 7–41, an image is clicked on a face to make wall art. The steps are:

1. Import as image.
2. Click on two corners to size and place.
3. Draw a rectangle around it.
4. Push/pull the image forward to give it thickness.

The thickness will take on the color of the wall it's push/pulled from, but it can be painted a different color. Exploding the image (select, right-click, choose *explode*) turns it into a texture, and its thumbnail will appear in *In Model*.

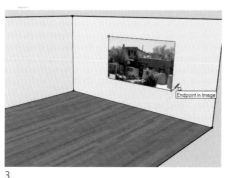

1.

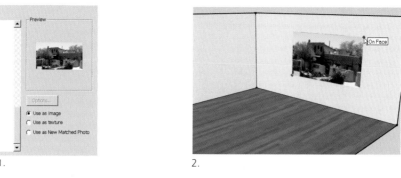

2.

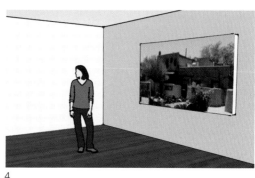

3.

4.

Figure 7–41: Import a file as an image to make a non-tiling piece of wall art. Draw a rectangle around it and push/pull it forward to add thickness.

In Figure 7–41 the image was applied on a face bigger than itself, so placing it wasn't a problem. However, applying it to a smaller face will cause it to extend past the face's edges. If your intent is to just display a portion of the image on that face, import it as a texture. Then right-click, select *Position*, and press the mouse's scroll wheel to pin it in place. The four pins that appear will be discussed later in this chapter.

Make a Picture Frame

Figures 7–42 and 7–43 show how to put a frame around that art. Import the file as an image, place it on the screen somewhere off the model, and explode (if the explode option doesn't appear when you right-click on an image, right-click on the image's border). Draw a frame profile perpendicular to the art, select the art as the path, then click the Follow Me tool on the profile to extrude it around the perimeter. This is the same process that made the crown molding in Chapter 6.

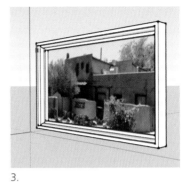

1.   2.   3.

Figure 7–42: Make a frame for wall art.

Triple-click to quickly select the art and frame, then hold the **Shift** key down and click on the art to deselect it. Click the Paint Bucket on the frame to paint it all at once. Then group and move it. If the art flashes when the picture is placed on the wall, open the group editing box and push/pull the photo a little bit forward.

Figure 7–43: Paint the frame

Image Placement Tips

Placing images directly on faces can be tricky, as sometimes, SketchUp gets confused about which to display, the image or the face. This results in the image disappearing into the face and displaying on the other side. Three workarounds are:

Explode the image and make it a component, specifying the face it should glue to (horizontal or vertical).

Draw a rectangle on the face, import the image as a texture, and fill the rectangle with it. You may need to group the face before painting the image on it.

Import the image somewhere off the model, work on it there, and then move it into place.

Figure 7–44 shows an image imported for use as a rug. It flashed on the face; this was fixed by push/pulling it up a bit.

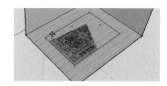

Erase an Image

To erase an image, select it. Just the edges will be selected; you won't see highlighting dots on its face. Right-click and choose *erase* (or hit the delete key). Erasing images on faces can be tricky because even though the image is completely visible, it may really be partly buried in that face. Solve by zooming in closely to find an edge, and then select that edge for erasing. Scaling the face down in size will aid in finding an image edge.

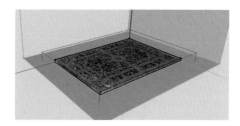

Make and Link a Local Textures Collection on the PC

On the PC (but not on the Mac), you can create and link to a local textures collection (Figure 7–45). Make a folder on your desktop called *Wallpaper and Draperies Textures* and put some files in it. Open the Materials browser, click the Details arrow, and choose *Open or create a collection*. Browse to that

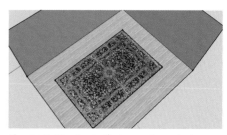

Figure 7–44: A rug photo was imported as an image, exploded, and turned into a component. It was then moved to the floor, where it flashed (top graphic). The editing box was opened, and the rug push/pulled up a bit to stop the flashing.

folder. Click *ok*. Click the *Details* arrow again, and choose *Add collection to favorites*. It will now be listed with all the other collections.

Here's where the process differs from making a local components collection. The folder is empty; each texture must be imported. Go to **File>Import** and paint a texture onto a face (Figure 7–46). Then open the bottom pane, scroll to *Wallpaper and Draperies Textures*, and drag the texture down into it.

After you add each texture, an *skm* (SketchUp Materials) file gets created for that swatch inside the desktop folder. Don't delete the *skm* file, because it is the link between the local collection and the SketchUp software. As an aside, earlier in this chapter a *Reset* button was mentioned as a way to restore an altered color or texture swatch on the PC. There is no *Reset* button for the Mac, but thumbnails on it can be restored by finding the thumbnail's *skm* file and clicking on it.

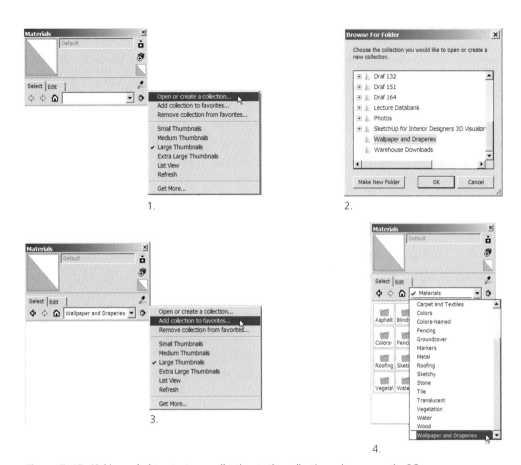

1.

2.

3.

4.

Figure 7–45: Linking a desktop textures collection to the collection submenu on the PC.

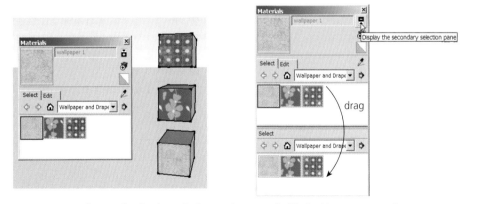

drag

Figure 7–46: After a collection is made, it must be manually filled with texture swatches.

Import and Replace a Color or Texture with *Load* on the Mac

The Mac has a feature on its Edit panel called *Load.* Click on a color or texture you want to replace. In the *Texture* field, scroll to *Load* (Figure 7–47). A navigation browser appears. Find the new file, and click *Open.* That file will import and replace the current one. Load defaults to the last place it retrieved a texture from.

Figure 7–47: Use *Load* to import and replace a file in one step.

Drag Textures into the Model

An alternative way to import materials on both the PC and the Mac is to drag a texture from the local collection folder right into the model. It enters as an image and must be exploded to become a texture. On the PC, it enters attached to the Scale tool. Click it on a face and adjust the top and side grips to fit the face. This often results in the tile size defaulting to the height and width of the face—but not always; file size and resolution also impact the tile size.

One more tip: If you import a texture from another model and want to save that texture to your local collection, right-click on its *In Model* swatch and choose *Export Texture Image* (Figure 7–48). It will export at the same resolution it was imported in.

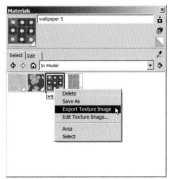

Figure 7–48: A texture can be exported to a local collection.

Position with Fixed and Free Pins

Textures can be changed with tools called *Fixed* and *Free Pins.* Select a texture on the model, right-click, and choose **Texture>Position**. Four fixed pins appear. Drag each pin to move, scale/shear, scale/rotate, or distort. The texture changes around the pin's location. The thumbnail in the Materials browser doesn't change, just its appearance in the model. Relocate the pin by clicking on it, moving the cursor (don't drag, just move)and clicking again to place. Pins only work on textures, not images.

Figure 7–49 shows changes made to a tile pattern floor by holding down the green pin and dragging the mouse. Rotate the pattern randomly or incrementally along the protractor, and move the cursor up and down to enlarge or reduce it. Drag the blue pin to shear the pattern (Figure 7–50); drag the yellow pin to warp it. Drawing a rectangle or circle on the floor will protect the area inside from the pattern change, which is useful for something like preserving a medallion in the middle.

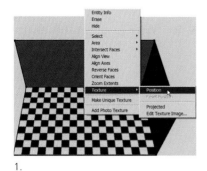

1.

2.

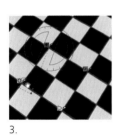

3.

4.

Figure 7–49: Rotate the tile pattern by dragging the green pin; enlarge/reduce it by dragging the cursor up and down.

Drag the red pin to reposition the texture—useful for a design that will be displayed behind a smaller window. Figures 7–51 and 7–52 show a texture painted onto a wall that has different proportions from the design. When the second endpoint is clicked, the portion of the design above the ceiling disappears. It's still there; it just doesn't have a face to display on. Grasp the red pin, move the design around, and click into place.

Figure 7–53 shows how to make a texture a piece of wall art. Paint the texture on the wall. Draw a rectangle the art's size and reposition the texture if needed. Paint the wall outside the rectangle a different color and then push/pull the rectangle forward.

Figure 7–50: Shear the pattern by dragging the blue pin.

1.

2.

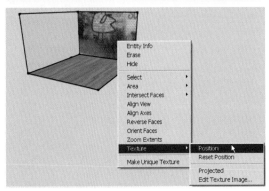

3.

4.

5.

Figures 7–51 and 7–52: Repositioning a texture and turning it into wall art.

1.

2.

3.

Figure 7–53: Give the image thickness to finish it as wall art.

After the texture is positioned, click somewhere off the model to exit the *Position* function. Alternatively, right-click and choose *Done* from the **Texture>Position** context menu (Figure 7–54). While there, note its other options. *Rotate* is useful for changing a texture's orientation, such as that of wood grain (Figure 7–55). *Flip along* mirrors a texture. *Reset* reverts the texture back to the original.

Clicking the *Fixed Pins* entry toggles to *Free Pins* mode, in which you can stretch the texture between four yellow pins (Figure 7–56). Click and release a pin to select, and then just move it with the cursor; don't drag it. Free pins enable you to straighten a skewed image or stretch one instance of a repeating pattern over the whole face. Figure 7–56 shows one black square stretched over the floor. Although this particular example offers no advantages over just painting the floor black, the technique can be useful for more elaborate patterns. You can also make one repetition cover the floor by enlarging the tile size, but finding the right size takes trial and error.

Figure 7–54: Access this context menu by right-clicking within the **Texture>Position** function.

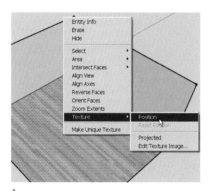

1.

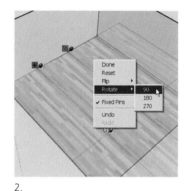

2.

3.

Figure 7–55: The *Rotate* option from the context menu in Figure 7–54 changes the texture's direction.

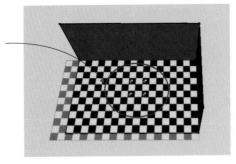

1.

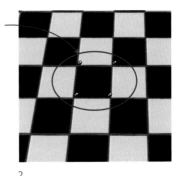

2.

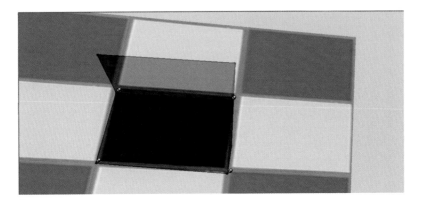

3.

Figure 7–56: Stretch one square over the whole floor by moving the Free Pins to the corners of one square. Then move each pin to a room corner.

Generally, Fixed Pins work best on tiled textures, and Free Pins work best on skewed images. Multiple toggles between both modes may be needed to achieve the desired result. Figures 7–57 to 7–59 show how an angled view of the Berlin Wall was straightened and then used as wall art.

Figure 7–57: A photo of the Wall was imported as an image, placed on the screen, and exploded to make it a texture. To skew the Wall horizontally, it was stretched with the Free Pins and then dragged some more with the yellow Fixed Pin. The texture was then made unique.

Figure 7–58: In *In Model* we see thumbnails for both the skewed Wall and the straightened Wall. Paint the straightened texture on the face to be the wall art. We see that the texture has tiled. We want just one tile, so click the thumbnail to bring up the editing box, and input larger numbers until one tile completely fills the face. If the design or text shows up backward after being painted onto the face, fix by reversing the face orientation and/or flipping along the axis.

Figure 7–59: Finally, push/pull the face for thickness, group, and move it into the model.

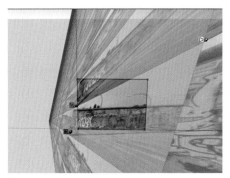

1.

2.

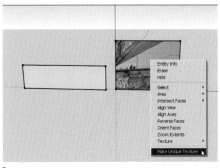

3.

Figure 7-57: Import the image, stretch it with Fixed and Free Pins, and then make the stretched image unique.

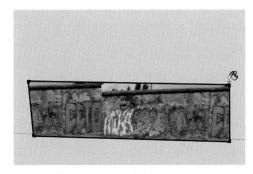

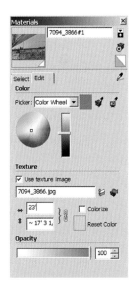

Figure 7-58: Paint the new texture onto a face and then edit its scale.

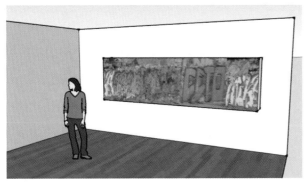

Figure 7–59: Give the straightened image volume to make it a piece of wall art.

So far, we've only painted textures onto flat surfaces. Painting textures on curved surfaces is a technique useful for applications such as adding a pattern to draperies or a logo to a curved sign. We'll do both now.

Project a Texture on Curved Surfaces: Draperies and a Cylinder

Figures 7–60 and 7–61 show how to paint a fabric swatch onto draperies. The draperies are a Warehouse model and originally consisted of multiple nested components. I exploded everything and replaced the existing color with the default color. Then I made three groups: one for the bar and one for each set of draperies. This enables new color to be easily applied. Remember, paint can be applied to a closed group, but if anything in the group is already painted, the group's editing box must be opened.

1. Make a face. It can be any size and located anywhere on the screen. Then paint the texture on it. Adjust the texture size in the Materials browser editing box, if needed.
2. Select the texture, right-click, and choose **Texture>Projected**.
3. Sample the texture. (Click the Paint Bucket and then press and release the **Alt** key on the PC; on the Mac, press and release the **Command** key.)
4. Paint the texture on the draperies.

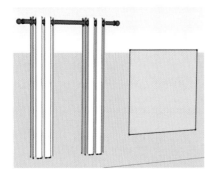 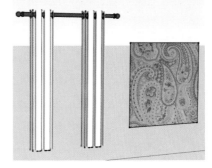

Figure 7–60: Paint the fabric texture on a face.

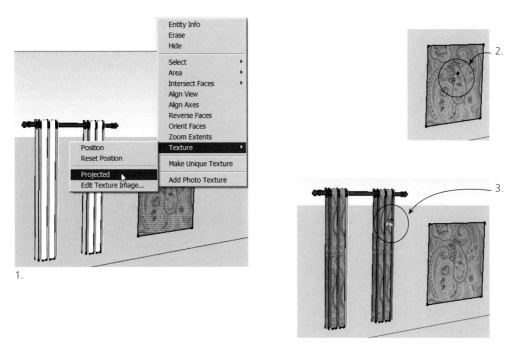

Figure 7–61: Paint the projected fabric onto the draperies.

In Figures 7–62 and 7–63, a raster image of letters is projected on a cylinder; the letters could represent a corporate logo; the cylinder a kiosk, curved sign, or desk. The only difference is that you must paint the texture on a face that is the exact size and shape as the item it will be projected to. The easiest way to ensure this is probably to project lines from the item forward, then draw a face between those lines. Note that the face doesn't have to be right in front of the item; it can be anywhere on the screen. If the texture tiles after being applied to the item, adjust the tile size in the editing box until the desired appearance is achieved.

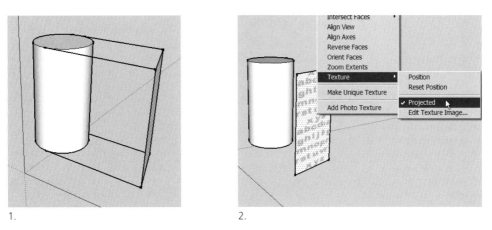

Figure 7–62: Paint the letters onto a face the same size as the cylinder.

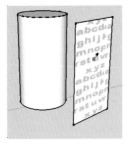

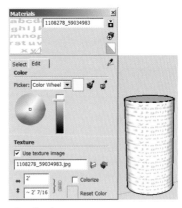

Figure 7–63: Paint the projected word texture onto the cylinder and adjust the tile size as necessary.

Photo-Match an Interior Space

So far we've imported photos as textures and images. There's a third option: import as a photo-match. This enables us to paint three-dimensionally on a model instead of on just one face. Photo-matching is a tool to study existing conditions three-dimensionally. The photo must be a two-point perspective view, with two perpendicular walls.

Figures 7–64 to 7–69 show the process.

1. *Import the Photo.* Go to **File>Import**, navigate to it, and click the *Use as New Matched Photo* radio button. The photo will import with red and green vanishing point bars on it and an open Match Photo dialog box. In that dialog box, select the first graphic under *Grid*. This tells SketchUp to photo-match an interior space. The middle grid is for an aerial view, and the last one for an exterior one. If your match doesn't work, you may have selected the wrong grid. The spacing field underneath is for inputting the distance between grid lines. The default of 5′ is fine. Then minimize the dialog box by clicking on its top blue bar to get it out of your way.

   If you inadvertently close the Match Photo dialog box, get it back at **Window>Match Photo**. And if you inadvertently import a photo-match when you meant to import an image or texture, exit by clicking *Done* on the Match Photo dialog box and/or right-clicking and deleting the tab that appears in the workspace's upper-left corner when a match photo is imported. It's dark blue and displays the photo's name.

Figure 7–64: Import as a photo-match (image obtained from **http://www.sxc.hu/**).

Figure 7–65: Select the first graphic (interior grid).

2. *Align the photo's perspective to SketchUp's camera view.* Grabbing the bars by their end grips, move the red ones onto two converging lines on one wall and the green ones onto two converging lines on a perpendicular wall.

3. *Align the photo's scale to SketchUp's scale.* Grab the grip at the scale figure's feet and move the figure to the origin. This should be the back corner, where two walls and the floor meet. Drag the mouse up and down that corner to scale the figure relative to the photo. When it looks good, maximize the Match Photo dialog box by clicking on its blue bar, and click *Done*. The Pencil appears. Minimize the box again to get it out of the way.

4. *Trace a model over the photo.* Here you need to draw faces onto which the photo will be projected. Trace the walls, floor, and ceiling. Know that you aren't likely to trace the photo exactly, because of discrepancies between it and SketchUp's perspective.

   Tracing the model can be tricky and take multiple attempts. Drawing parallel to the axes is critical; watch for inferences. When the surface turns filmy, a face has formed. If a face doesn't form, the edges aren't coplanar. Press the mouse's scroll wheel to activate Orbit, which causes the photo to disappear. You can then study the model for problems. Erase bad lines, and then click on the Pencil to reactivate it. Bring the photo back by clicking the dark blue Match Photo tab.

5. *Project the photo.* Maximize the Match Photo dialog box, and click *Project textures from photo*. Two more dialog boxes will appear; "Yes" is typically the correct answer to both. Voila: the photo-matched model.

Figure 7–66: Adjust the perspective bars and scale figure.

Figure 7–67: Trace the walls.

Figure 7–68: Trace the ceiling and floor.

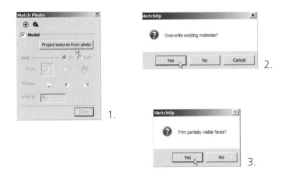

Figure 7–69: Project the photo onto the model.

Summary

In this chapter we used the Materials browser and learned painting techniques. Along with applying native colors and textures, we imported raster images as textures, images, and photo-matches, and manipulated them with editing and positioning tools. Such techniques add visual interest and realism to a SketchUp model (Figure 7–70).

In Chapters 1–7, we learned how to make and embellish a model. In Chapter 8, we'll learn ways to present it.

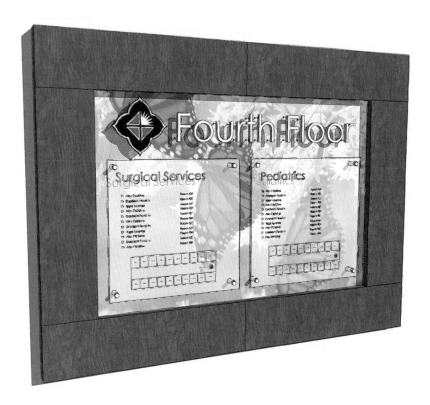

Courtesy Matthew Kerr, IIDA, ASAI, Zimmerman Architectural Studios, Milwaukee, WI

Figure 7–70: This model utilizes an imported background image and material texture, as well as opacity settings.

Courtesy Matthew Kerr, IIDA, ASAI, Zimmerman Architectural Studios, Milwaukee, WI
Figure 7–71: This model utilizes SketchUp's built-in colors plus a large imported image positioned behind the model for the view. It was achieved by making a cylinder, erasing the front half, and then projecting the photo onto the curved back half.

Further Resources

Download a free digital imaging program here: www.irfanview.com/

Site with links to lots of textures to practice with: http://sketchupdate.blogspot.com/2011/09/treasure-trove-of-textures.html

Site with thousands of free images uploaded by users: www.sxc.hu/

Video on fixed and free pins: www.youtube.com/watch?v=vO16eaFpBF0

Website with a free Photoshop-like application. Google "portable gimp" to find places to download a GIMP app: www.gimp.org/

Exercises

www.wiley.com/go/sketchupforinteriordesign

1. Import the paperback books file (Exercise 7–1) and paint on a face. Then use Push/Pull and the Pencil to model the stack of books. Paint their tops with plain colors from the color palette/color picker. The result should look like Figure 7–72.

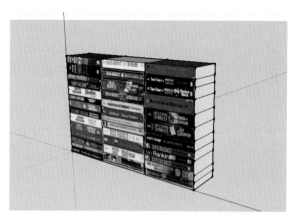

Figure 7–72

2. Open the Small Kitchen model (Exercise 7–2). Import finishes from the Materials folder and paint them on the model. Rotate, enlarge, and make other modifications of your choice to those files. Alternatively, take photos of your kitchen cabinet doors, resample to make them small files, and import them as images. Then paint them onto the model's cabinet doors.

3. Import the Berlin Wall photo (Exercise 7–3) and straighten it out.

4. Import the graffiti image (Exercise 7–4) and position it behind a window with different proportions.

5. Import the letters (Exercise 7–5) and project them on a cylinder.

6. Import the draperies (Exercise 7–6) and project a pattern from the Materials folder on them.

7. Import the wallpaper files in the Materials folder and edit their colors.

8. Photo-match Living Room 1 (Exercise 7–7. Image obtained from http://www.sxc.hu/).

9. Photo-match Living Room 2 (Exercise 7–8. Image obtained from http://www.sxc.hu/).

10. Model a room in your home. Include:

   ▶ windows

   ▶ doors

   ▶ trim (base, crown molding)

   ▶ built-ins (e.g., cabinets, fireplace)

11. Paint the model using imported photo files of the room's finishes.

Enhancing and Presenting the Model

I n Chapters 1–8, we learned how to create a SketchUp model. Here, we'll discuss techniques to polish and creatively display it.

Annotate the Model: Dimensions and Text

Most drawings benefit from some *annotations*, which are notes and dimensions. Annotations should go on their own layer so they can be hidden as needed. Make a layer for them (see Chapter 6), and then make it active. All annotations will then be created on it until a different layer is activated. Annotations are made with the Dimension and Text tools.

The Dimension Tool

Activate the Dimension tool (Figure 8–1). The mouse turns into an arrowhead. To dimension an edge, click somewhere along its length (not on a midpoint or endpoint), and drag it out. A *stringer*, which is a dimension line with visible endpoints and a note, appears. The note describes the line's length. Raise the stringer to the desired height (Figure 8–2). Make a second stringer the same height by clicking it on the first stringer's endpoint (Figure 8–3). Sometimes the stringer won't move along the axis you want; for instance, instead of moving vertically it may stubbornly move horizontally. Orbiting around the geometry to dimension it from another angle may solve that.

You can also dimension an edge by clicking on two separate points: endpoints, midpoints, and intersections. The second click must be on a point, because the Text tool won't click a second time on a random place along the line. If a random place is what you want, put a guide point or guide line there (see Chapter 4).

Objective: This chapter discusses tools and techniques for enhancing a SketchUp model and presenting it to an audience.

Tools: Dimensions, Text, 3D Text, Walk, Position Camera, Interact with Dynamic Components, Polygon

Concepts and Functions: apply leader text, screen text, dimension stringers, styles, shadow and settings, make a watermark, create scenes and animations, present different design schemes, export to 2D and 3D formats, dynamic components, make SketchUp run faster, polygon count, develop the model with other software and hand-rendering

Clicking the Dimension tool on an arc yields a dimension note prefaced with *R* for radius (Figure 8–4). Clicking on a circle yields a dimension note prefaced with *DIA* for diameter. To notate an arc with *DIA*, or a circle with *R*, right-click on the note (not on the arc or circle), and choose *Type*. Be aware that exploded or extruded arcs and circles won't show size information. Edit dimension notes by double-clicking and overtyping. Erase them with the Eraser, or select and hit **Delete**.

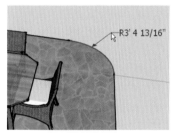

Figure 8–1: The Dimension tool.

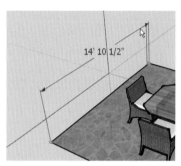

Figure 8–2: Click a line's edge or endpoints and move the resultant stringer up.

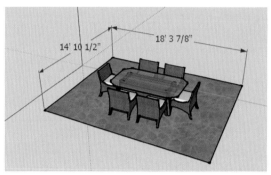

Figure 8–3: Click the second stringer on an endpoint of the first to align them.

Figure 8–4: Click on an arc for a radius dimension note.

Edit the Stringer

To edit the stringer, select it, right-click, and open its *Entity Info* box (Figure 8–5). Click the arrow in the upper-right corner to open the bottom pane, if it doesn't automatically open. Here, you can change text position, alignment, and endpoint style. Click the *Change Font* button to open the screen in Figure 8–6, and choose font style, color, and size. Change units at **Window>Model Info>Units**, and scroll through the *Format* field (Figure 8–7). Precision (how many numbers after the decimal) is also changed there. These settings affect all annotations on the model.

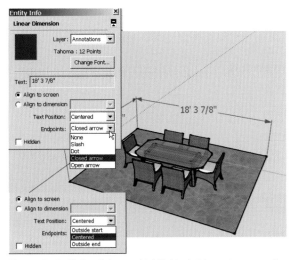

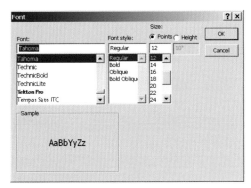

Figure 8–5: Right-click on a highlighted stringer to access its Entity Info box.

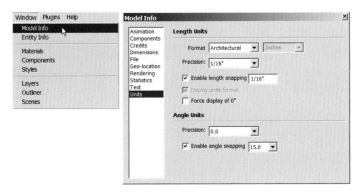

Figure 8–6: The Font dialog box.

Figure 8–7: Change units at **Window>Model Info**.

Text Size: Points vs. Height

The Font box offers two size options: *points* and *height.* Points describe a font's physical size. Choosing points sets the text's on-screen size, and that size never changes, even when zoomed in or out. Height lets you choose the size in inches, and its appearance scales with the model. That is, zooming in and out makes it appear larger and smaller. Since this size is true scale like the rest of the model, you might have to set a number such as 10′ (feet, not inches) to make it readable on a large floor plan.

If text continues to appear tiny, you may have inadvertently checked some settings causing that. Go to **Window>Model Info>Dimensions**, and click on *Expert Dimension Settings* (Figure 8–8). Is *Hide when foreshortened* or *Hide when too small* selected? If so, deselect. Those options should be clicked only if the text appears cluttered but you don't want to completely turn it off.

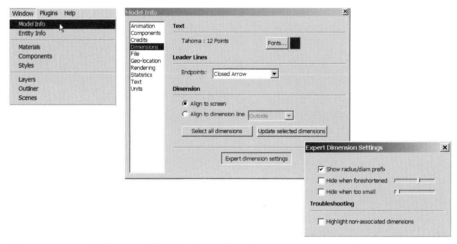

Figure 8–8: At **Window>Model Info>Dimensions** there are more options for dimension settings.

The Text Tool

The Text tool (Figure 8–9) creates freestanding notes. They have the same font, color, and size options as dimension text. There are two types of text: *screen* and *leader* (Figure 8–10).

Figure 8–9: The Text tool.

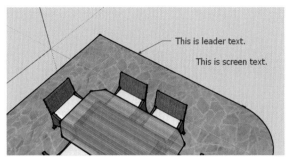

Figure 8–10: *Leader* text is attached to the model with a leader line. Screen text is a note placed anywhere.

Screen Text vs. Leader Text

Screen text is placed on a specific location anywhere on the screen and stays there. No matter how much you pan, zoom, or orbit, it stays fixed in place. It is only set with height, not points, and can be relocated with the Move tool. Double-clicking the Text tool on any face creates screen text that reveals the face's area.

Leader text has a leader (a line with an arrow at one end and a note at the other) that points to, and is attached to, a face. It moves with the model. Leaders are automatically made when the Text tool is clicked on a face, and its text can be set in height or points. Depending on the geometry clicked, a different default note appears. Clicking on a point reveals its coordinates; clicking on a face reveals its area; clicking on a line reveals its length; clicking on a component reveals its name. Double-click to overtype your own note. Exit by clicking outside the box or by hitting Enter twice.

As discussed in Chapter 4, a way to verify if a face is coplanar is by clicking leader text on each endpoint to see the coordinates. One coordinate must be the same on each endpoint. If all are different, the face is not coplanar (Figure 8–11).

Pushpin vs. View-Based Leaders

Leaders are either *pushpin* or *view based.* *Pushpin* leaders rotate and orbit with the model. This is useful for presentations that use animated fly-bys. View-based leaders always face the camera, such as the scale figure. This is useful for presenting still images (slide shows). Choose them through the leader's Entity Info box (Figure 8–12) or by right-clicking on the leader, selecting *leader* from the context menu, and then

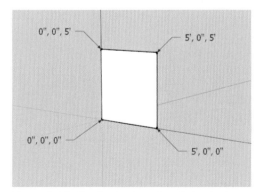

Figure 8–11: Check a face's coplanarity by viewing its endpoint coordinates. If a face is coplanar, all its endpoints will have one identical coordinate. This vertical face's endpoints have the same *y* coordinate.

clicking *Pushpin* or *View based.* There you'll also find an option to hide the leader line and just show its note.

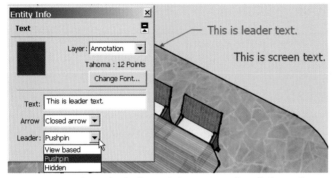

Figure 8–12: Select a leader line to bring up its Entity Info box, where edits can be made.

Color, font, and size can also be changed. Make those changes at **Window>Model Info>Text** (Figure 8–13) or **Window>Model Info>Dimensions** to apply to all annotations on the model. There you can also select all text and update it. The *Select all text* option is also handy for moving the text to a different layer, if that wasn't done at the outset.

To make these settings apply to all SketchUp files, put them in a custom template, as discussed in Chapter 3.

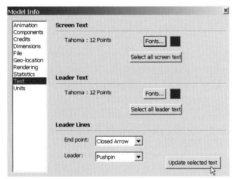

Figure 8–13: Text and dimension changes made through the Model Info window affect all the model's annotations.

Dimension a Floor Plan

The rudimentary annotations in Figure 8–14 were made by switching to the plan view, setting the numbers precision to ½", the endpoints to slashes, and the text aligned with/above the stringers. I made guidelines for dimensioning to the center of openings where needed.

SketchUp Make is inadequate for detailed dimensioning. For instance, you can't place a hyphen between the foot and inch symbol, and dimensions in tight areas are displayed poorly on a printout. Producing plans drawn and drafted to National Kitchen and Bath (NKBA) standards is problematic, since there are no hidden and center lines. The workarounds and plugins for this are time-consuming.

Instead, many designers import their Pro models into AutoCAD, Revit, or 20–20 when transitioning from the design to construction document phase. Plans, elevations, and sections import at a 1:1 scale and components and layers are preserved. Different line types and dimension stringers are then easily added.

However, LayOut, a Pro feature, may be an option for creating construction drawings, depending how detailed they must be, as it has some line types and additional dimensioning capabilities. It's discussed in Chapter 9.

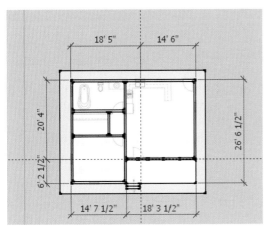

Figure 8–14: SketchUp has rudimentary dimensioning capabilities.

3D Text

The 3D Text tool (Figure 8–15) makes text components. These are edited and manipulated like any other component. Click the 3D Text tool on the screen. A dialog box appears; type the note, and choose the settings. The *Extruded* option controls the letters' thickness. Then click *Place*, and move the 3D text where desired.

Figure 8–15: The 3D Text tool.

Placing 3D text along a specific axis can be tricky. A tip is to draw a small face and place the text on or near it, which helps the 3D text snap to that orientation (Figure 8–16). Alternatively, use the Rotate tool to position it.

Figure 8–16: Drawing a face and clicking the 3D Text tool on or near it makes it easier to align the text with a specific axis.

Styles

Styles are display settings that give aesthetic appeal to a model and may eliminate its "cartoony" look. SketchUp has native collections in its Styles browser. Go to **Window>Styles** (Figure 8–17) to bring it up. On the *Select* tab, see *Default Styles* in the text field and their thumbnails below. To date, we've just modeled with the first thumbnail's style. Click on another thumbnail, and the model will automatically update with new settings. Then scroll the text field to a different collection and click on its thumbnails (Figure 8–18). Some styles show the model in black and white, which is great for making prints to use as an underlay. Others have plain white backgrounds or show the model with sketchy lines. To restore the default style, go back to the default collection and click the first thumbnail.

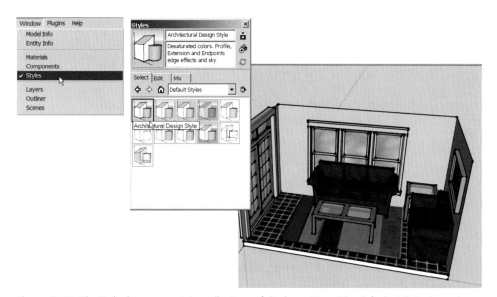

Figure 8–17: The Styles browser contains collections of display settings. The default style is shown here.

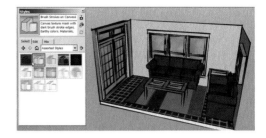

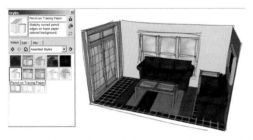

Figure 8–18: Click on a style collection, then on a style's thumbnail to apply it to the model.

Like components and textures, every style clicked on the model remains in it, increasing the file size. Purge unused ones via the Styles browser's *Details* arrow (Figure 8–19).

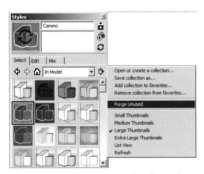

Figure 8–19: Purge unused styles to keep the file size down.

SketchUp lets you mix and match native styles to create your own. Click the *Create new Style* button (Figure 8–20) to make a new thumbnail, and then click the Mix tab to mix and match existing styles to make a new one.

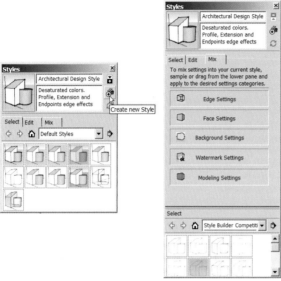

Figure 8–20: Click the *Create new style* button to make a new thumbnail, and edit it with options on the *Mix* tab.

Drag the thumbnail for a new style to the bottom pane of the Styles browser to put it in the SketchUp software. Or save it in a collection on your computer and link to it. Review the discussion in Chapters 6 and 7 about doing this with components and textures, as the process is identical.

SketchUp Pro's *Style Builder* feature offers the ability to make entirely new styles that aren't assembled from existing ones.

Make a Shortcut to the Default Style

When experimenting with styles, navigating back to the default all the time is tedious. Figure 8–21 shows how to make a shortcut to it. Go to **Window>Scenes**. A dialog box opens; type *Home* in the name field and a description of the scene in the field below. A dark blue tab that says *Home* is now visible in the upper-left corner of the workspace. There's no *ok* button to push; close the dialog box. You've just created a *scene tab*, a shortcut to a view with preserved properties. Clicking on it returns the default setting. We'll talk more about scene tabs later in this chapter.

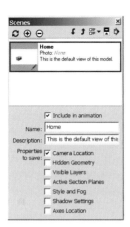

Figure 8–21: Creating a shortcut to the default setting.

More Style Options: Remove the Sky and Make a Watermark

Click the Edit tab of the Styles browser. The five cubes at the top each access a different dialog box. We've used the first two in past chapters to adjust edge settings and face colors.

The third cube lets you remove the sky from the model's background (Figure 8–22). SketchUp models have a ground and sky. What you're seeing, however, is a blue sky on top of a background color. The ground color is disabled by default. This is an issue when printing the model, because background colors don't print. Hence, you'll get a blue sky on top of a white "ground." To print the ground color, check its box. Change the sky and ground colors by clicking the boxes next to their names.

The fourth cube creates watermarks (Figure 8–23).

Figure 8–22: The Styles/third cube edit tab. Uncheck the sky to remove it from the model, and check the ground to add it to a print.

Figure 8–23: The Styles/fourth cube edit tab accesses the watermark dialog box.

Import a Title Block with the Watermark Function

Use the watermark function to display an already-made title block. Here's how:

1. Go to **Window>Styles>Edit** and click the fourth (watermark) cube.
2. Click on the plus sign. A navigation browser appears; find the title block, and double-click to bring it into the model (Figure 8–24).

 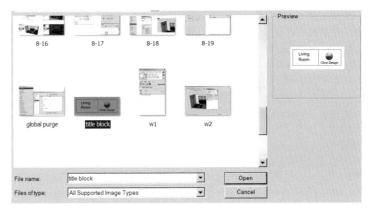

Figure 8–24: Click the plus sign and navigate to the title block.

3. The title block and a dialog box appear. Click the radio button in front of *Background* (Figure 8–25).

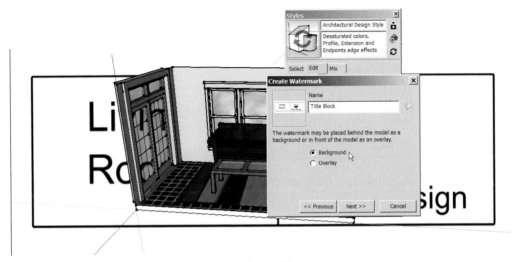

Figure 8–25: Name the title block, and click the *Background* button.

4. Two more dialog boxes appear (Figure 8–26). The first has an opacity slider at the bottom; if you want to make the title block translucent, move it to the left. I kept it as is. The second asks how and where to position the block. I clicked *Positioned in the screen* and chose the bottom-right corner. I also made the title block smaller with the slider at the bottom.

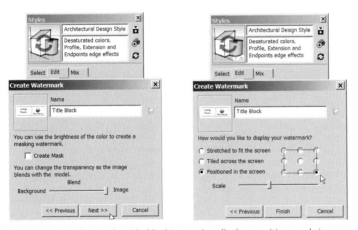

Figure 8–26: Choose the title block's opacity, display, position, and size.

5. The title block (Figure 8–27)! It's fixed in place and won't pan, orbit, or zoom.

Figure 8–27: A watermark used as a title block.

To change its display, position, or scale, go back to the watermark cube's Edit tab, select the title block entry, and then click on the gears (Figure 8–28). To delete it, select the title block entry and click on the minus sign. To hide it, uncheck *Display watermarks*.

Figure 8–28: Make changes to the watermark at **Styles>Edit**.

Shadow Settings

At **View>Shadow** splash some sunlight onto the model (Figure 8–29). Interior spaces are lit by artificial light, though, not sunlight, for which rendering programs are needed. Such programs have a learning curve and consume a lot of computer resources. A workaround for simulating interior light is to select the ceiling, open its *Entity Info* box, and uncheck *Cast Shadows*. That brings sunlight into the space. Further adjustments can be made in the **Window>Shadows** dialog box (Figure 8–30). There you can specify the month and time of day, and use sliders to make the shadows and surrounding surfaces lighter or darker (Figure 8–31). The shadow function in the **View** menu must be turned on for the display options at the bottom of the dialog box to work. Animated shadow studies can be made with the *Scenes* function, discussed next.

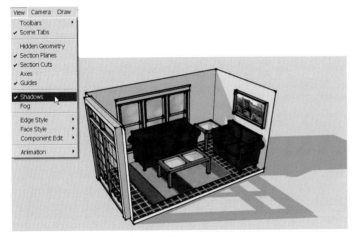

Figure 8–29: **View>Shadows** adds shadows to the model.

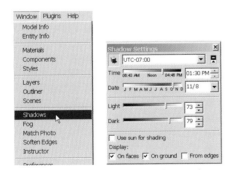

Figure 8–30: At **Window>Shadows** adjust the shadow settings.

Figure 8–31: This space was modeled from an AutoCAD floor plan. The black-and-white style, opacity, and shadow settings lend drama. Making all furniture groupings, table lamps, and pendants the same (see the latter two in Figure 8–61) was an efficiency that contributed to its completion in three hours.

Scenes

Earlier in this chapter, we made a scene tab for use as a shortcut to the default style. Scenes are saved views of a model. Scene tabs are the links or bookmarks that take you to the scene. They preserve property (display) changes. Specifically, scenes preserve:

- ▶ Camera settings (viewer position, angle, zoom, type of perspective)
- ▶ Shadows
- ▶ Hidden settings
- ▶ Layers
- ▶ Section planes
- ▶ Styles (including edges, faces, endpoints, and display settings)
- ▶ Global axes visibility
- ▶ Field of view

Geometry, color, and texture changes are not preserved, since they are model changes, and all scenes show the same model. Hence, changes made to those aspects will appear in all scenes, not just the scene they're made in.

If you want to show different furniture, colors, and textures (which is geometry, not properties), combine layers with scenes to different models. This technique makes both the design and presentation processes more efficient, because it enables studying and viewing different solutions by just clicking their tabs. Let's do that now.

Make Scenes of Different Designs

You have three designs and want to show two views of each (six scenes total) one at a time, in one file. Here's how:

1. *Make three new layers*, called Design 1, Design 2, and Design 3 (Figure 8–32).

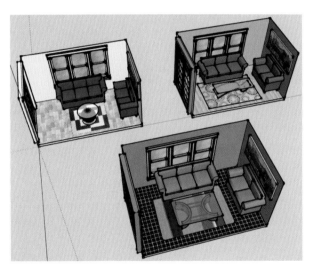

Figure 8–32: Make a layer for each design.

2. *Group each design*, open their Entity Info boxes, and move them to their respective layers (Figure 8–33). Then place (overlap) all three at the origin. This is possible because, unlike loose geometry, groups can occupy the same space. They may flash; this is okay.

3. *Make the first scene tab and scene* (Figure 8–34). Click on **Window>Scene**s to open the Scenes Manager dialog box. If the box doesn't display all the options shown in Figure 8–30, click the arrow in its upper-right corner to open the bottom pane. Next, click on the plus sign to make a tab. Type *Design 1, first view* in the *Name* field. Hide Designs 2 and 3 by unchecking their *Visible* boxes, and orbit/zoom to the view desired. Change any other properties in the preceding bullet list. Right-click on the scene tab, and choose *Update*.

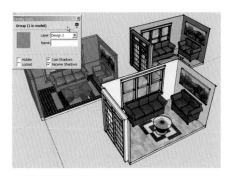
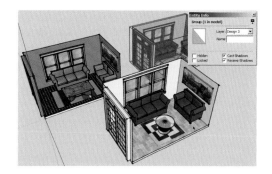

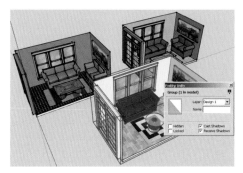

Figure 8–33: Group each design, move them to their respective layers, and place all of them at the origin.

Figure 8–34: At **Window>Scene** make a scene tab, create the scene, and then update the tab.

4. *Make the second scene tab and scene* (Figure 8–35). Go to **Window>Scene** again, or right-click on the first scene tab and choose *Scene Manager*. Call the tab *Design 1, second view*. Orbit/zoom to choose another view, and adjust other properties. Then right-click on the *Design 1 second view* tab, and choose *Update*.

5. *Make the third scene tab and scene* (Figure 8–36). Call the tab *Design 2, first view*. Hide Designs 1 and 3. Orbit/zoom to the view desired, and change other properties. Right-click on the scene tab, and choose *Update*.

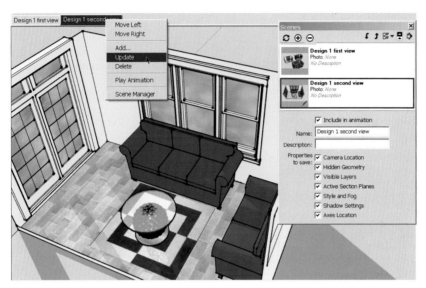

Figure 8–35: Create a second scene tab and scene, and then update the tab.

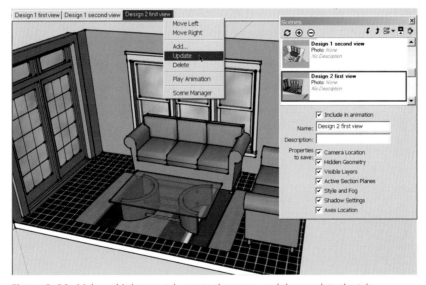

Figure 8–36: Make a third scene tab, create the scene, and then update the tab.

6. *Make the fourth scene tab and scene* (Figure 8–37). Call the tab *Design 2, second view.* Orbit/zoom to the view desired, and change other properties. Right-click on the scene tab, and choose *Update.*

7. *Make the fifth scene tab and scene* (Figure 8–38). Call the tab *Design 3, first view.* Hide designs 1 and 2. Orbit/zoom to the view desired and change other properties. Right-click on the scene tab, and choose *Update.*

Figure 8–37: Make a fourth scene tab, create the scene, and then update the tab.

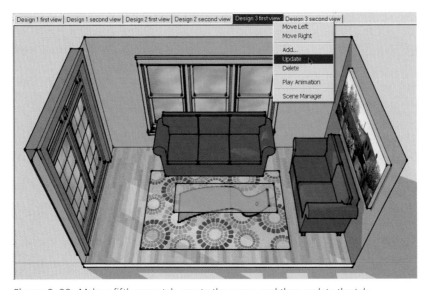

Figure 8–38: Make a fifth scene tab, create the scene, and then update the tab.

8. *Make the sixth scene tab and scene* (Figure 8–39). Call the tab *Design 3, second view*. Orbit/ zoom to the view desired, and change other properties. Right-click on the scene tab, and choose *Update*.

Figure 8–39: Make a sixth scene tab, create the scene, and then update the tab.

Change a scene by clicking on its tab, adjusting the properties on the model, and then updating the scene tab. If you want another scene to have the same changes, right-click and update its tabs at the same time. Update all scenes at once by selecting them all in the Scenes Manager and then right-clicking. Remember that geometry changes must be made inside the group they're in or they'll affect every scene.

You may have noticed that new tabs default to the left of older ones. Move a tab by right-clicking it and choosing *Move Left* or *Move Right*. Delete a scene by right-clicking it and choosing *Delete* (Figure 8–40).

If you want a scene that shows the model as a two-point perspective instead of SketchUp's three-point default, go to **Camera>Two- Point Perspective**. You might do this when you're ready to print the scene. Orbiting will kick you out of two-point perspective mode and back into three-point.

Components can't display scenes, even if they contain them. If you've downloaded a Warehouse

Figure 8–40: Right-click on a scene tab to move or delete that view.

model into your open model and want to display its scenes, open it in a new instance of
SketchUp.

▶ A creative use for scenes is to make step-by-step tutorials. Search for tutorials in the Warehouse, where
many uploaders show off different techniques.

Make an Animation of the Scenes

SketchUp animations are multiple scenes displayed in succession. The transition between
them is animated by default. Adjusting is done at **Window>Model Info>Animation**
(Figure 8–41). Right-click any scene tab, and choose *Play Animation* to start (Figure 8–42);
click it again to stop.

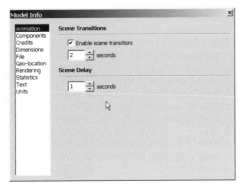

Figure 8–41: Adjust animation settings in the Animations dialog box.

Figure 8–42: Click *Play
Animation* to both start and stop
the display of scene tabs.

Animated transitions might show parts of the model you don't want shown, such as unfinished areas. In this case, use still transitions instead of animated ones by unchecking the
Enable scene transitions box. That way you'll cut to each image
instead of travel to it (that is, make a slide show rather than an
animation). Time between transitions and scene delay are also
editable. If the viewer travels a large distance between scenes, you
might set a longer transition time than the two-second default, to
avoid "dizziness." The time setting applies to all scenes and cannot
be adjusted between scenes. Make one scene appear to display longer by making multiple, consecutive copies of it.

Scene Delay is the time SketchUp pauses on each scene before
moving to the next. Set it to zero to create a movielike quality,
useful for shadow studies, or to animate scenes made with the
Walk-Through tools discussed next. Remove scenes from the animation by selecting them in the Scenes Manager and unchecking

Figure 8–43: Remove a scene
from an animation by unchecking the *Include in animation*
option in the Scenes Manager.

Include in animation (Figure 8–43). This is useful for excluding "not ready for prime time" parts of the project.

Turn the animation into a movie at **File>Export>Animation**. SketchUp automatically creates an *mp4*, *avi*, or *webm* file of your scenes. Present to the audience on a laptop or tablet.

▶ Think like a producer when making a movie. Write a storyboard or outline detailing what should be shown and in what order. How many wide-views vs. close-ups? Should the viewer travel between transitions or see a slide show? Which scenes should be displayed longer? Which should be rendered or left black and white? How long should the movie be? Import it into the free Movie Maker or iMovie software that comes with PCs and Macs, and add music and photos.

The Walk-Through Tools

SketchUp's Walk-Through tools display a model as though you were walking inside or around it and swiveling your head. Find them on the **Camera** toolbar (activate it on the toolbar dialog box). There are three Walk-Through tools: *Position Camera*, *Look Around*, and *Walk* (Figure 8–44).

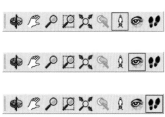

Figure 8–44: From top to bottom: *Position Camera*, *Look Around*, and *Walk*.

You might want to widen the field of view before using them, to see more of the model (**Camera>Field of View**, then over type a larger angle than the default in the measurements box).

The Position Camera and Look Around Tools

Position Camera puts you in a location from which the space is viewed (Figure 8–45). Activate it and click on the floor. Your eye level defaults to 5′-6″ above it; if you want a different height, type it and hit **Enter**. That eye level is consistent; for example, when climbing stairs, it adjusts to 5′-6″ above each tread.

After you click on the floor, Look Around is activated. In it, you are stationary and swiveling your head. Drag the mouse up, down, left, and right to view those directions.

Panning or orbiting will change your eye level—look at the measurements box to see how your eye level has changed. If you can remember to just drag the mouse, you'll stay at the same 5′-6″ eye level and really will get a better view of the space. But if you do inadvertently pan or orbit, just overtype the new eye level and hit **Enter**.

Position Camera also lets you see the view from a specific location (Figure 8–46). Click it on the scale figure's face, and drag it to the item you want to view. Release the mouse. The view will move to the starting point of the item you clicked on. Again, if you inadvertently orbited or panned, the eye level height will change and you'll get a mess of a view (too high or too low). Overtype and hit **Enter**.

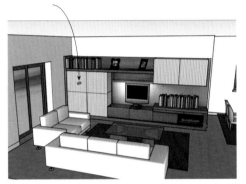

Figure 8–45: *Position Camera* was clicked on the floor, and then the mouse dragged left and right to view the space. (This house is a derivative of a Warehouse model.)

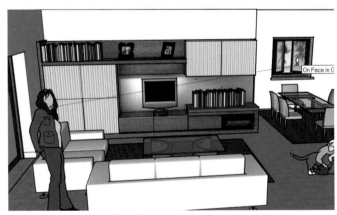

Figure 8–46: Click *Position Camera* on the scale figure's face, and drag the mouse to whatever you want her to look at. Then release. The model will shift to that view.

While inside Position Camera, you can go to **Camera>Field of view** and drag the mouse up and down to make the field of view wider or narrower. Releasing the mouse makes the current field of view active.

The Walk Tool

The Walk tool lets you walk inside your model at a constant eye level, as opposed to Pan and Orbit, which constantly change your eye level. Walk only works in perspective mode.

Activate it, and then type the eye-level height wanted. Click on the floor. A small pair of crosshairs appears, indicating your location (Figure 8–47).

Now walk! Hold the cursor down and drag it up to go forward, down to go backward, left to go left, and right to go right. The farther you move from the crosshairs, the faster you walk; the closer you are to the crosshairs, the slower you walk. There's a built-in collision detection so you can walk up stairs and not through walls. If you want to walk through walls, hold the **Alt** key down while dragging the mouse.

Hold the **Shift** key down to raise or lower eye height. Alternatively, type a new eye height, and hit **Enter**. Height is always from the red/green axis plane. If you are on a second floor or a higher level, add the height of that floor or level to whatever eye height you enter. Holding the mouse's scroll wheel down will switch to the Look Around tool.

Figure 8–47: Click the Walk tool on the floor, then drag the cursor in the direction you want to walk.

Using Walk, make a series of scenes, each with an incremental movement. The resultant animation will be a smooth movie of the viewer walking through the space. Remember to uncheck the Enable scenes transitions box.

What Are Dynamic Components?

A *dynamic component* (DC) is geometry that has *attributes*, or special features. Examples of attributes are:

- ▶ Stored parts and price numbers
- ▶ A staircase adding steps when height-adjusted with the Scale tool (wouldn't that have been handy in the Chapter 6 living room!)
- ▶ A closet system showing configurations and calculating price
- ▶ Window trim retaining its width when the window is stretched
- ▶ Colors changing
- ▶ Lights turning on and off
- ▶ Doors opening and closing

Such attributes can make the workflow faster and the presentation more interesting. There's a collection of DCs in the Components browser and more in the Warehouse, identified by the ➡ symbol. Manufacturers create DCs of their products (Figure 8–48), the SketchUp team has created a bunch, and casual users have created even more. SketchUp Make users can download and manipulate existing ones, but only Pro users can create and edit them.

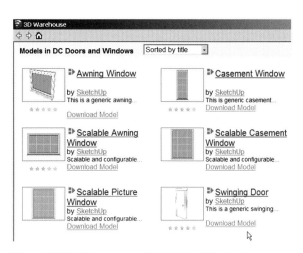

Figure 8–48: The green symbol indicates the window component is dynamic.

Find and Download Dynamic Components

Download a dynamic component through the Components Browser into an open file, not directly to the desktop. Its features may not work when directly opened, because of options selected when the component was modeled. If the DC is already on your desktop, import it into an open file at **File>Import** (remember to scroll the *Files of Type* field at the bottom to *SketchUp Files*). Figure 8–48 shows dynamic windows from the Warehouse; Figure 8–49 shows a dynamic furniture search made through the Components browser. Be aware that not all modelers describe their DCs as dynamic, so this search will miss some.

Figure 8–49: Search for dynamic furniture through the Components browser.

Figure 8–50: Open the Dynamic toolbar at **File>Views>Toolbars**. The toolbar is at the bottom.

How to Use Dynamic Components: The DC Toolbar

Open the DC toolbar at **View>Toolbars>Dynamic Components** (Figure 8–50). Its three icons are *Interactive Tool*, *Components Options*, and *Components Attributes*. Manipulate a DC by using the Interactive Tool and/or the Options box. Pro users can edit the DC through the Attributes box.

The Interactive tool: When Interactive touches a programmed part of a DC, a yellow glow appears. Click it on the scale figure to see him talk (Figure 8–51). Yes, the scale figure is a dynamic component! The Interactive tool mostly just clicks doors open and closed, turns lights on and off, and changes colors.

Figure 8–51: The scale figure is a dynamic component who talks.

The options box: This is where you can do the more complex operations the modeler programmed the DC to do, such as resize and reconfigure. The component must be selected for the options box to display the options.

Figure 8–52 shows the options box for another scale figure. Clicking on it changes the sweater color. Scroll to a new color, and click *Apply*. The component will update. Figure 8–53 shows a Warehouse bench and its options box; size and material choices are offered.

Most changes to DCs are made through the options box or by scaling. If grips appear when you click the Scale tool on a DC, it's scalable.

Figure 8–52: The scale figure's sweater color can be changed through its options box.

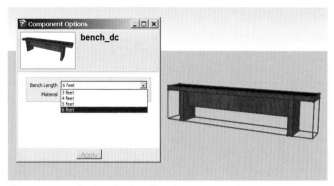

Figure 8–53: This bench's length and material can be changed through its options box.

As with any other component uploaded by casual users, some DCs have problems, but they may be fixed with a little editing. For instance, if an options box appears blank, try exploding the DC once, because its interactive features may be nested inside a group (if the interactive part itself is exploded, the programming will be lost—undo to get it back). The bench in the example here didn't work until the component was repainted with the default paint first.

Any component can be made dynamic. The process involves inputting formulas in spreadsheets. See Further Resources at the end of this chapter for links to websites that show how to make them.

Save vs. Export

Saving a file preserves its data in its native format, with all layers, features, and selections intact. It can be imported or reopened in the program that made it.

Exporting a file compresses and converts its data into a completely different data format. It cannot be turned back into the original format or re-imported into the software that made it. This is because the layers and information needed to do that are gone. When exporting a file, you choose a format to *save as* and a location to *save to*, but you don't save it in the original format. Exporting is how *skp* files are turned into files that can be printed or imported into other software programs.

To turn the model into a hard copy, first decide how you want that hard copy to look. Change its appearance from a three-point perspective to a two-point at **Camera>Two-Point Perspective** (Figure 8–54). To print a saved scene, activate that scene. Everything on the screen will print, so hide the axes and any guide lines or geometry you don't want to show. Choose a style and appearance—such as black and white, sketchy edges, blue pen, plain white background, hidden edges—appropriate for what you plan to do with the print.

Figure 8–54: At **Camera>Two-Point Perspective**, change the model from its default three-point appearance to a two-point.

Export the Model as a 2D Graphic

Figure 8–55 shows the following sequence. Go to **File>Export** and choose *2D Graphic*. With SketchUp Make, the options are *jpg*, *png*, and *tif*. With Pro, they're *jpg*, *png*, *tif*, *pdf*, *eps*, *bmp*, *epx*, *dwg*, and *dxf*. A navigation browser appears. Click *Options* in the browser's lower-right corner to get a dialog box that enables resolution setting. Uncheck *Use view size* to customize the number of pixels in the image size. A publishable 2D image needs to be 300 ppi (pixels per inch), but 200 ppi is enough for use as an underlay. A 5″ × 7″ image needs a pixel size of about 1000 × 1400.

That said, note that number of pixels is just one measure of resolution. SketchUp Make does not generate the same quality 2D or animation exports that Pro does.

The printout may not look exactly like the screen. Some adjustment of the zoom, text size, and font type may be needed to get the print desired. Once you get all the settings right, save the file as a scene to easily return to it. Some adjustments to the paper and scale size in the printer's *Page Setup* might also be needed.

SketchUp Make doesn't offer a *pdf* export option, which is the best option, because a *pdf* is a vector file, hence scalable. A workaround is to download a *pdf* printer emulator. Some, like *CutePDF* and *PDF995*, are free (see Further Resources at the end of the chapter for download links).

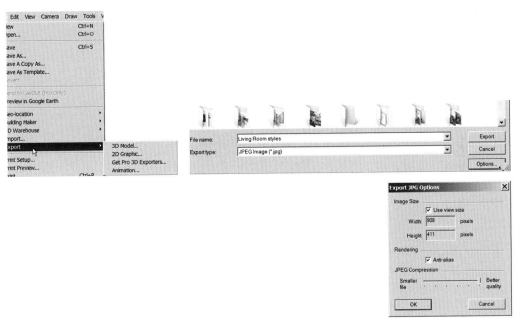

Figure 8–55: At **File>Export** choose *2D Graphic*, then *Options*, and then customize the resolution as needed.

Export the Model as a 3D File

Turn the model into a 3D file to import into another program. At **File>Export>3D model**, the options in SketchUp Make are *dae* (COLLADA) and *kmz* (Google Earth). The options for Pro are *dae, kmz, 3ds, obj, vrml, xsi, dwg, dxf, and fbx.* The last three can be directly imported into AutoCAD or Revit.

COLLADA is a go-between program that converts *skp* files into *dae* files, which can then be imported into other 3D programs. Direct import/export is possible between SketchUp Make and 3dsMax, Maya, and Blender. However, a *dae* file needs to be converted into an *fbx* file to work with AutoCAD and Revit. See Further Resources, at the end of the chapter, for a download link for that software.

On the COLLADA options box, check *Export Two-Sided Faces* if you plan to render the model in another program (Figure 8–56).

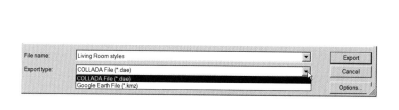
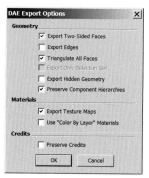

Figure 8–56: At **File>Export** choose *3D graphic*, then *Options*, and choose the ones wanted.

Enhance with Other Software

Many designers import a SketchUp print or model into other software programs to enhance or render it. Photoshop for enhancing prints and 3dsMax for enhancing models are popular for this purpose.

Even just a limited knowledge of Photoshop will enable you to refine presentation materials. You can add light glows, text, arrows, highlights, entourage, and paint daubs; color-correct; clean up; slightly alter; compose a group of images and text; and attach a title block to the composition. With 3dsMax, you can give the model a photorealistic treatment, complete with reflections. Plugins, which are add-on software (discussed in Chapter 9), are also popular for enhancement.

Enhance with Hand-Rendering

Good hand-sketching skills are still valuable even in today's digital world. The fastest modeling software may not be as fast, or produce sketches as intriguing, as the old-school pen and paper. Computer rendering may actually take longer or be counterproductive if the software is too strong for an older computer or has a steep learning curve. A practiced hand can represent textures faster with marker. Hand-drawing also offers more control over focus and visual weight.

Figure 8–57: A model with an applied sketchy lines style, and the same model imported into Photoshop to experiment with color schemes.

Combine the best of both worlds by making fast, accurate line models with software and tracing or coloring over hard copies for a hand-drawn look. The only rule for a presentation image is that it looks good, communicates the design, and gets the client emotionally involved in the space. Generally, perspective trumps any orthographic drawings, and color trumps everything.

Figures 8–58 through 8–64 show SketchUp models enhanced with Photoshop, 3DMax, and hand-drawing. Figure 8–65 shows a space modeled from an imported AutoCAD plan, and then hand-colored with marker. Hand renderings were printed on bond paper and colored with Prismacolor markers, Sharpie Ultra Fine Point, and a Pentel Sign Pen.

The photorealistic renders were done in 3dsMax by Terry Sandee of REDgraphx, Inc., from models provided by Matthew Kerr of Zimmerman Architectural Studios, Milwaukee, WI. Matthew Kerr does workshops for both students and professionals, showing techniques for creating those fabulous pieces! To learn more, contact him at Matthew.Kerr@zastudios.com.

Courtesy Matthew Kerr, IIDA, ASAI, Zimmerman Architectural Studios, Milwaukee, WI

Figure 8–58 A sketchy-line style model and the same model printed on bond paper and hand-rendered with ink and marker.

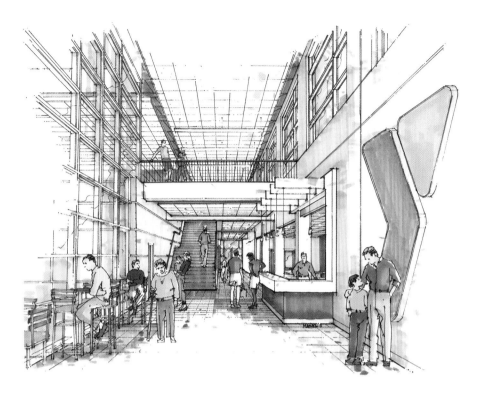

Figure 8–59: A model printed on bond paper, hand-rendered with ink and marker, and rendered photo realistically in 3dsMax.

Figure 8–60: A model with a black-and-white style and shadows applied, and rendered photo-realistically in 3dsMax.

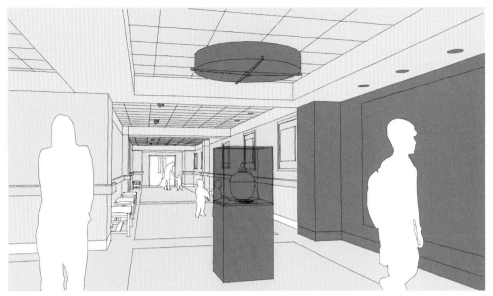

COURTESY MATTHEW KERR, IIDA, ASAI, ZIMMERMAN ARCHITECTURAL STUDIOS, MILWAUKEE, WI

Figure 8–61: A model with Photoshop color filters applied.

COURTESY MATTHEW KERR, IIDA, ASAI, ZIMMERMAN ARCHITECTURAL STUDIOS, MILWAUKEE, WI

Figure 8–62: A model printed on bond paper and hand-rendered with pen and marker.

Courtesy Matthew Kerr, IIDA, ASAI, Zimmerman Architectural Studios, Milwaukee, WI

Figure 8–63: A model printed on bond paper, then traced and hand-rendered with pen and marker. An imported image was used as wall art.

Courtesy Matthew Kerr, IIDA, ASAI, Zimmerman Architectural Studios, Milwaukee, WI

Figure 8–64: A model made from an imported AutoCAD plan; the printed model was hand-rendered with pen and marker.

Why SketchUp May Run Slow

By now you've probably experienced SketchUp slowdowns, freezes, and display abbreviations, where bounding boxes are shown instead of components, and details/textures are lost. This affects presentation as well as workflow—no presentation is enhanced by a frozen model. Slowdowns are caused by bloated geometry, which means an excessive number of polygons (the plane figures that make up a SketchUp model). This isn't necessarily the same thing as a large file size. A large file size can certainly reflect bloated geometry, and indicates complexity, but it's possible to have a small file size and a large polygon count (the number of polygons in a model).

File size is really just an issue when e-mailing the model. Check its size by right-clicking the model's icon and choosing *Properties* (Figure 8–65). The Warehouse doesn't accept uploads larger than 10 MB, so that might be a guide. That said, some architects routinely generate residential models that are 40 MB or larger.

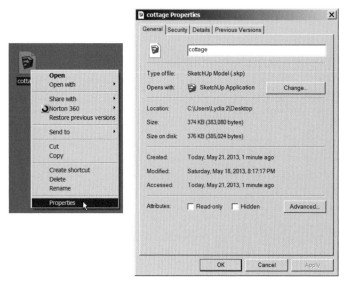

Figure 8–65 Right-click on the model's icon, and then Properties, to see its file size.

Make SketchUp Run Faster by Keeping the Polygon Count Down

SketchUp has to calculate each polygon when panning, orbiting, and zooming, so modelers should try to keep the polygon count down. Start by being cognizant of how much geometry the shapes you create have. As an example, look at Figure 8–66. It shows two circles with the hidden geometry option

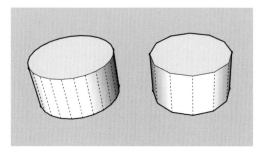

Figure 8–66: Turn on **View>Hidden Geometry** to see the smoother circle's larger amount of geometry.

turned on. The left is made with the default 24 sides, the right with 12 sides. The left one looks smoother, but you can see how much more geometry it has. If the circle isn't a large, important part of the model, will a 12-sided one suffice?

SketchUp also makes hidden lines when autofolding, creating curves, and even using Follow Me (the path line gets left behind). Some of this can be erased. Examine the model in hidden and x-ray modes (**View>Face style>X-ray**) to find extraneous geometry. You may find parts stuck into each other—not deliberately intersected, just stuck (Figure 8–67). Erasing them reduces the polygon count and keeps the model clean.

At **Window>Model Info>Statistics**, the amount of geometry is displayed. Over 100,000 edges will cause slowdowns. The following section provides strategies to manage the polygon count, which will make SketchUp run faster.

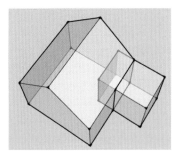

Figure 8–67: X-ray mode shows erasable interior pieces.

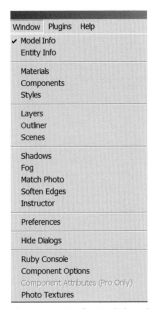

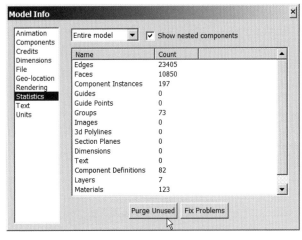

Figure 8–68: The Statistics window shows how much geometry the model has. Click the purge button at the bottom to remove all unused files at once.

Strategies to Make SketchUp Run Faster

Purge unused files. We've discussed managing file size by separately purging unused components, materials, and styles. At **Window>Model Info>Statistics**, click the *Purge Unused* button at the bottom (Figure 8–68). This removes all unused components, materials, and styles at once as well as unused layers and stale metadata accumulated during the modeling process.

Use images instead of textures when only one instance is needed. Images take less space than textures. Choose *jpgs* or *pngs* when possible, because they take the least space.

Use appropriate sizes for imported images. Is the image a major part of the model? Must it display in high resolution? If not, import a small file (e.g., 512k × 512k) or resample an already imported file with digital software inside SketchUp, as discussed in Chapter 7.

Download components to the desktop and purge unused/unneeded items before copy/pasting them into the model.

Be aware of imported component size. In the Components Browser, highlight the component and click the *Statistics* tab to see its polygon count (Figure 8–69).

Use components for multiple copies. Components take less space than groups. Use groups for single instances only.

Model minor items simply. A small, intricate model takes up as much as space as a large one. When zooming in to work on it, it's easy to lose sight of its relative importance. But small items should be simpler than large ones, and background items even simpler.

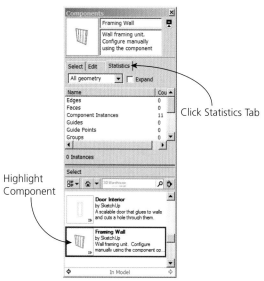

Figure 8–69: The Statistics window shows how much geometry the model has. Click the purge button at the bottom to remove all unused files at once.

Model half of symmetrical items. Make it a component and copy/flip along axis to complete. This is more time-efficient and takes up less space than a fully modeled component.

Place groups and components on layers, and turn off ones not needed. Turned-off layers don't get calculated. Until you're ready to print, does entourage need to be displayed?

Use 2D components for people, cars, and trees that "always face camera" (check that setting in their editing box). If a plan view isn't needed, use 2D plants, too. Put them in 3D pots to look more convincing.

▶ Tip: Here's how to make your own 2D components. Import a photo into Photoshop, cut out its background, set the background to transparent, and save as a *png* file. It shouldn't be larger than 1024 × 1024 at 96dpi. Open SketchUp, click on the front view and **Camera>Parallel Projection**. Draw a rectangle the size of the component, import, and paint the png file onto the rectangle. Adjust the rectangle's size with Move and use Freehand Line to trace around the image, adding interior holes where needed. Hide edges. Select everything, make it a component, and check *Always face camera*.

Model with textures off. Textures are calculated with each pan, orbit, and zoom. Click **View>Face Style>Monochrome** after you're done painting. Make a scene with the *Shaded with textures* face style to quickly view it as needed.

Turn off edge profiles, depth cue, and extensions at **View>Edge Style** (uncheck their boxes). At **Styles>Edit**, uncheck every box except *Edges*. All these settings are on by default, but they add little and slow the model down a lot. Set edge color to *All the same*, and hide all watermarks.

Model with the default style. Don't model with elaborate styles, because they take longer to recalculate when rendering, panning, orbiting, and zooming.

Turn off shadows when modeling. They slow the model down and are only needed when studying, adjusting, or when printing a hard copy.

Summary

A SketchUp model can be annotated with text and dimensions, and you can replace its default appearance with artsy display styles. Present different design schemes by utilizing scenes and layers. The Walk-Through tools simulate a person's view of the space from a constant eye level. Make animations of multiple scenes for maximum audience visualization.

Dynamic components add interest to a presentation with their ability to click animated features on and off. They also add function by performing programmed tasks. SketchUp models can be exported as 2D graphics for printing or as 3D models for development in other software. Always be mindful of a model's polygon count and the size of imported files because both contribute to slowdowns.

Further Resources

Download CutePDF, a free pdf emulator: www.cutepdf.com/products/cutepdf/writer.asp

Download an *fbx* converter here: www.autodesk.com/products/fbx/overview

Download free SketchUp styles: www.sketchupartists.org/presentations/sketchup-styles/

Download PDF995, a free pdf emulator: www.pdf995.com/download.html

Dynamic Component Functions: http://support.google.com/sketchup/bin/answer.py?hl=en&answer=108144

Video about the Dimensions tool: www.youtube.com/watch?v=xKLc3hb9Crk

Video about dynamic components: www.youtube.com/watch?v=fsBpIPnF31A

Video about the Position Camera and Look Around tools: www.youtube.com/watch?v=XekVjYzzy84

Video about Scenes: www.youtube.com/watch?v=qEYmiKh-sqs

Video about Text and 3D Text: www.youtube.com/watch?v=ClHdYWFczgU

Video about the Walk tool: www.youtube.com/watch?v=5Nai-cOHiik

Three-part Video Series on Dynamic Components:

Getting oriented: http://support.google.com/sketchup/bin/answer.py?hl=en&answer=116817

Making components that animate: http://support.google.com/sketchup/bin/answer.py?hl=en&answer=116822

Making components that copy: http://support.google.com/sketchup/bin/answer.py?hl=en&answer=116821

Exercises

www.wiley.com/go/sketchupforinteriordesign

1. Model a space for a specific activity, such as an office lobby, a gym exercise room, or a classroom. Use components, layers, and entourage. Add a title block.
   - ▶ Make scenes of the space, setting the camera at different heights and angles.
   - ▶ Use the Position Camera tool to stand in a location and look in a specific direction.
   - ▶ Export a 2D image of the model in a style conducive to use as an underlay or for coloring by hand (e.g., black-and-white wireframe).
2. Download a living room from the Warehouse.
   - ▶ Copy it twice and change geometry and properties in copies' design schemes.
   - ▶ Make scenes of each design by grouping and layering them.
   - ▶ Export an animation of the scenes.

3. Model the image in Exercise 8–1 (the triangular shape was made with the Polygon tool; activate it, type the number of sides, and click on the screen to place. Click a second time to set its size or type a number).

  ▶ Color each shape differently.

  ▶ Use the Walk-Through tools to walk through it.

4. Download an entire city from the Warehouse and use the Walk-Through tools to view it.

CHAPTER 9

Plugins and LayOut

This chapter discusses how to extend SketchUp's native capabilities with plugins. It also introduces *LayOut*, a Pro feature with which construction drawings are made.

What's a Plugin?

A *plugin*, also called an *extension* or *script*, is a simple text file with an *rb* or *rbs* extension that "plugs in" to SketchUp to extend its native capabilities. Think app on a smart phone. Developers use the Ruby programming language to make plugins, which is why plugins are also called *rubies*. Each plugin performs a specific task. Examples are: render (Figure 9–1); make Bézier (French) curves; put all loose geometry on the 0 layer; adjust scene transition times individually; perform energy analysis; add manufacturer information to a component; send the model to a 3D printer; identify too-large textures; cut openings through double-face walls; find the center of an arc . . . if it's a useful function, someone has probably written a plugin for it. Plugins work with both SketchUp Make and Pro.

Objective: This chapter discusses how to find and install plugins, and how to make a simple construction document in LayOut.

Tools: Get Extensions, Export to LayOut

Concepts and Functions: Extension Warehouse, plugin, extension, script, rubies, Ruby Console, install plugins, find plugin folder, prepare the model for LayOut, link the model to LayOut, viewport, copy and resize a viewport, grips, annotate and dimension, use symbols from the Scrapbook tray, export to raster or vector file

COURTESY MATTHEW KERR, IIDA, ASAI, ZIMMERMAN ARCHITECTURAL STUDIOS, MILWAUKEE, WI

Figure 9–1: A SketchUp model rendered with a free plugin called Kerkythea.

At **System Preferences>Extensions** are four native plugins: *Advanced Camera Tools* (Pro only), *Dynamic Components*, *Sandbox Tools*, and *Photo Textures* (Figure 9–2). All others must be found, downloaded, and installed. Many are free; others cost anywhere from 99¢ to $200. Most plugins perform their function in a stand-alone manner; however, others serve as exporters to a different software package. And some plugins require additional software before they can function.

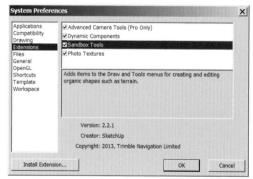

Figure 9–2: SketchUp has four native plugins. The Sandbox Tools plugin is highlighted, with its description underneath.

Plugins are scattered across many websites. However, the most reliable and convenient place to obtain them is the SketchUp Extension Warehouse (EW). Plugins from the EW are installed automatically. Plugins found elsewhere must be installed manually.

The Extension Warehouse

The Extension Warehouse is a website containing hundreds of plugins written by both the SketchUp team and third-party developers (mostly the latter). It is integrated with the SketchUp software. Click the Get Extensions tool (Figure 9–3), or go to **Window>Extension Warehouse**. Only IE or Safari will access it from within SketchUp. You can go to it directly at http://extensions.sketchup.com/ with any browser, but accessing it within SketchUp enables installation with just one click.

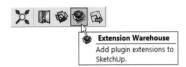

Figure 9–3: The Get Extensions tool.

Browse the categories (Figure 9–4) or type a specific query in the search field. When you find a plugin you like, click the red *Install* button (you'll need to sign in to your Google account first). Let's browse and install a few plugins now.

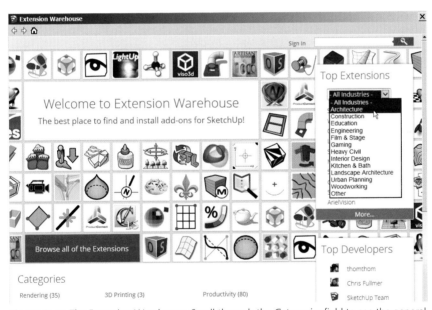

Figure 9–4: The Extension Warehouse. Scroll through the *Categories* field to see the general areas.

Install a Smattering of Plugins

Figure 9–5 shows a free plugin that optimizes texture size. Looks good, let's get it! Click the *Install* button. You're asked to confirm the installation. Click *Yes*. The plugin installs, confirmed by another message.

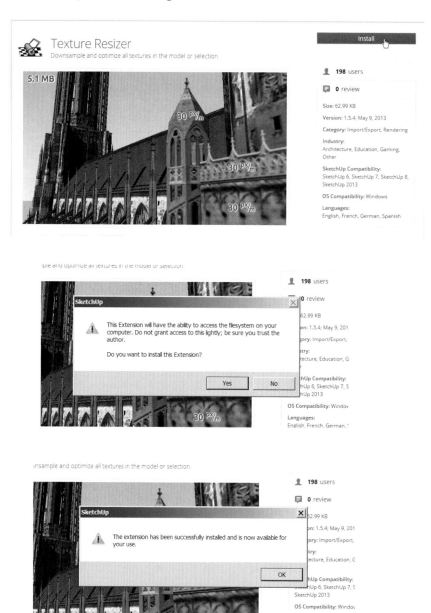

Figure 9–5: Installing a texture resize plugin.

Figure 9–6 shows a plugin that exports the model into a program that has enhanced camera tools. Downloading and clicking on the plugin yields a message giving the program's website address. At that website, you can either purchase the program or download a free trial.

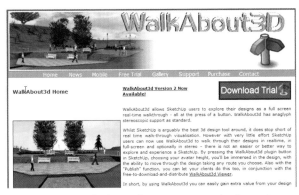

Figure 9–6: An exporter plugin to a for-pay program of enhanced camera tools.

Figure 9–7 shows two popular plugins for rendering SketchUp models. Shaderlight provides photorealistic material and lighting effects, and Podium has thousands of render-ready components. Note that their red buttons say *Get Extension*. Clicking takes you to their websites, where you can purchase them or download a limited free version.

Figure 9–8 shows a free plugin for editing 3D text. After you download and click, a message will appear saying that another program must be downloaded for the plugin to work, and giving a link to it.

Figure 9–7: Shaderlight and Podium are popular programs for enhancing the appearance of interior models.

Figure 9–8: This free 3D text-editing plugin requires another piece of software to work.

Figures 9–9 and 9–10 show eight free plugins: Select Outer Edges, Window Maker, Keyframe Animation (to animate objects), Simplify Contours Tool, SketchThis Kitchen Design, Construction Line (converts edges from solid to dashed), Artisan Organic Toolset (models organic shapes), and Architect Tools.

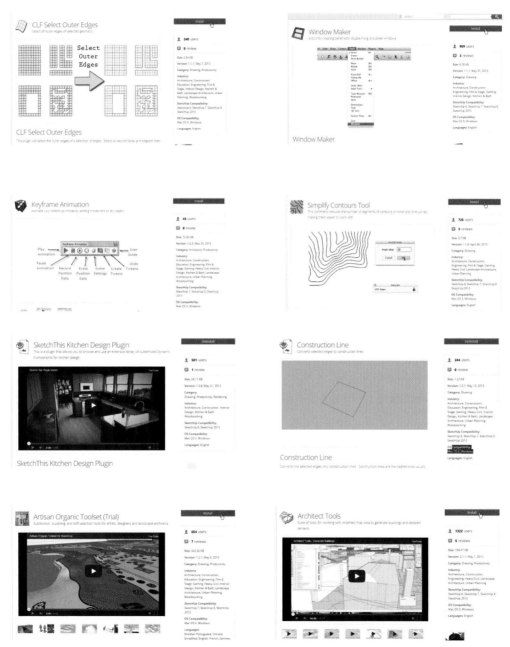

Figures 9–9 and 9–10 Eight free plugins that perform diverse functions.

If you're experiencing problems installing plugins, ensure that you're logged in as an admin and that all security permissions on the plugins folder are set to *Allow*. Locating the plugins folder is discussed later in this chapter.

If you visit the plugin page after installation, you'll see that the red button now says *Uninstall*. There's also a *Your Extensions* page showing all plugins you've downloaded, with *Uninstall* and *Disable* buttons for each. This is convenient when upgrading plugins, as it's often best to uninstall the existing one before installing an upgrade.

Find the Installed Plugin

Finding the installed plugins can be somewhat of a *Where's Waldo?* search, because they appear in different locations, depending on how the programmers wrote them (Figure 9–11). Although looking in the **Plugins** menu is the most intuitive, they don't always appear there. A plugin may appear as an entry in the **Tools** or **Draw** menu at the top of the screen, or as a submenu under one of them. Sometimes a toolbar will appear in the workspace upon installation; at other times, it must be activated first at **View>Toolbars** or **Preferences>Extensions**. A plugin might even appear in a context menu when the appropriate geometry is right-clicked.

If you can't find the toolbar, go back to the plugin's EW details page and read whatever instructions the developer put there. You could also open the plugin file in a text editor such as Notepad and look for code about menus and toolbars, which is typically near the top or bottom of the script. Of course, you'll have to find the plugin file first.

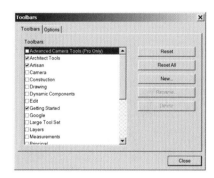

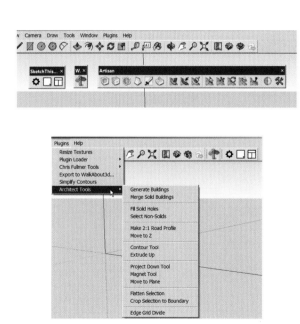

Figure 9–11: Plugins appear in different places after installation.

Find the Plugins Folder

Plugins are downloaded into their own folder in SketchUp's program files. On the PC, go to **My Computer>Program Files (x86)>SketchUp>Plugins** (Figures 9–12 and 9–13). As an aside, the *x86* program files is where 32bit software lives; the other program files is where 64bit software lives.

1.

2.

3.

4.

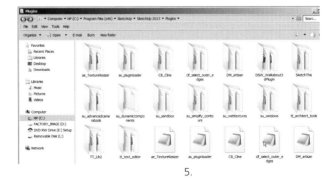

5.

Figure 9–12 and 9–13 Finding the plugins folder on the PC.

On the Mac, the plugins folder is in the user library. Go to **Macintosh HD >Users [User]> ~/Library>Application Support>SketchUp 2013>SketchUp>Plugins**. The user library is invisible in OS X; press the **Option** key to make it appear in the Home folder menu. A quicker way, however, is to press **Shift+Command+G** to access the Finder's Go To window, and type *~/Library* (Figure 9–14). Then click *Go*. It will take you right to that folder.

Figure 9–14: On the Mac, the Finder's *Go To* window can help locate the plugins folder.

The Ruby Console

The Ruby Console is the window in which plugins are developed. You can also use it to find the plugins folder. Go to **Window>Ruby Console** and type this script in the bottom text field:

UI.openURL("file://#{Sketchup.find_support_file("Plugins")}")

Then hit **Enter** (Figure 9–15). That will take you right to the folder.

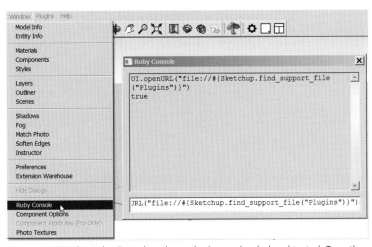

Figure 9–15: The Ruby Console, where plugins are loaded and tested. Type the script shown in the bottom field and hit Enter to find the plugins folder.

Place a shortcut to the plugins folder on the desktop to make it easier to access (Figure 9–16). On the PC, right-click on the folder and choose *Create Shortcut*. Make sure the small, curved arrow appears on the new icon, indicating that the folder is, indeed, a shortcut; a simple copy/paste doesn't make a shortcut. On the Mac, make an alias (shortcut) by holding down the **Command** and **Option** keys while dragging the folder onto the desktop. Again, look for the small, curved arrow indicating that the new icon is an alias and that you didn't inadvertently drag the original folder out.

Figure 9–16: Shortcut icons to the plugins folder (PC on the left, Mac on the right).

▶ If you want to try your own hand at making plugins, go to your plugins folder, right-click a plugin, and open it in Notepad. Study how it's written.

Install Plugins from Non-EW Websites

Why bother finding the plugins folder? Because many good plugins are hosted on other sites, such as **www.smustard.com**, and need to be installed manually. Here's how:

Download and save the plugin to the desktop. Following are three options for installation; if one doesn't work, try another.

▶ Go to **Preferences>Extensions**, click the Install Extension button at the bottom (Figure 9–17), navigate to the plugin, and click Open. Be aware that this only works for rbz files (zipped Ruby files).

▶ Move unzipped files—just the files, not their enclosing folder—into the plugins folder (or its shortcut). Leave their file structure alone; that is, don't remove files from subfolders.

▶ Unzip a zipped folder yourself (right-click, choose *Extract*), and move the contents into the plugin folder (again, leave their file structure alone and take them out of the enclosing folder).

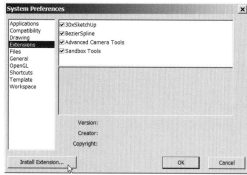

Figure 9–17: Install plugins from sources besides the EW by clicking the Install button at **Preferences>Extensions**.

LayOut

LayOut (a Pro feature) is construction documentation software, and installs as a separate program. Think of SketchUp as the modeling software and LayOut as the drafting software. With LayOut, you can display multiple views of a model simultaneously (Figure 9–18). It's similar to AutoCAD's *paper space* mode, if you're familiar with that. The model is exported directly to LayOut, and the live link between them enables easy updating of the LayOut views after the model is changed.

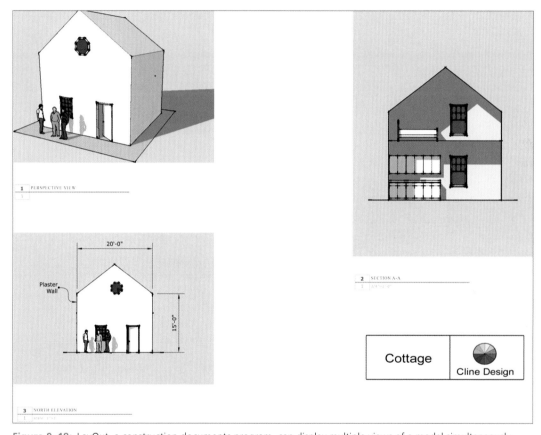

Figure 9–18: LayOut, a construction documents program, can display multiple views of a model simultaneously.

Prepare the Model for Export to LayOut

Here are some steps to take before exporting the model to LayOut. They aren't required, but make working in LayOut easier.

1. *Create scenes of the views you want in the LayOut document* (Figure 9–19). Change the camera to *parallel projection* for orthographic views, and use the Section tool to cut any needed sections (Figure 9–20). You can place multiple sections on a model, but only one will be active. Toggle the inactive section(s) off with the *Display Section Cuts* tool to make the entire model visible again before inserting another one (Figure 9–21). But don't erase the inactive section, because you'll lose the view it created.

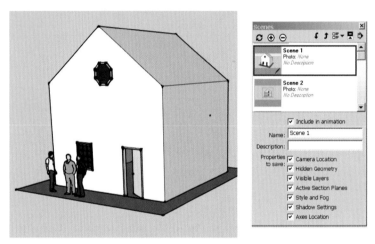

Figure 9–19: Create scenes for each view to be displayed in LayOut.

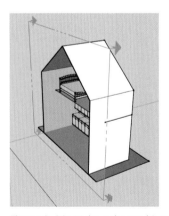
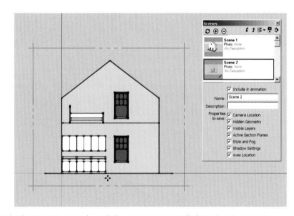

Figure 9–20: Make orthographic sections with the Section tool and the camera *parallel projection* setting.

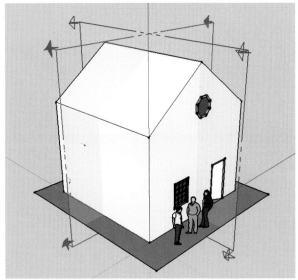

Figure 9–21: Toggle the inactive section cuts off, but don't delete their cutting planes.

2. *Create a new style with appropriate settings* for the model's display in LayOut (Figure 9–22a). Settings may include turning off the axes, sky, and cutting planes, and adjusting the profile settings. If you don't want the color background, the engineering style in the default styles collection has a white background (Figure 9–22b), which will blend in with the LayOut background.

3. *Save the model.* The model must be saved for the changes to appear in LayOut. Any subsequent changes must also be saved before updating in LayOut.

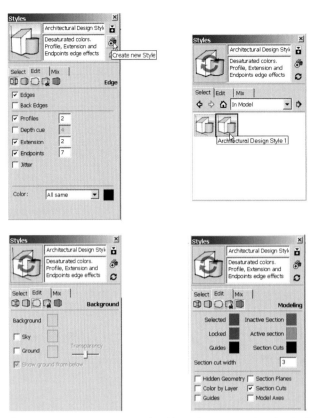

Figure 9–22a Create a new style with settings appropriate for the LayOut display.

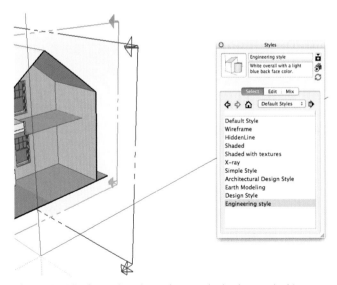

Figure 9–22b The engineering style turns the background white.

SketchUp for Interior Design

4. *Export to LayOut.* Click the *Export to LayOut* tool (Figure 9–23). Models can also be imported from within LayOut, using its Insert function.

LayOut opens and presents template choices (Figure 9–24). Select one, click *Open*, and the model will open inside that template as the last view saved. Keep both SketchUp and LayOut open to make toggling between them easier, because you'll probably want to make some changes to the model while developing the LayOut document.

Figure 9–23: Click the *Export to LayOut* tool to send the model to LayOut.

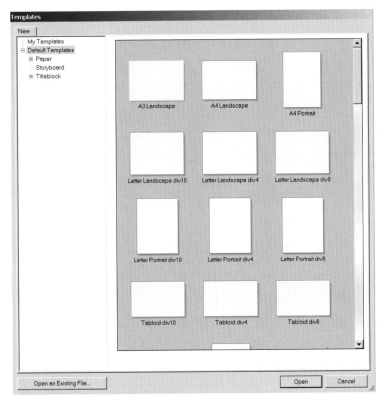

Figure 9–24: Upon opening, LayOut presents template choices.

Make a LayOut Document

The LayOut workspace consists of a large drafting window, a top toolbar, and trays on the right. By default, most of the trays are collapsed.

1. *Click on the model to reveal a blue bounding box.* This is a *viewport*, a framed area that displays the model or other information. The triangular tabs are *grips*; drag them to resize (Figure 9–25). Dragging a corner and holding the **Shift** key will preserve the viewport's proportions.

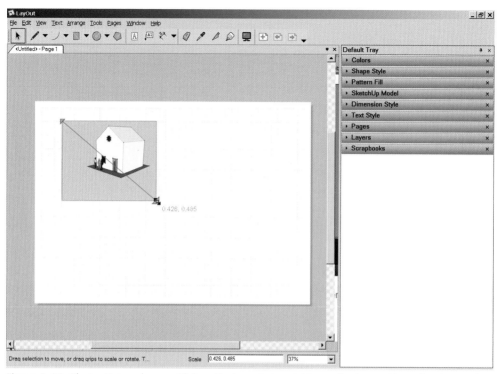

Figure 9–25: The LayOut workspace. Click on the imported model to see its viewport bounding box, and then resize it by dragging the grips.

2. *Copy the viewport* (Figure 9–26). Select and drag it with the Move tool plus the **Control** key. Note that inference lines appear; use them to align the copies. Since we made three scenes of the model, we'll make three copies. Adjust the viewports to the size/shape wanted.

3. *Link each viewport* to a scene by right-clicking inside it and choosing *Scene* (Figure 9–27).

   To change how the model appears in one or more viewports, go back to SketchUp and adjust the appropriate scene(s). Don't forget to save. Return to LayOut, right-click the appropriate viewport(s), and choose *Update.* The saved model changes will appear (Figure 9–28).

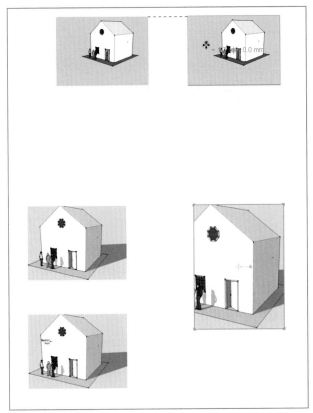

Figure 9–26: Copy the viewport with Move plus the Control key, using inference lines to align them. Adjust size and shape with the grips.

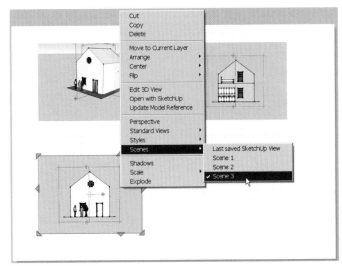

Figure 9–27: Reference Each Viewport to a Scene.

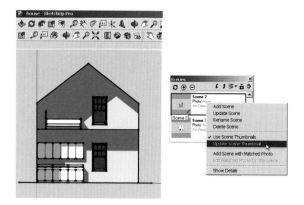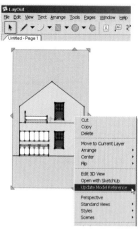

Figure 9–28: Shadows were added to all three SketchUp scenes and saved. All three LayOut viewports were then updated.

4. *Scale the orthographic views* by right-clicking inside the viewport and choosing *Scale* (Figure 9–29).

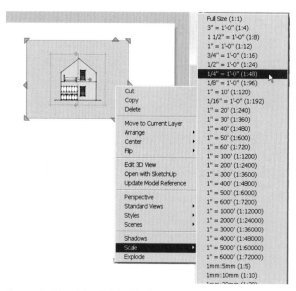

Figure 9–29: Right-click inside the viewport to scale orthographic views.

SketchUp for Interior Design

5. *Annotate and dimension inside the viewports.* Click the Dimension tool (Figure 9–30) on the model's endpoints. Note that LayOut automatically places hyphens between feet and inches. Click the Text tool (it's immediately left of the Dimension tool) inside the viewport to type notes. Make curved leader lines by typing the Text tool on the model and click-dragging the second endpoint (Figure 9–31).

Figure 9–30: The Dimension tool.

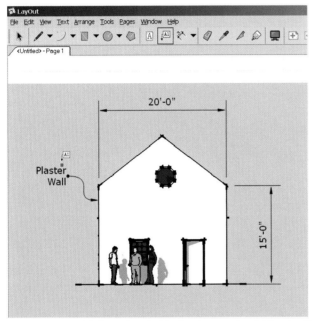

Figure 9–31: Add dimensions inside the viewport by clicking the Dimension tool onto the model's endpoints; click the Text tool on the model and click-drag it to make a curved leader line.

6. *Edit text and dimension notes* by double-clicking on them (Figure 9–32).

Look at the nine trays on the right of the workspace now. They are: *Colors, Dimension Style, Shape Style, Pattern Fill, SketchUp Model, Text Style, Pages, Layers,* and *Scrapbooks.* Click on each to expand, and see their functionalities. Figure 9–32 shows the open Dimension Style tray, where units and alignment are chosen.

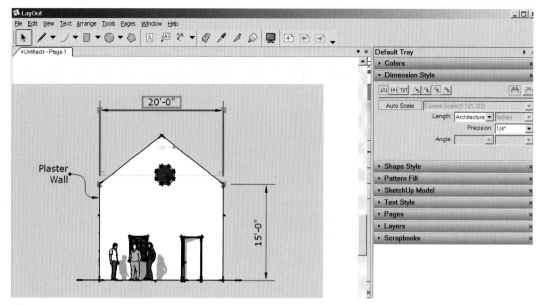

Figure 9–32: The open Dimension Style tray.

Figure 9–33 shows pattern fills. There are four categories: *Material Symbols*, *Geometric Tiles*, *Site Patterns*, and *Tonal Patterns*, over one hundred total. Click the material symbols on plans, details, elevations, and section views of the model to poché them. Most of the files are *pngs* with transparent backgrounds, which enables the addition of colors, and they can be rotated and scaled. You can also import your own.

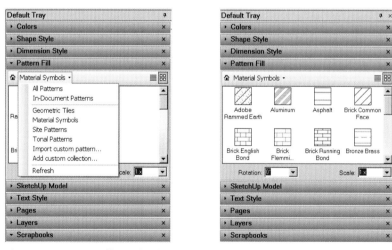

Figure 9–33: Pattern fills can be clicked on construction drawings.

Figure 9–34 shows the Scrapbook tray, which contains symbols that can be dragged directly into the viewports. In Figure 9–35, an ID label was added to a scene, and then overtyped with a new name. You can add your own symbols to this collection as well.

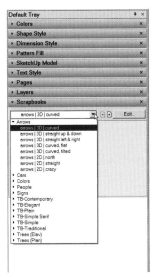

Figure 9–34: The Scrapbook tray contains symbols.

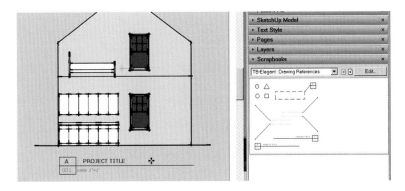

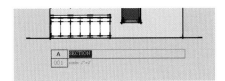

Figure 9–35: Drag symbols from the scrapbook into the viewport.

At **File>Insert**, navigate to a title block or other file that you want to bring in. Size it, and move it into place (Figure 9–36).

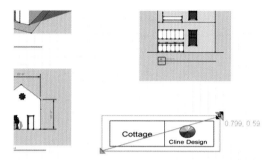

Figure 9–36: At **File>Insert** a title block was brought into the document, sized, and moved into place.

Finally, make a *pdf, dwg/dxf,* or raster image of the document via **File>Export** (Figure 9–37).

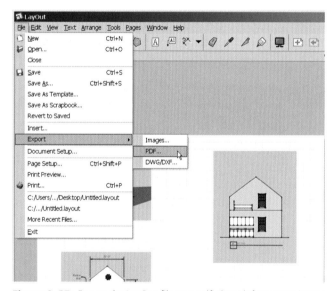

Figure 9–37: Export the LayOut file to a *pdf, dwg/dxf,* or raster image.

More LayOut Capabilities

Other noteworthy capabilities LayOut has are:

- ► *Editable lines*, including configurable dashed lines.
- ► *Numbered Pages,* which enables you to print or export specific pages.
- ► *Copy-Array,* which makes multiple, arrayed copies of elements in the viewports.
- ► *Vector rendering*, which means you can render the model in vector mode instead of raster mode. This is faster and results in sharp, clear lines that export to a *pdf* that, in turn, can be printed any size without loss of quality.
- ► *Export* to pdf for printing or to *dwg/dxf* for export into other software.
- ► *Spell checker* for Mac users.

SketchUCation Forum

If you haven't found it on your own yet, point your browser to www.sketchucation.com (Figure 9–38). This is a great resource for SketchUp news, discussion, plugins (free and low-cost), and tutorials. But its best feature is the busy community forum, with its knowledgeable, helpful moderators and posters who suggest solutions to those stuck on specific problems. The website also has a for-pay premium membership that offers extra help and access to more content.

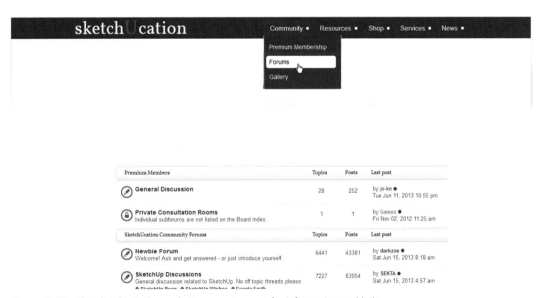

Figure 9–38: The SketchUCation website, a great source for information and help.

Summary

SketchUp's native tools and functions are enhanced with plugins—pieces of code that add tools and functionality. Plugins downloaded from within SketchUp via the *Get Extensions* tool will install automatically; plugins found elsewhere must be installed manually. LayOut is a Pro feature with which construction documents can be made from the model. This is achieved by making multiple viewports, each displaying a different model scene. Help with all things SketchUp can be obtained at SketchUCation.com, a forum for SketchUp users.

Further Resources

Advanced SketchUp tips: https://sites.google.com/site/sketchupsage/

Compete against other SketchUp users to show off skills: www.sketchup3dchallenge .blogspot.com/

Information on the Ruby console and making plugins: www.sketchup.com/intl/en/developer/ docs/tutorial_console.php

Message boards at SketchUCation: http://sketchucation.com/forums/

Plugin for adding manufacturer product information and some BIM capability to a SketchUp model: http://igloostudios.com/productconnect/learn-more

Tutorials and examples of high-end SketchUp models: www.sketchupartists.org/

Video about using LayOut: www.youtube.com/watch?v=Z3xUOAicq-Y

Exercises

www.wiley.com/go/sketchupforinteriordesign

1. Do a Google search for a specific plugin you'd like (type *sketchup plugin* + the query).

2. Download and install plugins you might use from the Extension Warehouse and smustard.com.

3. Export a model you've made into LayOut,

   ▶ Make a construction document of it.

   ▶ Create multiple viewports.

   ▶ Dimension and annotate it.

   ▶ Insert symbols from the Scrapbook tray.

   ▶ Insert poché from the Pattern Fills tray.

Index

Paint Bucket tool, 171
    sampling color, 172–173
navigating to default style, 218–219
nested group, 49
non-EW websites, installing plugins from, 264
non-filling face, 51–52
normal, defined, 45
numbered pages, LayOut, 277
number units, entering, 30
NVIDIA GTX 600 series video card, 14

O

offsetting
    faces, 63–64
    perimeter wall, 91
Offset tool, 63–64
On Face inference, 68
operating system requirements, 13
Orbit tool, 31
orientation, faces, 162–164, 180
origin, axes, 21
orthographic views, 3–4, 32–35, 116–117, 272
Outliner tool, 164–166

P

Paint Bucket tool, 171
painting
    adding colors and texture to software,
        178–179
    checking face orientation, 180
    defined, 169
    importing colors, 181–182
    importing images, 188–202
    importing swatches, 178
    importing texture, 183–188
    Native SketchUp Materials, 169–173
    photo-matching, 202–205
    with textures, 174–177
    workflow, 182
Pan tool, 31

paper sketch, drafting plan from
    importing door through Components
        Browser, 105–107
    overview, 102–104
    Trimble 3D Warehouse, 104–105
paper space mode, AutoCAD, 265
paraline view, 32, 33
parallel inference, 155
Parallel Projection view, 117
pasting
    importing swatches from other models,
        178
    between SketchUp files, 110–111
pattern fills, LayOut, 274
PC
    Colors Palette, 170
    customizing toolbars, 38–39
    menu bar, 20
    modifier keys, 32
    plugins folder, 262
Pencil (Line) tool, 46–47
perspective view, 32, 34
photo-matching, 202–205
photos, incorporating into models, 11
Photoshop, 15, 238
Photo Textures plugin, 254
picture frames, 191–192
Place option, 3D Text tool, 215
planar inference, 28
plan view, 34, 116–117
plugins
    Extension Warehouse, 255
    finding, 261
    installing, 256–261
    from non-EW websites, 264
    overview, 253–255
    Plugins folder, 262–263
    Ruby Console, 263–264
Plugins folder, 262–263
png file format, 85
Podium plugin, 258